Objects and Others

DR. H. M. SAMPATH
92 Waterfordbridge Road
St. John's, Newfoundland
Canada, A1E 1C6
Phone: (709) 579-5778

HISTORY OF ANTHROPOLOGY

Volume 1
Observers Observed
Essays on Ethnographic Fieldwork

Volume 2
Functionalism Historicized
Essays on British Social Anthropology

Volume 3
Objects and Others
Essays on Museums and Material Culture

Volume 4
Malinowski, Rivers, Benedict and Others
Essays on Culture and Personality

Objects and Others

ESSAYS ON MUSEUMS
AND MATERIAL CULTURE

Edited by

George W. Stocking, Jr.

HISTORY OF ANTHROPOLOGY
Volume 3

THE UNIVERSITY OF WISCONSIN PRESS

The University of Wisconsin Press
114 North Murray Street
Madison, Wisconsin 53715

The University of Wisconsin Press, Ltd.
1 Gower Street
London WC1E 6HA, England

Library of Congress Cataloging in Publication Data
Main entry under title:
Objects and others.
(History of anthropology; v. 3)
Includes bibliographies and index.
1. Anthropological museums and collections—History—
Addresses, essays, lectures. 2. Anthropology—History—
Addresses, essays, lectures. 3. Material culture—Ad-
dresses, essays, lectures. I. Stocking, George W.,
1928–   . II. Series.
GN35.O25 1985   306   85-40379
ISBN 0-299-10320-X
ISBN 0-299-10324-2 (paper)

HISTORY OF ANTHROPOLOGY

EDITOR
George W. Stocking, Jr.
Department of Anthropology, University of Chicago

Contents

Contents

Objects and Others

ESSAYS ON MUSEUMS AND MATERIAL CULTURE

The two halves of our volume title—"Objects and Others" and "Essays on Museums and Material Culture"—imply overlapping but somewhat different enterprises. The latter suggests, and did in fact elicit, a series of institutionally oriented studies, focusing on what has been called the "Museum Period" in the history of anthropology (Sturtevant 1969:622). The former—which suggested itself only later in our volume planning—implies a more generalized metahistorical, philosophical, or theoretical consideration of two defining categories (or category relationships) of human existence, and therefore of anthropological inquiry in the broadest sense.

Given the announced bias of *History of Anthropology* toward studies grounded in primary historical materials, it is not surprising that the essays in this volume are, for the most part, more obviously related to its subtitle than to its title. Particularly in the early stages of the historiography of any field, institutional (and/or biographically oriented) topics provide a convenient focus for research grounded in documents, which tend to collect around individuals and institutions. But despite the embeddedness of the present essays in documentary historical material, they do in fact raise important broader issues: the problematic interaction of museum arrangement and anthropological theory; the tension between anthropological research and popular education; the contribution of museum ethnography to aesthetic practice; the relationship of humanist culture and anthropological culture, and of ethnic artifact and fine art; and most generally, the representation of culture in material objects—to mention only some of the more obvious focusing themes.

Nevertheless, they are far from exhausting, even by glancing allusion, the range of issues implicated in our title—in either of its parts. In order to suggest something of this still-unrealized context of significance, this volume is framed by two brief essays, each taking one-half of the title as its point of departure.

Etymologically, a museum is a place dedicated to the muses. Although astronomy and history were perhaps more at home there than dance and erotic poetry, the force of that etymology was clearly manifest two thousand years

3

ago in the Mouseion of Alexandria (Alexander 1979:6–7). Modern museums, too, have been called secular temples, and the spirits of certain of the muses still inhabit and sometimes inspire them; but the common denominator of modern definitions of "the museum" is distinctly material. Museums are institutions devoted to the collection, preservation, exhibition, study, and interpretation of material *objects*. Insofar as they are "anthropological" museums, in the broader Anglo-American sense of the term, they are the archives of what anthropologists have called "material culture." Characteristically, these objects of material culture are the objects of "others"—of human beings whose similarity or difference is experienced by alien observers as in some profound way problematic.

As objects—things thrown in the way of the observer or actor—the pieces preserved in museums exist in a three-dimensional space encompassing both object and viewer. It is this complex three-dimensionality that distinguishes the museum archive from essentially two-dimensional repositories of linear texts—although linear thinking long characterized much museum practice. But as the word "archive" suggests, there is a fourth dimension that bears a peculiarly problematic relation to the museum. In general, the objects preserved in museums come from out of the past, so that the observer experiencing them in three-dimensional space must somehow also cross a barrier of change in time. Paradoxically, however, those objects are at the same time timeless—removed from history in the very process of embodying it, by curators seeking (among other goals) to preserve objects in their original form. Removed, however, from their original contexts in space and time, and recontextualized in others that may or may not seek to recreate them, the meaning of the material forms preserved in museums must always be acutely problematic. This is even more the case inasmuch as the objects viewed by museum observers are "survivals" not only of the past from which collection wrenched them, but from those later pasts into which any given act of exhibition has placed them. Museums, in short, are institutions in which the forces of historical inertia (or "cultural lag") are profoundly, perhaps inescapably, implicated.

Whatever the contingencies of their specific histories, the three-dimensional objects thrown in the way of museum observers from out of the past are not placed there by historical accident. Their placement in museums, their problematic character, and indeed, their "otherness," are the outcome of large-scale historical processes. In the case of some "anthropological" objects—e.g., a paleolithic stone ax—these processes may be the very long-term ones of geological, climatic, and human evolutionary change. But the historical processes that led to the collection of archeological objects in museums are much more recent: they have to do on the one hand with the forces of economic development and nationalism that transformed Europe in the nineteenth century (cf. Trigger, in this volume), and on the other with those of imperial domination (Silberman 1982). As far as ethnographic objects are concerned, there is a large subcategory of anthropological objects (those of "folklore" or *Volkskunde*) generated by processes of industrial development and social change internal to particular national states. Such processes, however, have in some instances been appropriately characterized as processes of "internal colonialism," and certainly in the case of the bulk of traditional ethnographic objects, the most important historical processes have been those of colonial domination.

This brief historical excursus confirms what is in fact implicit in the etymology of the word "object": that there is inherent in the museum as an archive of material objects a fifth dimension beyond the three of materiality and the fourth of time or history. Since the objects thrown in the way of observers in museums were once those of others, there are relations implicit in the constitution of a museum which may be defined as relations of "power": the expropriation (not only in an abstract etymological sense, but sometimes in the dirty sense of theft or pillage) of objects from actors in a particular context of space, time, and meaning and their appropriation (or making one's own) by observers in another (cf. Foster 1984). From the observer's perspective, however, the power involved in that appropriation is largely external, since she or he neither "owns" the objects in a literal sense nor defines the parameters of their recontextualization. Within these parameters a multitude of individual recontextualizations may occur, but within them also the recontextualized objects may be said to exert a power over their viewers—a power not simply inherent in the objects, but given to them by the museum as an institution within a particular historical sociocultural setting.

The issue of "ownership" suggests a sixth dimension to the constitution of the museum as an archive of material objects: that of wealth (though some might regard this as simply an aspect of the dimension of power). Even before the political processes of modern nationalism defined it as such (cf. Handler, in this volume), material culture was, in a literal economic sense, "cultural property." The very materiality of the objects of material culture entangled them in Western economic processes of the acquisition and exchange of wealth. While many ethnographic objects were acquired by expropriative processes involving no element of exchange, many others were acquired by barter or purchase, so that the development of museum collections has always been heavily dependent on the commitment of individual, corporate, or national wealth (cf. Chapman and Stocking, in this volume). And while the detritus of the shell heap has never been given a value commensurate with the labor expended in its recovery, its aesthetic-cum-economic valuation in relation to objects higher on the scale of "culture" has been a factor affecting the allocation of resources for its collection and preservation (cf. Hinsley, in this volume). From the beginning, market processes have been potent influences on the constitution of museums as archives of material culture—the more so insofar as the objects therein have been regarded, or come to be regarded, as objects of fine art, rather than as artifacts (cf. Wade, in this volume).

This suggests one further—and for present purposes, final—definitional dimension: the aesthetic. Despite its history of exclusion from museums devoted to the fine arts, and of negative evaluation by universal humanistic or evolutionary aesthetic standards, the material culture of non-Western peoples has undergone a process of aestheticization since its original emplacement in museums. This has resulted in part from the relativization (and universalization) of Western aesthetic standards (cf. Williams in this volume), and in part from processes which have recontextualized the production of traditional items of material culture. Items that once had multiple functions, so that their aesthetic element could only be isolated by abstraction, have often had their functions reduced in scope by processes of acculturation, with the more utilitarian functions transferred to the products of Western technology. Insofar as they continue to be produced, items of traditional material culture are reconceptualized from both the native and the western perspective in aesthetic terms—whether those of curio kitsch or fine art. Thus objects of "material culture"—which in traditional contexts often had spiritual value—are respiritualized (in Western terms) as aesthetic objects, at the same time that they are subjected to the processes of the world art market. As their productions become entangled in the market nexus, some of those who were or might have been native craftsmen are transformed into artists in the Western sense. But whether defined as "art by metamorphosis" or created as "art by designation," objects that once went into museums of ethnography as pieces of material culture have become eligible for inclusion in museums of fine art (cf. Wade, in this volume, and Cannizzo 1982:10).

It is within the context of such issues of definition—considered both etymologically and historically—that the institutionally focused histories of museum anthropology included in this volume take on broader meaning.

Although the museum has been called "the institutional homeland" of anthropology (Lurie 1981:184), it took a long time for anthropology to find that homeland, and its presence there was, even in the so-called "Museum Period," always somewhat problematic. The renaissance humanist "cabinet of curiosities"—the commonly accepted prototype of the modern museum—emerged contemporaneously with the age of discovery and exploration; from the time Cortez sent back pieces from Mexico after the Conquest, both "artificial" and "natural" curiosities from the New World and the East found a place in them (Sturtevant 1969:621; cf. Hodgen 1964:111–23; Mullaney

1983). Along with the dodo, the marine unicorn (or narwhal), and the stirrups of Henry VIII, the collection of the Tradescants, which formed the basis for the Ashmolean Museum established at Oxford in 1683, included "*Pohaton*, King of *Virginia's* habit all embroidered with shells" (Alexander 1979:43). It was some time, however, before ethnographic objects began to be treated as a distinct category. When the British Museum, the first great national museum, was founded in 1753, its three departments were devoted to "Printed Books, Maps, Globes and Drawings," "Manuscripts, Medals, and Coins," and "Natural and Artificial Productions"; a fourth, added in 1807, was devoted simply to "Antiquities"—although by that time the Museum's ethnographic materials had been greatly augmented by the expeditions of Captain Cook (Alexander 1979:45).

During the first half of the nineteenth century, however, a number of museums of a more clearly anthropological character were established, or evolved out of previously existing collections, along several different lines. In the case of the National Museum established in Denmark in 1816—where Christian Thomsen's categorization of the contents of Danish burial chambers, kitchen middens, and bog-sites provided the basis for the "three-age" system of archeological periodization—the anthropological dimension emerged as an aspect of an interest in the history of the nation itself (Daniel 1943); it was only in the 1840s that a specifically "ethnographical" collection was established. In the case of the ethnographic museum of the Academy of Sciences in Petrograd, whose independent existence has been dated to 1836, the anthropological element derived from an interest in the peoples of an internal empire. In the case of the National Museum of Ethnology founded in Leiden, customarily dated from the opening of von Siebold's collection to the public in 1837, overseas imperial interests were implicated from the beginning, although the Siebold collection itself focused on Japan (cf. Ave 1980).

Although the "Museum Period" has been described as extending from the 1840s to 1890 (Sturtevant 1969:622), the designation seems somewhat anachronistic for the earlier portion of those years. In three of the major national anthropological traditions, a more characteristic institutional setting was perhaps the "Ethnological Society"—founded in Paris in 1839, in New York in 1842, and in London in 1843. While ethnographic materials were by that time included in museum collections in each of these countries, the establishment of their major anthropological museums began only with the founding of the Peabody Museum of Archaeology and Ethnology in 1866 (cf. Hinsley, in this volume).

Internationally, the great foundation period of museum anthropology extended over the rest of the nineteenth century. Some museums followed the pattern of the Peabody, focusing on prehistoric archeology and ethnology;

others, especially in continental Europe, were museums of national and peas-
ant culture in the Volkskunde tradition. In some cases, anthropological exhibits were a department of a general national museum, or—especially in
North America—of a museum of natural history; others were the outgrowth
of international fairs or exhibitions (cf. Chapman, Jacknis, and Williams in
this volume). Many of the earlier foundations, however, took some time to
reach institutional maturity; from the point of view of both the employment
of anthropological personnel and the support of field research, the great period of museum anthropology only really began in the 1890s. By that time,
the university was already emerging as a complementary, but in the longer
run alternative (and dominating) institutional setting (cf. Sturtevant
1969:623; Jacknis and Stocking, in this volume).

   If we may judge from the essays in this volume, it is hard to locate the
historical moment when the situation of anthropology within the institutional "homeland" of the museum was not intensely problematic. In programmatic statements or retrospective analyses, it may be possible to specify
clearly the theoretical notions or ideological messages that were intended to
be or seem to have been conveyed through the arrangement of material objects for viewing by diverse audiences. The explicitly stated theoretical and
ideological agendas of General Pitt Rivers and of Franz Boas contrast sharply
in this respect: the one arranging objects linearly, in terms of externally defined formal or functional qualities, to convey an ethnocentric message of
conservative evolutionary gradualism; the other arranging them contextually,
seeking to preserve the multiple functions and inner meanings of a given
form, to convey a message of liberal relativism. But in both cases, program
was frustrated by the pragmatics of museum practice, and by the perhaps
inherent contradictions of museum purpose. Even before the institutionalization of anthropology in museums had peaked—in terms of numbers of jobs
and resources for field research—Boas had already become acutely conscious
of "the limitations of the museum method of anthropology"—just as he had
previously argued the "limitations of the comparative method of anthropology" (cf. Jacknis, in this volume).

   Museum collections remained important for certain research purposes, especially in relation to the culture area and distributional concerns of the
diffusionist schools that continued to flourish into the 1920s. More generally,
the museum tradition in its Volkskunde form has continued strong on the
European continent (cf. Hofer 1973). But in the Anglo-American tradition,
the shift toward a more behaviorally oriented anthropology, reinforced by
substantial funding from foundation philanthropy, had by the outbreak of the
second World War left museum anthropology stranded in an institutional,
methodological, and theoretical backwater (cf. Stocking, in this volume).

Except in archeology, material culture studies and museum collections were no longer important for anthropological research. Surveying major anthropological journals for ethnological papers "concerned (at least in part) with material culture," and the fraction of these "based (at least in part) on museum collections," William Sturtevant found in 1969 that although the timing and duration of the peak of museum anthropology had come at different times in England, France, Germany, and the United States, the general trend after 1930 had been uniformly down, reaching a low point in the United States in the 1960s, when both lines nearly touched the bottom of his graph (1969:626). At the last point in history when it would be possible to collect and document "hand-made traditional artifacts," few field ethnographers were still interested in collecting; two-thirds of recent acquisitions at the U.S. National Museum had been collected "under non-scientific conditions by untrained people" (632–33). In a context where "at least 90% of museum ethnological specimens [had probably] never been studied" at all, the research function of museums had atrophied, and the professional status of curators drastically declined. Collections were increasingly inaccessible to researchers, and often inadequately cared for; many "important ethnographic specimens" were in fact being sold at public sales desks, to socialite "friends" of museums, or on the recently inflated market in "primitive art" (634; cf. Reitlinger 1963:292, 543). A century after anthropology entered its "institutional homeland," the question could be seriously posed "Does anthropology need museums?"

Despite his bleak portrayal of its twentieth century history and current state, Sturtevant was not ready to abandon to archeologists the museum study of material culture. Appealing to the definition of man as "preeminently the tool-using animal," to the "material basis" of other aspects of human social life, to the utility of dated artifacts for historical reconstruction, and to the evidential value of artifacts as less subject to "both informants' and recorders' biases," he pointed to various trends within anthropology that might revivify "ethnological research on material culture": an increasing attention to "classification, semantics, and symbolism" and a "variety of structuralist methods"; the heightened interest in "diachronic studies"; the difficulty of access to foreign areas for ethnographic fieldwork; even the "explosive increase in the number of anthropologists who must publish or perish" (639–40; cf. Sturtevant 1973).

Writing in 1981, another leading museum anthropologist, Nancy Lurie, offered an account of "museumland revisited" that provides a convenient benchmark for evaluating developments since 1969. Granting that museums had become almost "totally irrelevant for sociocultural anthropologists"—

whole generations of whom had "now completed professional careers without ever having had to set foot in a museum"—Lurie nevertheless took as her starting point the fact that "the museum business in the United States is big and growing": at that time it was estimated that there were 5,500 museums with half a billion annual individual visits and operating budgets totalling a billion dollars. Given the push toward accreditation within "the museum profession," she was optimistic about future museum career prospects for those with graduate degrees in anthropology, and felt that the formation of the Council for Museum Anthropology in 1974 might contribute to breaking down their isolation from anthropological colleagues.

However, unlike Sturtevant, for whom the community of scholars in the Alexandrian Mouseion represented the museum ideal, Lurie found her classic roots in the "peripatetic education" of Aristotle—accompanied, perhaps, by as many of the nine muses as could be lured back into the museum. Rather than seeing exhibition as a potential intrusion "on the time and support for curator's research," her primary concern was "the kind of paring down to basics needed for effective exhibits" (1981: 185; cf. Sturtevant 1969:645). Working in the Milwaukee Public Museum, which (along with the National Museum of Anthropology in Mexico City) had been the site of the latest in six major advances in "anthropological exhibit techniques" listed by Sturtevant (643–44), Lurie was an advocate of the "now widely copied 'Milwaukee style.'" It featured "color, light, sound effects, open dioramas with unobtrusive 'natural' barriers rather than glass fronts, and exhibits the public actually enters . . .[along with] miniature dioramas and attractive specimen groupings to . . . stave off 'museum fatigue'" (Lurie 1981:184). The Milwaukee style had only slightly lengthened the nine to fifteen second attention span which the first time-and-motion study of museum visitors discovered back in 1924 was the average for a single exhibit (Alexander 1979:165); Lurie gave a figure of thirty seconds. Nevertheless, the Milwaukee style well exemplified the "new museum technology" which, even against the great inertial force of all those objects long in situ, was having revolutionary impact in the museum world.

Technology, however, is not the only recent revolutionary force. Like other elite cultural institutions of the later nineteenth century (cf. Harris 1981), museums have felt the impact of major social and political changes in the twentieth—slowly at first, but with increasing momentum in the last several decades. True, recent demographic studies (at museums in Milwaukee, Toronto, Albany, Washington, Belfast, and Dundee) suggest that—despite General Pitt Rivers' agricultural laborers and Franz Boas' urban mechanics—museum audiences are today predominantly white, upper-middle-class, and above average in education (Alexander 1979:166–67). But since the late 1960s others—specifically, the non-European "others" whose objects have traditionally filled exhibit halls and cases—have come forward as actors in the world of museum anthropology.

The emergence of new national consciousnesses in the aftermath of the colonial era, during a period of heightened domestic radicalism in the centers of Euro-American power, called into question the traditional relationship of objects and others in the museum environment. Both the physical ownership of objects and the right of representing their meaning became issues of contention. For anthropologists in the United States, these came to the fore in 1970 in the controversy between the New York State Museum at Albany and the Onondaga Indians (and other militant Indian supporters) over the rightful ownership of Iroquois wampum belts. Reacting perhaps to the closing off of field sites by new nations critical of the colonial involvement of social anthropology, and reflecting the heightened consciousness of ethical issues in the human sciences generally, many nonmuseum anthropologists took a stand "in favor of returning 'native property.'" On the other hand, museum anthropologists, appealing to the role of their institutions in preserving the "material heritage" of native peoples from destruction, were concerned that "great collections might be dismantled and lost to scholarly use and public instruction" (Lurie 1981:186). Although that fear has not been realized, the issue of the repatriation of cultural property has been the subject of international concern since the 1970 UNESCO convention on the prohibition of its illicit transfer (Tymchuk 1983). No longer is it possible for museum anthropologists to treat the objects of others without serious consideration of the matter of their rightful ownership or the circumstances of their acquisition—which in the colonial past were often questionable (cf. McVicker 1984).

It is not, however, simply a question of the ownership of "cultural property," but also of who should control the representation of the meaning of the objects in the Western category, "material culture." Although it may appropriately be regarded as an "invention" of modern Western culture, the museum is no longer exclusively a Euro-American preserve. Non-European others, both in postcolonial "new nations" and within the Euro-American sphere, have established museums of their own—as witnessed in the United States by such institutions as the Seneca-Iroquois National Museum, or more generally by the Association of American Indian Museums founded in 1979. While it seems likely that their mode of representation, like that of Western anthropological museums (cf. Jacknis, in this volume), will be governed largely by pragmatic considerations, the outcome should not be prejudged. Certainly, in Western museums there has been some rethinking of problems of representation. Not only radical critics, but establishment museologists now raise questions about the situation of non-European others along with animals and plants in museums of natural history, or their segregation from the rest of world history in museums of ethnography (Sturtevant 1969:642–

43). Increasingly, Western museologists are calling into question the romantic exoticism that has in fact motivated much of anthropological museology; increasingly, they have insisted on the need to represent the problems of present day life in the Third World (Ave 1980; Reynolds n.d.).

Despite these changes over the last several decades, the issue that most concerned Sturtevant—the role of the museum in anthropological research—seems little closer to positive resolution than it did in 1969. Lurie estimated that only 240 of the more than 5,000 individuals listed in the American Anthropological Association's *Guide to Departments of Anthropology* for 1980–81 were "actually employed full-time in museums." And among the many aspects of anthropological inquiry covered by about 200 articles in the *Annual Review of Anthropology* during the last decade, only two (Plog's "Analysis of Style in Artifacts" in 1983 and Silver's "Ethnoart" in 1979) dealt with topics close to museum anthropology. Recent writers on museum anthropology seem more concerned with issues of exhibition and popular education than research; while noting optimistically that the "concept of museums as static institutions" with essentially archival responsibilities is being replaced by a "dynamic" approach reflecting "contemporary concerns," a recent evaluation of museums of human history predicts that "original scholarly research will continue to decline, except in selected institutions" (Reynolds n.d.).

On the other hand, some of the "revivifying" factors that Sturtevant identified in 1969 are still potentially operative. Although the demographic explosion in the anthropological profession was soon thereafter perceived more as threat than promise, this very fact reflected the increasing sense that anthropology had entered a phase in which the unexamined optimism of its "classic" period could no longer be taken for granted. Ethnographic field work in the mode of participant observation may continue for some time to be the hallmark of anthropological inquiry; but the changing circumstances of the "others" who have traditionally been its subject/object, and their changing relationship to the European world, have already changed the character of field work and reduced its relative importance. Although sociocultural anthropology has not since 1969 been reoriented to issues of evolutionary development and material base, there are indications that its rehistoricization may be under way (cf. Fabian 1983). In this context, the privileged position of observational evidence seems likely to be modified. The rediscovery of the textual mode has already begun, and it seems not unlikely that objects—conceived in symbolic as well as material terms—may become important to other anthropologists besides archeologists. A small sign of that development is the recent appearance of the journal *Res: Anthropology and Aesthetics.* "Dedicated to the study of the object, in particular cult and belief objects and objects of art," it is published by the doyen of American anthropological museums: the Peabody Museum of Archaeology and Ethnology.

Although the present volume has achieved a certain thematic unity, there are many aspects or ramifications of our topic that remain here unpursued. We would have liked an article that would treat systematically the development of Western notions about the "object," and about the objects of "others"—the idea of the icon, or the fetish, or the respective relations of "savage" and of "civilized" man to the material world. We would have liked an article on the actual processes of collection of objects, and on the recent movement for their repatriation. We would have liked to be able to treat other alternatives within museum anthropology, including the continental Volkskunde tradition, or its modern congener, the museums of erstwhile "native" peoples. We would have liked to explore other modes of "displaying humankind," including the anthropology of world's fairs and of modern touristic cultural performances. And we would have liked to have an article reflecting more directly the modern radical perspective on all these issues. At the very least, however, the essays here on "Museums and Material Culture" may help to open discussion on some of the broader issues implicated in the relation of "Objects and Others."

Acknowledgments

Aside from the editor, the editorial board, the contributors, and the staff of the University of Wisconsin Press, several other individuals and organizations facilitated the preparation of this volume. The Editor's efforts were sustained in part by a fellowship from the John Simon Guggenheim Memorial Foundation. A continuing grant from the Wenner-Gren Foundation for Anthropological Research, Inc. supported editorial expenses. The staffs of the Department of Anthropology (especially Kathryn Barnes), the Morris Fishbein Center for the History of Science and Medicine (Elizabeth Bitoy) and the Social Science Division Duplicating Service of the University of Chicago provided necessary assistance. Charles Stanish served as editorial assistant; Martha Lampland translated an article from Hungarian; Ira Jacknis and Neil Harris offered bibliographic advice; Françoise Weil, of the Museé de l'Homme, was especially helpful in obtaining some of the pictures. Our thanks to them all.

References Cited

Alexander, E. 1979. *Museums in motion: An introduction to the history and functions of museums.* Nashville.

Ave, J. 1980. Ethnographical museums in a changing world. In W. R. van Gulik et al., *From field case to show case: Research, acquisition and presentation in the Rijksmuseum voor Volkenkunde, Leiden,* 11–28. Amsterdam.

Cannizzo, J., et al. 1982. Old images/new metaphors: The museum in the modern world. Transcript of three programs of the Canadian Broadcasting Company, November 29–December 26. Toronto.

Cole, D. 1982. Tricks of the trade: Northwest Coast artifact collecting, 1875–1925. *Can. Hist. Rev.* 63:339–60.

Daniel, G. 1943. *The three ages: An essay on archaeological method.* Cambridge.

Fabian, J. 1983. *Time and the other: How anthropology makes its object.* New York.

Foster, S. 1984. Appropriating the primitive. Draft manuscript.

Harris, N. 1981. Cultural institutions and American modernization. *J. Lib. Hist.* 16:28–47.

Hodgen, M. 1964. *Early anthropology in the sixteenth and seventeenth centuries.* Philadelphia.

Hofer, T. 1973. A Neprajzi Muzeum tudomanyos es muzeologiai kapcsolatai [The Scientific and museological aspects of the ethnographic museum]. *Negrajzi Ertesito* 55:73–86 [with German translation].

Lurie, N. 1981. Museumland revisited. *Human Org.* 40:180–87.

McVicker, D. 1984. Exploring, collecting, and expeditioning: Frederick Starr in Mexico, 1894–1904. Unpublished typescript.

Mullaney, S. 1983. Strange things, gross terms, curious customs: The rehearsal of cultures in the late Renaissance. *Representations* 3:40–67.

Plog, S. 1983. Analysis of style in artifacts. *Annual Rev. Anth.* 12:125–42.

Reitlinger, G. 1963. *The economics of taste. Vol. 2. The rise and fall of objet d'art prices since 1750.* London.

Reynolds, B. 1982. Material culture: a system of communication. Address, South African Museum, Cape Town.

———. n.d. Museums of human history in contemporary society. Draft manuscript.

Silberman, N. A. 1982. *Digging for God and country: Exploration archaeology and the secret struggle for the Holy Land. 1799–1917.* New York.

Silver, H. 1979. Ethnoart. *Annual Rev. Anth.* 8:267–308.

Sturtevant, W. 1969. Does anthropology need museums? *Procs. Biol. Soc. Washington* 82:619–50.

———. 1973. Museums as anthropological data banks. In *Anthropology beyond the university,* ed. A. Redfield, (Procs. So. Anth. Soc. 7), 40–55.

Tymchuk, M. 1983. The repatriation of museum collections: An annotated bibliography. Typescript. St. Albert Place Museum, St. Albert, Alberta, Canada.

ARRANGING ETHNOLOGY

A. H. L. F. Pitt Rivers
and the Typological Tradition

WILLIAM RYAN CHAPMAN

In the history of anthropology, the name Pitt Rivers is indissolubly linked to a museum, and to the "evolutionary" principle of its organization—which like the name, was specified in the terms of a bequest.[1] Augustus Henry Lane Fox adopted the name Pitt Rivers in 1880 to fulfil the requirements of the will that made him master of a 25,000 acre estate. Four years later it was stipulated by Deed of Gift that the museum at Oxford University to which he gave that new name (along with his ethnographic and archeological collection) would retain his system of arrangement during his lifetime and be-

1. This article is based on research first presented in my Oxford doctoral dissertation (Chapman 1981). Pitt Rivers, unfortunately, left few records of his early life, and he destroyed many of his papers in old age. Many biographical details, therefore, must be reconstructed through judicious reference to military records, remarks in his published work, correspondence preserved in the papers of other figures or institutions, as well as the records of the scientific societies to which he belonged (see under "Manuscript Sources"). There is of course considerable biographical information in Thompson 1977, as well as in Blackwood 1970, Gray 1905, Penniman 1946, Thompson 1960 and 1979, and Tylor 1917. For biographical material on the other individuals mentioned, consult the *Dictionary of National Biography* and other standard sources. For a more complete bibliography and further documentation on all matters referred to, see Chapman 1981. Pitt Rivers' most important papers were collected after his death in *The Evolution of Culture* (PR 1906); but I have cited the original essays. Despite the slight anachronism involved, I have referred throughout this essay to its central figure by his adopted surname; readers consulting bibliographic entries by him prior to 1880 will of course find the author listed as A. H. Lane Fox.

William Ryan Chapman received his doctorate in anthropology at Oxford in 1982. He is employed by the United States National Park Service as a Historian in the Cultural Programs Office of the Mid-Atlantic Regional Office in Philadelphia. His current research includes further work on British anthropology and a study of Caribbean vernacular architecture.

15

yond—except for such changes in detail that might be "necessitated by the advance of knowledge" and did "not affect the general principle originated by the donor" (Oxford U. Gazette 5/13/84, p. 449).

The origin of the Pitt Rivers' collections and their principle of arrangement, as well as the development and fate of his ambitious plans for an anthropology based on their study, have yet to be adequately investigated. The distinction is commonly made between adherents of the so-called "geographical system" and those of the "comparative" or "typological" scheme, with the one strain leading in a predictably whiggish course to the field-intensive and geographically specific social and cultural anthropology of the early twentieth century, the other meandering on to the empty, armchair theorizing of late Victorian "evolutionism." But the picture is not wholly accurate, nor does it do justice to the complexity of the issues at hand. Nineteenth-century preoccupations with arrangement did not relate so straightforwardly to particular theoretical stances as later anthropological critics or historians of anthropology have tended to assume; nor was the relation of anthropology to museums unproblematic even in the so-called "museum age." Some of these complexities may perhaps be illuminated by a closer look at the career of Pitt Rivers and his collection.

From Muskets to Boomerangs in the 1850s

Stimulated, apparently, by the Great Exhibition of the Works of Art of All Nations, Pitt Rivers first began to collect objects of a broadly ethnographic kind around 1851. At the time he was a young military officer, assigned to testing the new rifles then being introduced to replace the older, smoothbore muskets. Struck by the "continuity observable" in small arms development, he began a collection of weapons to show their "slow progression" of development over time (PR 1888:826). That rifles were the result of slow advances in technology was in fact a standard historical view. Henry Wilkinson, with whom Pitt Rivers worked after he was assigned to the Hythe School of Musketry in 1853, had (among others) argued that early "missile weapons" developed from slings progressively through spears and other forms down to the military technology of the present age—a sequence which Pitt Rivers sketched in a training manual published in 1854, as well as in a lecture of 1858 (Wilkinson 1841; PR 1854, 1858).

Despite his developmental interest, Pitt Rivers' collection tended to emphasize the exotic rather than the antique. Supporting his wife and growing family largely on his army pay, he could perhaps more easily afford ethnographic objects, which were available in various port cities and some London shops—and could be obtained from friends returning from abroad. From an

General A. H. L. F. Pitt Rivers, F.R.S. Photograph by W. E. Gray from a life-size oil painting by Frank Holl, R.A., 1882 (reference number B1452Q, courtesy of the Pitt Rivers Museum, Oxford, and G. A. Pitt-Rivers).

early point in his collecting, he tended to emphasize two rather different organizing principles: one based on a "connection of form"; the other based on functional affinities (1874a:294). Series of the first type were the more ambitious: a typical early instance was his collection of boomerangs and throwing sticks, arranged to show "slow gradations" from straight to curved shapes (1883a). Other series, such as those on "primitive locks and keys," were organized by function or use (1883b); their status as "links in the chain of progress" depended on more general comparative considerations, rather than relationships of form (1858:455).

During the Crimean War, Pitt Rivers took advantage of his overseas service (which took him also to Malta, Turkey, and Bulgaria) to extend his collection. When a further tour of duty at Malta ended with severe criticism of his training methods, he returned to London in 1858. The next four years of enforced semiretirement from the military were largely filled by scientific activities. The Stanley family, into which he had married, was widely connected in the world of science. Through the Stanleys, Pitt Rivers already knew or soon met John Stuart Mill, the geologist Joseph Prestwich, the physicist John Tyndall, and the anatomist Richard Owen. (Mitford 1939; Russell & Russell 1937).

His first important organizational involvement was the United Service Institution, founded in 1831 "to foster the desire of useful knowledge" among the military (RUSI 1831). Pitt Rivers relied on the Institution's library for his own research, and regularly attended its lectures; his own lecture "On the Improvement of the Rifle" was the second one to be included in the journal the Institution began to publish in 1858. That same year he played an important role in the Institution's reorganization into five departments—one of them, which became the focus of his own activity, devoted to ethnography and antiquities (RUSI 1858). One of the most prominent features of the Institution was its museum, which included an ethnographic gallery among its displays of the progress of military technology (Altham 1931:235; Bosque-cillo 1849). Built up over the years chiefly through the donations of servicemen returning from posts throughout the empire, it was, in Pitt Rivers' words, "one of the best assortments of semi-civilized and savage weapons that are to be found in this country, or perhaps, in any part of the world" (1867b:612).

Pitt Rivers used his Institution connection to enlarge his collection wherever possible. He borrowed examples from the Institution's boomerang series to make copies for his own, and when the Institution decided to clear out some of its less essential exhibits beginning in 1861, he was one of the principal buyers (Chapman 1981:99; 593). He acquired other pieces from the members and guests of the Institution—returning military men, veterans of the Indian Mutiny, West African explorers, consular officers from South

America, etc. Among these acquisitions was the collection of John Petherick, consul in the Sudan during the 1850s and 60s, each piece of which was very well documented (Petherick 1860). From that time on, Pitt Rivers made a special effort to obtain objects from those who had actually come in contact with the exotic peoples who had manufactured them, rather than relying on shops and auction houses.

Early in 1859, Pitt Rivers' scientific interests took a more deliberate turn, when he joined the Royal Geographical Society—having been proposed by two Stanley family friends, the traveler/orientalist Henry Rawlinson and the Society's longtime president Sir Roderick Murchison (Mitford 1939; Rawlinson 1898). The new scientific connection was variously useful. In the Society's meeting rooms he encountered returning travelers, from whom he secured new objects for his collection—most notably from Richard Burton (another Stanley connection), who had just returned from West Africa. His sponsor Rawlinson offered advice on Middle Eastern antiquities, and provided notes for drawings and facsimiles (PR 1874b:175). The Society's library stimulated a wide range of geographic and ethnographic readings, which helped to contextualize the pieces in his collection. And it was through the Society that he established a network of contacts, both around the world and closer to home. Notable among them were Richard Dunn (an authority on Eskimo pieces) and the Quaker prehistorian, Henry Christy (whose ethnographic collection was to rival that of Pitt Rivers in the history of Victorian anthropology). Through these men and others, Pitt Rivers was to become increasingly involved in ethnological circles after 1860.

The Impact of Evolution and the Turn to Ethnology

Beyond his specific collecting interest, Pitt Rivers was clearly a committed scientific amateur—a typical member of what has been called the "scientific generation" (Buckley 1951:183). He was an avid reader of popular scientific works, open to new fashions in scientific and philosophical theory. Given his interest in the history of technology, with its implied emphasis on human inventiveness and the transmission of knowledge, he was especially interested in the development of the human mind. Through Mill's *Logic*, Lewes' history of philosophy, and the translations of Harriet Martineau, he seems to have been strongly influenced by Auguste Comte; Herbert Spencer was known to him personally, and phrases derived from Spencer's articles and books can be found sprinkled throughout Pitt Rivers' writings of the 1850s and 60s (PR 1858: 1861; 1867b; 1868a; 1869). His burgeoning family stimulated an interest in education, and in more general writings on the nature of man— including Locke, the Scottish philosophers, and the physiologist William

Carpenter (1854). The most notable of these was perhaps the phrenologist Charles Bray, who published books on education and human mental progress (1838; 1841). Pitt Rivers applied Bray's theories to his own family, as well as to his interpretation of human mental development (Russell & Russell 1937:121); the "nomenclature of phrenology," as Pitt Rivers phrased it, helped provide a unifying view for his writings on his collections (1867b).

In this context, it is not surprising that the publication of Darwin's *Origin* in 1859 had an immediate impact on Pitt Rivers. Like many of his Stanley relatives, he seems to have followed the controversy surrounding its publica-tion, and to have identified himself closely with the Darwinian camp (Russell & Russell 1937:72–73). He attended a number of popular lectures on Darwin during the 1860s, and clearly saw his own work as generally parallel; from that period on he portrayed his collecting efforts as equivalent to those of naturalists, and to Darwin's work in particular. Just as natural history collec-tions conveyed the order and evolution of the natural world, so his collection showed a parallel evolution within the realm of human technology. He later had a tendency to say that Darwin's work was simply confirmation of his own "principle of continuity."

Another pivotal influence in this period was the revolution in archeol-ogy—as embodied particularly in the work of the French archeologist Boucher de Perthes (1847–64; 1860; Daniel 1976; Laming-Emperaire 1964). Although De Perthes' work in the Somme Valley went back to the 1840s, it was only after 1858, after the discoveries in Brixham Cave in Devon and the findings of the British delegation to Abbeville, that it was given general cred-ibility (Evans 1859; Prestwich 1859). The realization that the span of man's life on earth could not be encompassed by the biblical chronology or inter-preted in the light of the biblical record had a sudden and often traumatic impact—in Pitt Rivers' case, the force almost of revelation (cf. Haber 1959). Just as Darwin had demonstrated the gradual nature of species change, the "long ridiculed discoveries" of De Perthes proved "the continuity of man's technical and intellectual development" by "the same laws which have been in force since the first dawn of creation" (1867b:614). Both Darwin and De Perthes confirmed Pitt Rivers in the belief that the world was somehow sub-ject to precepts beyond the scope of human intervention: the "great law of nature" was the final, determinant cause of all things. Having grown up in conventional religious belief, from the early 1860s on Pitt Rivers became a devoted evolutionist.

His conversion to evolutionism had an important impact on his other scientific activities, broadening the scope of his involvements considerably. He began attending lectures at the Geological and Zoological Societies, sub-scribing to their journals and extending the range of his readings. In all he read and heard, he looked for evidence of "the principle of continuity," and he tried to apply that principle more rigorously to his work, and particularly to his collection. New series were developed, including an important one on ornamentation, demonstrating an "unconscious selection" in the choice of ornamental motifs. Other series were refined by the addition of new objects to fill gaps and better convey the evolutionary message.

In the early 1860s, Pitt Rivers began also to seek a new audience for his collection, which until then had been essentially personal. Although he had used the weapons series in training soldiers under his command, it was no longer used for instructional purposes, except for an occasional lecture, usually at the United Services Institution; and the newer series had never been presented publicly. But in the aftermath of Darwin and De Perthes, his sense of purpose was to change.

The main focus of Pitt Rivers' hopes for his collection was the Ethnological Society of London, which he joined in 1861—attracted, perhaps, by the presence of other members of the Geographical Society, including his brother-in-law Henry Stanley and Henry Rawlinson, as well as military men such as C. H. Chesney, an authority on the history of firearms, whose work Pitt Rivers had drawn on (Chapman 1981:174, 616). At the time Pitt Rivers joined, the Ethnological Society was experiencing a period of profound reappraisal. Founded in 1843 as an offshoot of the Quaker-dominated Aborigines Protection Society, its underlying theoretical concern had long been the question of unity (monogenesis) or plurality (polygenesis) of the human species. For many of the early members, the issue was as much moral as scientific, rooted as it was in biblical assumption. Their general approach to the problem had been historical, in the sense that it sought to trace the existing races of mankind back through a history of migration and differentiation to a common root, on the basis of similarities of physical type, culture, and above all, language—with comparative philology, the queen science of the human disciplines, providing a model of genealogical development and a method for reconstructing it. When the biblical chronology was finally undercut in the late 1850s, confidence in the traditional ethnological approach was considerably eroded. With the gradual loss of many early members, and its sense of moral mission, the Society for a time almost ceased meeting altogether. But after 1859—partly as a result of the impact of Darwin and De Perthes, partly as the result of the activism of certain newer, younger members taking a more deterministic view of race—the Society began to grow again, its membership jumping from 50 to over 200 within a single year. Most of the new members, including Pitt Rivers, were interested in the new theories of evolution and the controversy surrounding man's antiquity and origin; but they were also very much interested in racial differences, and their implications for understanding human history—a tendency that was also to be reflected in Pitt Rivers' thought about the objects in his collection (cf. Stocking 1971).

At the time Pitt Rivers joined, however, the Society still lacked a unified program. Philology, which had offered the hope of reconstructing the history of mankind within a relatively short chronology, had largely collapsed as a programmatic tool with the greatly expanded timespan established by the new "prehistoric" archeology (Crawfurd 1863). A purely descriptive approach to race failed to answer questions of man's origins and differentiation, and the traditional appeal to the effects of environment had also been called into question (cf. Stocking 1971). Newer, more tangible types of evidence seemed called for. For some, these were the evidence of skeletal and cranial forms, either as measured or uncovered from the ground; for others, the evidence of archeology more generally; but for Pitt Rivers, the privileged evidence was to be that based on the comparison of artifacts.

Until Pitt Rivers and a number of other artifact-oriented members became active, the Ethnological Society had shown little interest in museums or in collections of exotic implements. What was later called "material culture" was treated simply as an aspect of physical description—clothing and ornament being subsumed with other attributes distinguishing different "races" (Hector & Vaux 1861). There had been no real attempt to develop a unified theory of technological development or systematically to relate the study of artifacts to the broader historical aims of ethnology. There had been some effort to encourage the development of a national ethnographic collection: the reorganization of the British Museum's collection of Natural and Artificial Curiosities in 1845 as an "Ethnological Gallery" was in part a response to suggestions by ethnologists such as Robert Latham and Ernest Dieffenbach (Dieffenbach 1843; King 1844). But the Society had never tried to establish a collection of its own, nor had it particularly encouraged "demonstrations" of artifacts at meetings, as was common among antiquarian and other scientific organizations.

Even so, the Ethnological Society did provide Pitt Rivers with new opportunities for collecting. Through Warren Edwards of the Niger Campaign, and Owen Stanley of HMS Rattlesnake, Pitt Rivers enlarged his West African and Pacific series (1874b:86, 127, 130, 149, 178). And during the period of his greatest activity, in late 1861 and early 1862, there were in fact several lectures featuring object presentations (Snow 1861; Spottiswood 1862). The most important of these for Pitt Rivers was that of Edward Belcher "On the Manufacture of Works of Art by the Esquimaux," which Belcher had studied in the early 1850s while commanding the search for the ill-fated expedition of Sir John Franklin. In addition to his Eskimo artifacts, Belcher's collection included many from the South Pacific and the Pacific Northwest, which he had visited during previous voyages. His lecture emphasized modes of manufacture and use—many of his harpoon and arrow points had been formed by natives in his presence, with chert taken in situ, using tools he then purchased. In a characteristically "ethnological" vein, Belcher conjectured a series of connections among the peoples represented in his collection, suggesting a regular commerce between western North America and the Pacific Islands (1861).

Pitt Rivers acquired forty of Belcher's artifacts; but more importantly, he seems to have borrowed from Belcher the notion that the manufacutures of modern peoples could be taken as evidence of common origin (1867a, 1874b:48). If the surviving artifacts of ancient man could be brought to reveal a previously obscure history—as archeologists were now proving—then so too could the artifacts of modern aboriginal races be brought together to reveal their often common histories. Through the "persistence of forms," as Pitt Rivers later phrased it, one could show that disparate peoples possessed common traits, and thus reestablish their past connections. Alongside his developmental, evolutionary interest, this more traditional "ethnological" concern was to become a major impulse behind Pitt Rivers' future efforts at enlarging and interpreting his collection.

"Geographical" and "Typological" Collections, c. 1860

Although motivated by traditional ethnological as well as by evolutionary concerns, the organizing principles of Pitt Rivers' collection did contrast sharply with those of other collections in Britain. The only large public ethnographic collection was that of the British Museum, which by this time had sixty-two cases devoted to ethnography (BM 1859). The core collection of Sir Hans Sloane was catalogued simply as "Miscellanea," but later eighteenth-century additions from the South Seas were grouped together; and when the South Seas Room was reorganized in 1808 to "illustrate particular Customs of different Nations," a de facto "geographical system" was established (BM 1808; cf. Braunholtz 1953). By Pitt Rivers' time, many of the objects were in poor condition; some had already been discarded because of deterioration (Miller 1973:41–48). Although other sectors of the Museum—notably the Department of British and Medieval Antiquities, under the supervision of A. W. Franks—had begun to burgeon in the 1850s, the effect was for a time to shift space and curatorial attention away from ethnographic materials (Clarke 1843–56). Pitt Rivers himself described the British Museum as an "ethnological curiosity," suggesting that it was in a "molluscus state of development"; as a research tool in a place of educational value, he felt it was "useless" (1874a:296; 1888:827).

In looking for models of ethnographic presentation, Pitt Rivers was better served by museums in other countries. There were important ethnographic collections in Berlin, Cologne, Frankfurt, Dresden, and Paris (Bahnson 1888; Farrington 1899; Murray 1904; Schasler 1868); but the largest and most significant was that of the Rijksmuseum voor Volkenkunde at Leiden, which incorporated the large personal collection of antiquities and curiosities given to the Dutch nation by the diplomat, traveler, and geographer P. F. B. von Siebold (Frese 1960; Wittlin 1949:140–41; Hudson 1975:52–55). All of these collections were known to Pitt Rivers by the early 1860s, who frequently made facsimiles of original pieces he saw in other collections. In later years he was to criticize the British government for not keeping up with governments and cities elsewhere in establishing an important central ethnographic museum (1888; 1891).

Most of these collections, too, were arranged according to place of origin. Insofar as this arrangement was systematically justified, the rationale was established by Siebold, whose scheme for a museum of modern "curiosities" (supplementing long-standing European collections of classical and national antiquities) set a precedent for ethnographical museums founded in mid-century. Following Siebold's example, the Leiden collection was arranged according to what were considered racial or cultural groupings—a method which, according to Siebold, gave the best impression of a "people's relative progress," "the condition of their arts," and the nature of past exchanges with other peoples (Siebold 1843). Siebold's scheme came to be known to Pitt Rivers and others as "the geographical system"; but in Siebold's hands, it was less an organizational tool than a means of reconstructing man's past, and as such was particularly salient to Pitt Rivers' interests. Whether he visited the collection is unrecorded, but Siebold's well-known work on Japanese arms was an important reference when he began his own collection of Japanese pieces (1874b:126).

The most carefully considered alternative to the "geographical system" was that propounded by E. F. Jomard. As conservator of the King's Library in Paris from 1828 on, Jomard had the responsibility of both the older royal collections of curiosities and the newer collections of exotic materials filtering into the national collections from the various exploratory voyages of the early nineteenth century (Hamy 1890). During the next few years Jomard devoted his attention to their reorganization, receiving support first from the Geographical Commission of Baron Georges Cuvier, and then from the Société Ethnologique de Paris—both of which had hopes that the ethnological collections, then housed in the upper floors of the Louvre, might form the core of a major museum. Jomard's "Plan d'une Classification Ethnographique" suggests a number of parallels to Pitt Rivers' later scheme (Jomard 1845; cf. 1831). Apparently influenced by Cuvierian comparative anatomy, Jomard

favored a comparative system of "classes," "ordres," "espèces" and "varietes"—
the first including ten functional categories (food, clothing, building materials, etc.), the next two divided by type of activity (agricultural tools, weapons, etc.; weapons of the chase, weapons of war, etc.); only the last introduced a geographical criterion. Although Jomard's scheme was never
implemented (Jomard 1862), it was known to ethnologists in Britain, and
Pitt Rivers must have met Jomard while making facsimiles at the Louvre.
Whether Jomard's ideas served him as a precedent is uncertain; by his own
account they merely gave support to a system he arrived at independently
(Chapman 1981:212, 628).

One of the few collections actually to embody an alternative to the "geographical system" was that of the German antiquarian Gustav Klemm, who
had begun to collect ethnographical and archeological pieces in the 1830s.
Klemm's collection was organized typologically; drawing parallels between
archeological and ethnographic pieces, it was intended to demonstrate a sequence of development in technology (Penniman 1965:61–62). His scheme
had been published in *Werkzeuge und Waffen* (1858), which was widely referred to by ethnologists and antiquarians in the 1850s and 60s (cf. Klemm
1843–52). Pitt Rivers himself cited Klemm's writings frequently, and took
illustrations from them to supplement his own series (1870; cf. Myres
1944:5–6). But although Klemm's publications suggested various avenues of
approach, as Pitt Rivers freely acknowledged, his basic principles of arrangement were probably arrived at independently.

If continental museums provided important exemplars, the most immediately relevant reference point for Pitt Rivers in the early 1860s was the collection of Henry Christy, his colleague in the geographical and ethnological
societies. Like Pitt Rivers, Christy had begun collecting around the time of
the Great Exhibition (Braunholtz 1953:90–93; Edwards 1870:697–99). Although his attention focused originally on Middle Eastern antiquities,
Christy traveled widely in Africa, Asia, and America during the 1850s, before becoming actively involved in prehistoric archeology at the end of the
decade (Christy 1863; Christy & Lartet 1875). During the early 1860s, the
two men were frequently at the same auction sales, occasionally bidding
against each other for the same items. They frequently exchanged pieces,
and offered each other advice on arrangement and organization. When
Christy's collection was left to the British Museum after his death in 1865,
Pitt Rivers continued to consult it in Christy's apartments, where it remained
housed until 1883; and as with other collections, he made a number of facsimiles for his own series.

Pitt Rivers was always careful to insist on the difference between their
approaches: "in the Christy collection the arrangement [is] geographical,
whereas I have from the first collected and arranged by forms" (PR

1874b:xiii). A catalogue prepared for Christy in 1862 by C. L. Steinhauer of the Danish National Museum generally confirms this assessment (Christy 1862). The collection was then divided into two major sections: "Antiquities" and "Ethnography"—the former divided into "early," "later," and post-Stone Age tools; the latter, into geographical regions (Greenland, the "Caribes," the ancient Peruvians, the ancient Mexicans, the modern Mexicans, the Eskimo, the North American Indians, etc.). But notwithstanding Pitt Rivers' characterization, Christy's goal was explicitly comparative, and he did allow for thematic considerations—including a special series entitled "War Weapons, and implements used in hunting, fishing and navigation." And when Pitt Rivers himself began to acquire more antique weapons, it is evident that Christy's collection was a stimulus.

The special character of Pitt Rivers' collection, however, reflected the fact that it was in the first instance one of comparative technology, not prehistoric implements. Even after he added prehistoric remains, the typologically organized ethnographic series remained the core; his purpose was not simply to help fill in an incomplete archeological series, but to offer a comparably effective historical tool for the study of the material culture of present exotic peoples.

Archeology and Race in Ireland

In the 1860s, Pitt Rivers' own scientific interests were, however, to turn increasingly to archeology. The prolonged inquiry into his training methods having ended with his exoneration, he resumed active military life in August 1862, when he took up appointment as Assistant Quartermaster General in the Cork Division of Ireland. Although he had done a bit of digging earlier on, and was friendly with a number of archeologists, his first formal involvement in archeology began that fall, when he witnessed a number of excavations in Cork, acquiring pieces for his own series (Thompson 1977:39–40). The following spring he was actively recording field sites; he went on to excavate a number of "raths" or Iron Age forts (PR 1866). He also became active in local antiquarian circles, joining the Royal Cork Institution and the Kilkenny and Southeast Archaeological Society, predecessor to the Royal Society of Antiquaries of Ireland—at the same time that his connections with ethnologists and geographers in London were necessarily curtailed.

In this context, developments in prehistoric archeology took on much greater salience for Pitt Rivers. He had been previously familiar with the "Three Age" system developed by the Danish antiquaries early in the century, and had typically listed objects in his collection in the categories "stone," "bronze," and "iron" (Hermansen 1941; Daniel 1943; Birket-Smith 1952; PR

1874b:v–viii). After 1865 he began also to employ John Lubbock's division of stone tools into palaeolithic and neolithic (Lubbock 1865). But his Irish experience underlined the importance of such an approach: what had been simply an organizational system became a means by which history could be rewritten. The same thinking, in turn, was applied to his own collection.

At this time, the most important archeological collection in Ireland was that of the Royal Irish Society in Dublin (Armstrong 1920). Organized during the early nineteenth century, and reorganized by George Petrie in 1853, the collection was taken over by Sir William Robert Wills Wilde, a local physician/antiquarian (and father of Oscar). Stressing that a strictly chronological arrangement was not possible, Wilde divided the collection into broad categories based on materials, roughly approximating the Danish scheme, with further subdivisions into subsidiary groups on the basis of use. Within this context, he adopted, as had Jomard, a natural history model, categorizing objects "according to Class, Order, Species and Variety" (Wilde 1857–63).

Pitt Rivers, who visited the Museum in 1862, was later to adopt a similar terminology, and there are many other similarities both in the details of his categorization and his modes of display. But although he frequently referred to Wilde in his publications, it is not clear to what extent it was a matter of defining or simply of confirming his orientation. Wilde did show how a system derived from the natural sciences could be applied to materials traditionally treated in a less rigorous manner; but it is clear that Pitt Rivers was already interested in organizing his collection this way before he came to know of Wilde's work. At the same time, it seems likely that Wilde's system did provide ideas for Pitt Rivers, especially for the new archeological series.

In 1863, Pitt Rivers was elected to the prestigious Society of Antiquaries in London—his nomination having been supported by Henry Christy and John Evans (Mitford 1939; Evans 1956). The following year he was elected to the Archaeological Institute, an organization founded and still led by his wife's uncle, Albert Way. Occasional trips to London allowed him to attend meetings, meet other antiquarians, and renew acquaintances with geographers and ethnologists.

In part as a result of his excavations, which turned up human remains as well as artifacts, Pitt Rivers became increasingly concerned in this period with the study of skeletal remains, and with questions of race—although as we have already seen, problems of racial migration and origin had interested him for some time. Following speculations earlier advanced by Belcher, he wrote several papers conjecturing that ancient races represented in Irish archeological sites were identical to present-day Eskimos (1866; 1867a). Starting in 1862, he gradually began to add skulls and other skeletal remains to the other materials in his collection, and attempted to establish a series of representative types—relying on the advice of Richard Owen, the preeminent British authority on human morphology, on William Flower, Owen's assistant in the Natural History Department of the British Museum, and on John Thurnam, a physical anthropologist in the Ethnological Society (PR 1867b:412; 1874b; Owen 1853–55; Flower 1898). Pitt Rivers never attempted to form a comprehensive anatomical series, contenting himself with casts and drawings to supplement his other materials. Nevertheless, craniological evidence became more important to his work.

Pitt Rivers' experience in Ireland left him with a slightly different attitude toward racial questions. He had long been interested in problems of race and development, and both his phrenological and Darwinian readings reinforced the interest. But he obviously felt the impact of his direct experience of Irish life, which seems to have reinforced a typically stereotypical view of the Irish as socially and intellectually inferior. Comparing Irish skulls and those of Australian aborigines and higher primates, he viewed the Irish "race" as occupying a low point in a hypothetical developmental hierarchy (1874b). These attitudes were reinforced by his activity as a military officer. During the autumn of 1865, he was appointed Prosecuting Officer for three noncommissioned officers charged with mutiny for their participation in the Fenian movement. Pitt Rivers saw the issue in racial rather than political or economic terms: Fenianism was "a war of the races," and social unrest in Ireland was due to "the social ethical and psichological [sic] condition of the people" (Chapman 1981:246, 637). Increasingly, Pitt Rivers was to view race in his anthropological work as a determining element in human progress.

From the Ethnological Society to the Anthropological Institute

By the spring of 1866, Pitt Rivers was reestablished in London, where he began a second period of semiretirement from the military on half pay. Resuming his involvement with the ethnological and geographical societies, he also participated actively in the Society of Antiquaries and the Archaeological Institute. He became better known to archeologists, including Evans, John Lubbock, A. W. Franks (with whom he had some dealings when transfering inscribed stones from Ireland to the British Museum [PR 1866; Franks 1867]), and J. L. Westwood, an authority on Irish art and ornament. Within the ethnological community, Pitt Rivers' contacts were also becoming more diverse. Through Albert Way he was introduced to George Rolleston, the Linacre Professor of Anatomy and Physiology at Oxford, a fellow Yorkshireman and veteran of the siege of Sevastopol, who was interested in skull types and cerebral development, and assisted Pitt Rivers in a number of excavations (PR 1868b; 1881). Equally important was Thomas Huxley, Hunterian Professor at the Royal College of Surgeons, and author of the first major evolutionary statement on *Man's Place in Nature* (1863), whose speculations on the representative value of modern races for understanding ancient ones also formed a central theme of Pitt Rivers' ethnological thought (Huxley 1865). By the late 1860s it is clear that Huxley's Australian Aborigines had supplanted the modern Eskimos in Pitt Rivers' imagination as the "best representatives of primeval man." Through his earlier innovative work at the Museum of Practical Geology, Huxley was also the exemplar of the popular scientific teacher (Bibby 1959).

Huxley's model may have helped to redirect Pitt Rivers' own museum efforts. By this time, his collection had begun to take over his home—especially after he reclaimed pieces that had been placed in storage during his stay in Ireland. He continued to buy original pieces from travelers and at auction sales, and to supplement these with facsimiles. E. B. Tylor, who had come to know him by this time, later said that Pitt Rivers' collection extended from the basement to the attic of his home, with labelled objects displayed on walls and cabinets in all the principal rooms (1917). When properly introduced, those who were interested were allowed to view the collection on appointment; but on these terms it could scarcely have the impact of a museum open to the public.

Outside his home, Pitt Rivers played an increasing role in the promotion of museums as an ideal. Especially after Christy's death, he helped out Franks at the British Museum, playing a role in Franks' reorganization of the prehistoric collection beginning in early 1866 (Franks 1870). Franks and Pitt Rivers also collaborated on exhibits at the Society of Antiquaries, encouraging that organization to increase its commitment to the promotion of archeological collections, especially at the British Museum. Increasingly, Pitt Rivers established himself as the leading expert on archeological and ethnological collections. In the spring of 1869, he was the main force behind a series of special exhibitions held at the Museum of Practical Geology (Chapman 1981:308–9). But although he was an active organization man in the Society of Antiquaries, the Archaeological Institute, and the Ethnological Society, he did little to promote his own collection to museum status—perhaps because he still sensed a lack of receptivity in these more traditional scientific societies.

Seeking therefore to extend the scope of his own involvement, he became active in this period in the Anthropological Society of London, which he had joined in 1865, while still in Ireland. The "anthropologicals" had split off from the Ethnological Society in 1863, opposing what their leader James Hunt regarded as the latter group's conventionality on a variety of issues— including Hunt's definition of anthropology as a science that would recognize man as one (or many) species in the animal world, his attempt to link science and racialist political ideology, and his insistence on excluding women from frank discussions of sexually related topics (Stocking 1971; cf. Burrow 1963). Displaying a skeleton in the window of their meeting rooms, and calling themselves to order with a gavel in the shape of an African's head, the "anthropologicals" were somewhat disreputable mavericks in the scientific world; their leader Hunt was also, on what he regarded as scientific grounds, anti-Darwinian. Even so, their program had a certain scientific appeal, especially at a point when traditional ethnological orientations seemed no longer adequate, and Pitt Rivers was not the only Darwinian to maintain a dual allegiance. He shared the "anthropologicals'" broadranging scientific goals, and to some extent their views on racial issues, especially with regard to the Irish. And in the absence of clear support for his museological ambitions among the "ethnologicals," he would have been particularly attracted by Hunt's emphasis on the importance of collections as research tools, and his desire that the Anthropological Society should assist the British nation "in forming [an ethnographic museum] that shall be worthy of the country" (Hunt 1863:13; 1864:xcv).

The Anthropological Society, however, did not turn out to be the vehicle for achieving Pitt Rivers' goals. He gave several papers, displayed pieces from his collection, helped on several special exhibitions, and was active for a time in the leadership—serving on the Council and even being approached by Hunt to serve as president for 1868 (Chapman 1981:278–81). By that time, however, the lines between the two organizations had sharpened, and Pitt Rivers' commitment to the "anthropologicals" had become more hesitant. Refusing Hunt's offer, he was to play a leading role with Huxley on behalf of the "ethnologicals" in the struggles and negotiations leading to the formation of the Anthropological Institute of Great Britain and Ireland in 1871 (Chapman 1981:334–41). Although it came quickly under the control of erstwhile "ethnologicals," the Institute reflected the broadened conception of anthropology which was simultaneously the goal of the "anthropologicals" and the logical outcome of the Darwinian Revolution. But, despite the fact that Pitt Rivers himself was later to serve four years as its President, the Anthropological Institute served no better than its predecessors in achieving the institutionalization of his collection.

Primitive Warfare and the Evolution of Culture

Pitt Rivers' conception of his collection and his hopes for what a comprehensive research institution and museum might accomplish are best revealed in a series of three lectures on "Primitive Warfare" he delivered in June of 1867,

1868, and 1869 to general audiences (including anthropologists, archeologists, and ethnologists) at the United Service Institution. The first (PR 1867b) focused on the relationship of man and nature, and the way in which early tools and weapons were gradually developed in unbroken continuity from natural forms by a process of "unconscious selection." Governed by the same instincts—Pitt Rivers, reflecting Bray's phrenology, listed "alimativeness," "amativeness," and "combativeness"—men shared with animals a number of basic defensive and offensive mechanisms, and many of their weapons derived directly from animal forms (antlers serving as piercing weapons, turtle shells for shields, etc.). From these beginnings, however, each weapon could be shown to have a "history of its own," independent of the intentions of its makers, and reflected in its formal development (619).

Pitt Rivers' basic metaphor—common to both Darwinians and ethnologists—was that of the tree, with present races "taken to represent the budding twigs and foliage" (PR 1867b:615). The main stem led up to European man: "civilization" was "confined to particular races, whose function it has been, by means of war and conquest, to spread the arts among surrounding nations, or to exterminate those whose low state of mental culture rendered them incapable of receiving it"—as witness the fate of the Tasmanians (616). But contemporary aborigines, surviving in a state of "arrested development," could serve as living illustrations of those from which they sprang, "whose implements are found low down in the soil" (618). Just as a comparison of languages had been used to determine recent historical relationships among races, so could a comparison of artifacts establish more distant connections. Boomerangs and throwing sticks would serve the role of words; given their more substantial character, they were in fact truer tests of race. On such a basis, the whole history of the world could be reconstructed.

The second lecture (1868a) moved forward in that history to the stone age, dealing more systematically with the method of its reconstruction. Pitt Rivers focused now on the processes of change, emphasizing "variation" (e.g., through "errors in successive copies"), the countless unconscious adaptations involved in each advance, and the way in which forms were generated from similar forms that preceded them, or were still in use (404–5). He then undertook to reconstruct the course of technological development by examining particular historical sequences, using examples from his own collection and that of the Institution. Thus one section was devoted to the "Transition from Celt to Paddle, Spear, and Sword Forms" (437): pointing to close resemblances between the simplest polished celts and the ornate paddles found throughout the South Pacific, Pitt Rivers suggested that the latter were derived from the former, just as the boomerang, throwing stick, and parrying shield were also derived from a common prototypical form. Aside from his emphasis on formal criteria, there was another dimension of his

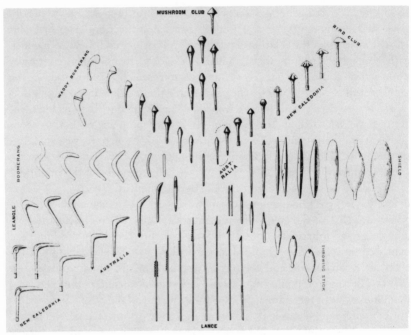

"Clubs, Boomerangs, Shields and Lances," an illustration from *The Evolution of Culture*, 1875 (reference number 2747B, courtesy of the Pitt Rivers Museum, Oxford).

argument worth noting: finding the same basic weapons distributed throughout the lands bordering on the Indian Ocean, Pitt Rivers was willing to apply his principle of continuity to ethnological as well as evolutionary purpose, arguing that it proved an underlying identity of race throughout the area (416–20).

The striking aspect of the third lecture is in fact its emphasis on historical, ethnological themes as well as what are commonly thought of as evolutionary ones (1869). Treating more systematically the association of the boomerang with specific races, Pitt Rivers noted the fit of his own earlier speculations with Huxley's recent argument that all the peripheral peoples of the Indian Ocean belonged to a single "Australoid" race—isolated near its primal state on the Australian continent (436; cf. Huxley 1870). He then turned to the "origin and development of metal tools," attempting to settle the dispute as to whether bronze tools had been independently reinvented, as some recent prehistorians were inclined to argue, or diffused from a single center, as more traditional antiquarians had held (PR 1869:516). Arguing by analogy to the issue of "polygenesis" and "monogenesis" of the human race, Pitt Rivers suggested that while the knowledge of metal production itself may have been established independently, the more refined techniques of admixture had been passed from one nation to another (520–21).

Embellishing it with conceptual and rhetorical flourishes from Herbert Spencer (who was the principal influence on his thinking after 1870), Pitt Rivers further elaborated his viewpoint in several later lectures (1874a), culminating in a general review of "The Evolution of Culture" (1875). But the basic rationale for his collection had been established by the late 1860s. Unified by the principle of continuity, or modification by small gradations— which could under some circumstances lead to degeneration instead of progress—it was essentially an approach to the classification of material artifacts in terms of criteria of external form. Progress, as he put it in 1874, was "like a game of dominoes—like fits onto like [and] we cannot tell beforehand what will be the ultimate figure produced by the adhesions; all we know is that the fundamental rule of the game is *sequence*" (1874a:307–8). From a broader perspective, however, his study might be called a "psychology of the material arts": what he sought to establish was "the sequence of ideas by which mankind has advanced from the condition of the lower animals." Writing to Tylor in the early 1880s, he argued that the value of his arrangement was not so much what it showed about the development of tools and weapons, but rather what it showed by analogy about the development of other "branches of culture which cannot be so arranged in sequence because the links are lost and the successive ideas through which progress has been effected have never been embodied in material forms, on which account the Institutions of Mankind often appear to have developed by greater jumps than has really been the case" (Chapman 1981:480).

The Institutionalization of Typological Arrangement

Although he continued to be involved in the activities of the Anthropological Institute, there is evidence to suggest that Pitt Rivers was somewhat discouraged by the reception of his museological ideas; after 1870, his interests turned increasingly to archeological field work. In 1873, he returned to active military service, partly in the hope that he might yet achieve the retirement pay of a lieutenant general, partly because a country posting would provide greater opportunities for archeological field work. His withdrawal from London raised the question of the disposition of his collection, which by this time included more than 14,000 pieces. Aware that the executors of Gustav Klemm in Leipzig had decided to open Klemm's collection— which was organized on similar principles—to the public, Pitt Rivers took steps to transfer his own to a museum (Chapman 1981:368–71).

In doing so, however, he did not wish to abandon his control, not only of the system of arrangement, but of the objects themselves, insofar as he might wish to add to, consult, or even to repossess them. He chose therefore the South Kensington Museum, which had a long tradition of taking collections on loan, and seemed likely to be amenable to his wishes (Chapman 1981:372–73). The collection officially opened in the new branch museum at Bethnal Green in the summer of 1874, with Pitt Rivers on hand to deliver a public lecture reiterating his "Principles of Classification" (1874a). Although the installation exemplified the newest ideas in display, the collection was relegated to the basement, and by 1878, when he returned to London, Pitt Rivers had pressed the South Kensington authorities into transferring it to the main museum building (Chapman 1983:188).

Actual authority for the collection remained curiously ambiguous. Technically, it was still Pitt Rivers' property, temporarily on loan. At the same time, it was in a real sense already in the public domain, subject to interpretation and revision by the South Kensington staff—although Pitt Rivers continued to exert an influence, through the periodic addition of new materials, and suggestions for different series, or for changes in display. Later complaints by Pitt Rivers suggest that disagreements were rather common; in late 1879 the parliamentary Council on Education, which oversaw the museum's educational work, informed him that he would have to give the Museum complete control if the collection was to continue on display there (Chapman 1983:190).

Early the next year, however, Pitt Rivers' inheritance of great fortune (and the name by which he has since been known) changed dramatically the framework of negotiation. He quickly let the South Kensington authorities know that he planned greatly to extend his collections, and was anxious to provide for them a more permanent foundation. For the time being, he needed "nearly double the space" he now had, and he offered to pay for a curator, if the Council on Education would accede to his other demands. In response, the Council appointed a special committee, chaired by John Lubbock, to consider the offer. It is evident from Pitt Rivers' correspondence with A. W. Franks that both were concerned about the collection's relation to that of the British Museum—which had previously delegated the care of Christy's collection to a sixteen-year-old custodian, and was in the process of absorbing it into the general ethnographic collection. Franks was in fact prepared to oppose the establishment of a permanent ethnographic collection in South Kensington, expressly on the grounds that it would compete with Bloomsbury. Pitt Rivers insisted that if he could not get more space at South Kensington, he was prepared to build his own museum: "if the nation will not accept my offer now on account of . . . rivalry between the two departments . . . I had rather leave everything to the United States" (where the Smithsonian Institution had recently established a National Museum, which was in fact to be organized along lines similar to those of Pitt Rivers' collection) (Chapman 1983:192–93).

After a compromise was proposed by which the collection would remain at South Kensington, but be attached to the British Museum, the special committee offered terms which satisfied Pitt Rivers' desire to retain control: although specimens were to become government property after six months, no part of the collection would be sold during his lifetime, or loaned without his permission, and he remained free to add to it or take from it at will, as well as to make such suggestions for the rearrangement of series as he saw fit. But when the Council on Education finally got around to deciding on the committee's proposal a year later, the whole negotiation was undercut: while they were anxious that Pitt Rivers' collection "should become the property of the nation," the Lords were not willing to establish a second permanent ethnographic collection in competition with that of the British Museum (Chapman 1983:194–96).

Although Pitt Rivers continued to add new materials to the South Kensington collection, by the end of 1881 the authorities there began to grow impatient. Preoccupied already with the management of his new estate, Pitt Rivers was reluctant to commit himself to building his own museum; instead, he turned toward the universities, which had been accepting private collections since the founding of the Ashmolean Museum at Oxford two hundred years before. Although Pitt Rivers apparently first thought of Cambridge, the fact that it had just taken steps to found its own archeological museum turned his attention rather to Oxford, where his recently deceased friend and collaborator George Rolleston had been a staunch advocate of scientific studies (Chapman 1983:197–98).

Toward the end of March 1882, Henry Moseley (naturalist on HMS Challenger, and Rolleston's successor as Linacre Professor) wrote to Franks stating that Pitt Rivers had offered his collection to the University. To help him persuade University authorities to accept, Moseley asked Franks, along with John Evans and E. B. Tylor, to provide documents for presentation to the Hebdomadal Council. So armed, Moseley made the offer to the University in late April 1882, under directive from Pitt Rivers as to the conditions, which were similar to those offered to the South Kensington. The University would be required to accept the collection as it was presently arranged, and he was to have the final say over its disposition until his death—although he no longer insisted on being allowed to borrow pieces at will. Moseley's efforts were successful, and on May 30, 1882, the Vice-Chancellor of the University delivered the Council's opinion that the offer should be accepted, and that £7,000 should be expended to build an annex at the east end of the existing University Museum. Although no formal stipulation was included for a lecturer, the Council felt that the museum could not "but prove useful in an

Henry Balfour in the upper gallery of the Pitt Rivers Museum, ca. 1890 (reference number B2219Q, courtesy of the Pitt Rivers Museum, Oxford).

educational point of view to students of Anthropology, Archaeology, and indeed every branch of history" (Chapman 1983:198–203). The terms of the gift were agreed to by all parties in May, 1883, and the University seal was formally affixed to the Deed of Gift a year later. By that time, the University had responded favorably to Pitt Rivers' suggestion "that a lecturer shall be appointed by the University, who shall yearly give lectures at Oxford upon Anthropology" (Oxford U. Gazette 5/13/84, p.449). E. B. Tylor, who in 1882 had written to Pitt Rivers about the possibility of lecturing at Oxford, and who had the following year been appointed Keeper of the University

Museum, was now given the added title of Reader in Anthropology (Chapman 1981:477, 481, 483).

Typological Museums for the Savants and the Masses

Tylor, like Pitt Rivers, learned to fashion stone tools, and had previously included chapters on material culture in his *Researches into the Early History of Mankind* (1865). By this time recognized as Britain's premier student of *Primitive Culture* (1871), he was in principle eminently suited to lecture on the collections. But material culture was in fact a secondary interest for him, and from the beginning much of the actual responsibility for setting up and managing the collections devolved on other men: notably Moseley, who had been given charge of the University's "ethnological collections" in 1882, and who was assigned to supervise the transfer of the Pitt Rivers materials from London (Chapman 1981:472, 488). Actual work on the construction of the building did not begin until 1885; for economic reasons it was staunchly utilitarian in character, and much smaller than required.

In the summer of 1885, Moseley and Tylor, with the assistance of Walter Baldwin Spencer (then a young research student in zoology and later to become an anthropological authority on Australian Aboriginals), supervised the packing of the collection in preparation for its transfer from South Kensington (Chapman 1981:489). Until the new wing was completed, the collection was stored in empty rooms in the University Museum and other buildings. To assist in the unpacking and eventual rearranging, Moseley selected a second research student, Henry Balfour, who was put to work that summer cataloguing the collection as it arrived, designing labels, and arranging objects on screens and in cases (490). He also handled the transfer of the ethnographic materials from the Ashmolean, including the famous Cook collection donated by Johann Reinhold Forster—which was "distributed throughout the Museum in accordance with its arrangements by subjects" (Blackwood 1970:11; PR Museum n.d.). Although much of the original Pitt Rivers collection had been put into place by the late 1880s, its opening to the public was delayed, as Balfour continued to work on labels, to revise series as new materials were added, and to work on the proposed catalogue (a task he never completed). While Pitt Rivers provided occasional advice on individual series, he left the management to Moseley and Balfour (who was at first "sub-" and then "assistant-" and finally in 1891, full "Curator") (Chapman 1981:493–95). Pitt Rivers did, however, occasionally admonish Moseley and Tylor that the work was going too slowly, and in 1888 his growing impatience came sharply to the surface.

The immediate cause of his annoyance was a visit to Oxford in the spring

of that year. He found much of the collection still not unpacked, and many
of the series changed from those originally proposed by him—although still
conforming to the general plan. He was not impressed with Balfour, and he
was upset that Tylor's lectures were focusing increasingly on problems in religion and mythology, rather than on the material culture studies they had
been instituted to promote (Freire-Marreco 1907). His irritation grew when
Balfour suggested in a paper "On the Structure and Affinities of the Composite Bow" (1889) that nothing had been previously written on the subject.
Outraged, Pitt Rivers demanded that nothing further be published on the
collection until he was through "publishing on it" himself. Balfour, following
Tylor's advice, concealed his own annoyance; but from that point on relations
between Pitt Rivers and those managing what was once his collection remained strained (Chapman 1981:518–24).

In the meantime, Pitt Rivers returned to his own archeological work,
which had largely preoccupied him since he acquired the estate in Dorset-
shire. His house there was virtually surrounded by remains, and shortly after
taking possession he started a series of excavations that were to become the
subject of his four volume *Excavations in Cranborne Chase* (PR 1881–98).
Through his work as Inspector of Ancient Monuments—a title Lubbock had
helped win for him in 1880—he was also involved in recording field remains
at other sites, including Stonehenge and Avebury (Chapman 1981:454–64).
Politics attracted his attention for a short time in the late 1880s; and much
of his time was involved in the daily affairs of county life and the management
of his vast property (509–17).

His museum interests also took a different direction. His new wealth made
it possible to collect on a much wider scale; yearly expenses that used to total
a few pounds now exceeded £1,000—including collections of paintings,
Chinese vases, and other Fine Art pieces, as well as a collection of folk
objects built up in the course of his travels as Inspector of Ancient Monuments. Beginning in 1883, Pitt Rivers had begun to assemble some of his
new acquisitions, along with a few series never transferred to Oxford, in a
new museum "calculated to draw the interest of a purely rural population ten
miles distant from any town or railway station." Set up in four rooms of an
abandoned school house on his estate, the museum at Farnham included an
archeological series, agricultural implements, folk costumes, and early pottery—all arranged by the "typological method" to illustrate the progress in
each art (Buxton 1929). By 1890, there was also a restored medieval building
known as "King John's House," a game park full of exotic animals, Sunday
concerts by his "private band," and a variety of pavillions for the use of visitors, who by then exceeded 15,000 annually (PR 1888: 1890; 1894).

In 1888, and again in 1891, Pitt Rivers restated what might be called his
"museum ideal." In his presidential address to the anthropological section of

the Bath meeting of the British Association, he called for the establishment of a national educational museum of arts organized as a "giant anthropological rotunda"—concentric circles being peculiarly adapted for "the exhibition of the expanding varieties of an evolutionary arrangement" (1888:828). Elaborating a theme he first articulated in the 1870s when his collection was put on display in the working class district of Bethnal Green, Pitt Rivers argued the need for a truly popular museum—or, as he put it in 1891, "an educational museum"—as well as one of "reference" or "research" (1891:115). The nation had thought it proper "to place power in the hands of the masses," whose ignorance of history lay them "open to the designs of demagogues and agitators." Fortunately, however, "the law that Nature makes no jumps" could be "taught by the history of mechanical contrivances, in such way as at least to make men cautious how they listen to scatter-brained revolutionary suggestions" (116). While he still insisted also on the virtues of typological arrangement for scholarly purposes, it was clear that Pitt Rivers felt that his museum ideals were better realized at Farnham than at Oxford. Shortly before his death in 1900, he wrote a letter complaining of the work of Tylor and Balfour, and of Oxford in general (Chapman 1983:202). Reflecting on his decision to present his collection to the university, he concluded:

> Oxford was not the place for it, and I should never have sent it there if I had not been ill at the time and anxious to find a resting place for it of some kind in the future. I have always regretted it, and my new museum at Farnham, Dorset, represents my views on the subject much better.

Conclusion

That Pitt Rivers was an "evolutionist" and his collection arranged to illustrate the principles and the course of human cultural evolution is undeniable. But as we have seen, his anthropological thinking was molded in the interaction of a variety of orientations toward several different anthropological issues. Grounded in a practical technological developmentalism, its basic principle was that of continuity of typical form—the development of one technological form from another by small gradations. Under the impact of Darwinism, his thinking took on more explicitly biological overtones, and the temporal range of his developmentalism was greatly expanded: the principle of continuity had now to establish links with the animal world. But Pitt Rivers was also strongly influenced by "ethnological" concerns of a more traditional sort: the attempt to trace all mankind back to a single source and to reconstruct the history of human racial differentiation and interconnection. Typological gradations thus served the purposes of two different kinds of diachronic re-

The main exhibition hall of the Pitt Rivers Museum, ca. 1970 (reference number PR255H, courtesy of the Pitt Rivers Museum, Oxford).

construction: generalized evolutionary sequences and localized historical sequences.

In this context, typological arrangement might in fact take on a sort of "geographical" character, as in Pitt Rivers' diagrammatic gradational arrangements of boomerang forms. Indeed, his later formulations of his museum ideal explicitly attempt to incorporate a "geographical" viewpoint. The concentric circles of his "anthropological rotunda" were designed to illustrate the major phases of evolutionary development: a spot in the actual center was left empty for "the relics of tertiary man, when he is discovered"; the inner-most circle was for the Paleolithic period; the next for the Neolithic, and then on through the Bronze, Iron, and Middle Ages—each larger than the last, because "the increased number of forms would require a larger area"—"until the outer circle of all would contain specimens of such modern arts as could be placed in continuity with those of antiquity." But by cutting the rotunda also into pie wedges, "separate angles of the circle might be appro-priated to geographical areas," and "where civilisations in the same stage of development are allied to one another, they might occupy adjacent angles within the same concentric ring." By following the radii, the "most unin-structed student" could reconstruct the history of any object and "trace like forms to their origin"; where "breaks in the continuity of any art must nec-essarily occur," signs might be posted directing viewers to the spot where "the threads of connection" might be picked up (PR 1891:117).

In the discussion of Pitt Rivers' paper, F. W. Rudler objected that if one walked around the Paleolithic circle, "one would never make any progress," and would actually have to pass "by a jump" to the Neolithic—thus violating the principle of continuity. The solution, Rudler suggested, was a spiral, which might perhaps be constructed in the Albert Hall, if "it could be cleared out" (PR 1891:122). A hundred years later, it is hard to say whether Rudler's tongue was in his cheek. Certainly, some very serious consideration has been given recently to implementing the rotunda idea. Around 1970, a very sim-ilar scheme was developed by the third Pitt Rivers Museum Curator, Bernard Fagg, and embodied by the architect Pier Luigi Nervi in the design of a yet unrealized new building to house the museum's collections, which since its opening had expanded from 15,000 to over a million specimens (Blackwood 1970:10). Although the plan was no doubt developed with an eye to the stipulations of the Deed of Gift, it departed somewhat from Pitt Rivers' ro-tunda. The principle of the geographical pie wedge was retained, as well as the concentric circles; but instead of being devoted to evolutionary phases, the circles were each devoted to objects of a single type, so that the visitor would follow the continuum of types not out along a radius, but around one of the rings. While the principle of typological continuity was thus pre-served, the general effect was to privilege geographical over evolutionary con-siderations—except in the case of certain archeological collections which would be arranged in evolutionary sequence along particular radii (9–10).

At the risk of imposing logical considerations upon the materials of history, one wonders whether Pitt Rivers' ideas of museum arrangement could, with-out compromise, be realized in the real world of museum display. It seems, however, to be historically the case that pragmatic considerations of museum display were in that period impelling both advocates and critics of typological

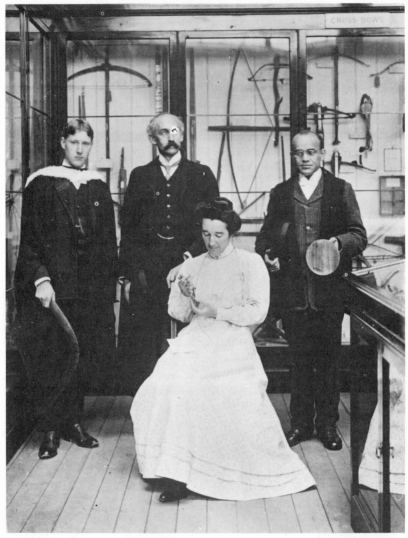

The first anthropology diploma students with Henry Balfour, 1908. *Left to right*: F. H. S. Knowles, Henry Balfour, Miss B. F. Marreco, A. Hadley (reference number B501Q, courtesy of the Pitt Rivers Museum, Oxford).

arrangement toward realistic life figure groupings exhibiting the mode of life characteristic of a particular geographical or cultural region (cf. Jacknis, in this volume).

Among these pragmatic considerations were those of audience response. Despite Pitt Rivers' hopes that typological arrangement might close working class minds to "scatter-brained revolutionary ideas," one suspects that those three hundred local agricultural workers who came to Farnham every Sunday may have been attracted more by exotic animals and band concerts than by typology. Certainly, an important factor in the shift of American typologists to life groups was their popularity with museum visitors. In short, typological arrangement may have been as problematic for the purposes of an educational museum as it was for the those of a research museum.

Nevertheless, despite its problematic character, and the General's disappointment, the Museum to which Pitt Rivers gave his adopted surname survived, and grew. His donation had placed anthropology in Britain for the first time within an academic setting. Tylor's appointment as Reader and later to a personal Professorship helped give the subject scholarly respectability and scientific status. Tylor's lectures were supplemented by those of Balfour on Arts and Industries, and in the 1890s, by those of Arthur Thomson on Physical Anthropology. And when a Diploma in Anthropology was finally introduced in 1907, the first class had its picture taken as a life group in its own academic geographical setting—in front of a display case in the Pitt Rivers Museum.

Acknowledgments

For their assistance at various points of the research and writing, I would like to thank B. A. L. Cranstone, Curator of the Pitt Rivers Museum, Wendy James (my advisor at Oxford), Godfrey Lienhardt, Dennis Britton, the late Beatrice Blackwood, Richard Bradley, Geoffrey Turner, Elizabeth Gunn, Major Frederick Myatt, Malcolm MacLeod, Anthony Pitt Rivers, Michael Pitt Rivers, and my wife Betty Ausherman—as well as all the archivists of the manuscript sources noted below.

References Cited

Altham, E. 1931. The Royal United Service Institution. *J. Roy. United Serv. Inst.* 76:234–45.
Armstrong, E. 1920. *National Museum of Science and Art, Dublin: Guide to the collection of Irish antiquities.* Dublin.

Bahnson, K. 1888. Ethnographical museums. *Arch. Rev.* 2:1–16.

Balfour, H. 1889. On the structure and affinities of the composite bow. *J. Anth. Inst.* 18:220–46.

Belcher, E. 1861. On the manufacture of works of art by the Esquimaux. *Trans. Ethn. Soc. London* 1:129–45.

Bibby, H. 1959 *T. H. Huxley: Scientist, humanitarian and educator.* London.

Birket-Smith, K. 1952. The history of ethnology in Denmark. *J. Roy. Anth. Inst.* 82:115–28.

Blackwood, B. 1970. *The origin and development of the Pitt Rivers Museum.* Oxford.

BM. See under British Museum.

Bosquecillo, ——. 1849. *A visit to the United Service Institution in 1849.* London.

Boucher de Crèvecoeur de Perthes, J. 1847–64. *Antiquités celtiques et antédiluvienes; Mémoire sur l'industrie primitive et les arts a teus origine.* 3 vols. Paris.

——. 1860. *De l'homme antédiluvien et des ses oeuvres.* Paris.

Braunholtz, H. 1953. History of ethnography in the museum after 1753. Pts. I and II. *Brit. Mus. Quart.* 18:90–93, 108–20.

——. 1970. *Sir Hans Sloane and ethnography.* London.

Bray, C. 1838. *The education of the feelings.* London.

——. 1841. *The philosophy of necessity; or the law of consequences; as applicable to mental, moral and social science.* London.

British Museum. 1808–1853. *Synopsis of the contents of the British Museum.* London (successive editions).

——. 1859. *A guide to the exhibition rooms of the departments of natural history and antiquities.* London.

Buckley, J. 1951. *The Victorian temper: A study of literary culture.* Cambridge, Mass.

Burrow, J. 1963. Evolution and anthropology in the 1860's: The Anthropological Society of London, 1863–71. *Vict. Studs.* 7:137–54.

Buxton, H. 1929. *The Pitt Rivers Museum Farnham.* Farnham, Dorset.

Carpenter, W. 1854. *Principles of comparative physiology.* Rev. ed. Philadelphia.

Chapman, W. 1981. Ethnology in the museum: A. H. L. F. Pitt Rivers (1827–1900) and the institutional foundations of British anthropology. Unpublished diss. Oxford Univ.

——. 1983. Pitt Rivers and his collection: The chronicle of a gift horse. *J. Anth. Soc. Oxford* 14:181–202.

Christy, H. 1862. *Catalogue of a collection of ancient and modern stone implements, and other weapons, tools, and utensils of the aborigines of various countries in the possession of Henry Christy, F. G. S., F. L. S., etc.* London.

——. 1863. On the prehistoric cave-dwellers of southern France. *Trans. Ethn. Soc. London* 3:262–72.

Christy, H., & E. Lartet. 1875. *Reliquiae aquitanicae; being contributions to the archaeology and palaeontology of Périgord.* London.

Clarke, H. 1843–56. *The British Museum; A handbook guide for visitors.* London (successive editions).

Crawfurd, J. 1863. On Sir Charles Lyell's "Antiquity of Man" and on Professor Huxley's "Evidences as to Man's Place in Nature." *Trans. Ethn. Soc. London* 3:58–70.

Daniel, G. 1943. *The three ages: An essay on archaeological method.* Cambridge.

——. 1976. *A hundred and fifty years of archaeology.* Cambridge, Mass.

Dieffenbach, E. 1843. The study of ethnology. *J. Ethn. Soc. London* 1:15–26.

Edwards, E. 1870. *Lives of the founders of the British Museum.* 2 vols. London.

Evans, Joan. 1956. *A history of the Society of Antiquaries.* Oxford.

Evans, John. 1859. On the occurrence of flint implements in undisturbed beds of gravel, sand, and clay . . . in several locations both on the continent and in this country. *Archaeologia* 30: 280–307.

Farringdon, O. 1899. Notes on European museums. *Am. Nat.* 33:763–81.

Flower, W. 1898. *Essays on museums and other subjects connected with natural history.* London.

Franks, A. 1867. Account of the additions made to the collections of British antiquities in the British museum during the year 1866. *Procs. Soc. Antiqs. London* 3:435–45.

———. 1870. *Catalogue of the Christy collection of prehistoric antiquities and ethnography formed by the late Henry Christy and presented . . . to the British museum.* London.

Freire-Marreco, B. 1907. A bibliography of Edward Burnett Tylor. In *Anthropological essays presented to Edward Burnett Tylor.* Ed. N. W. Thomas. Oxford.

Frese, H. 1960. *Anthropology and the public: The role of museums.* Leiden.

Gray, H. 1905. *Index to "excavations in Cranborne Chase," "King John's House, Tollard Royal."* Somerset.

Haber, F. 1959. *The age of the world: Moses to Darwin.* Baltimore.

Hamy, T. 1890. *Les origines du Musée d'Ethnographie.* Paris.

Hector, J., & W. Vaux. 1861. Notice of the Indians seen by the exploring expedition under the command of Captain Palliser. *Trans. Ethn. Soc. London* 1:245–61.

Hermansen, V. 1941. C. J. Thomsen and the founding of the ethnographical museum. *National Musees Skifter Ethnografish Raeke* 1: 27–58.

Hudson, K. 1975. *A social history of museums: What the visitors thought.* Atlantic Highlands, NJ.

Hunt, J. 1863. Introductory address on the study of anthropology. *Anth. Rev.* 1:1–20.

———. 1864. Presidential address. *J. Anth. Soc. London* 2:lxxx–xcv.

Huxley, T. 1863. *Evidences as to man's place in nature.* London.

———. 1865. On the methods and results of ethnology. *Fort. Rev.* 1:257–77.

———. 1870. On the geographical distribution of the chief modifications of man. *J. Ethn. Soc. London* 2:404–12.

Jomard, E. 1831. Rapport fait a la Société de Geographie, dans la séance du vendredi, 4 Mars sur la collection de dessins d'antiquites Mexicaines exécutees par M. Frank. *Bulletin de la Société de Geographie* 15:116–28.

———. 1845. *Caractère et essai de classification d'une collection ethnographique.* Paris.

———. 1862. Quelques mots sur l'ethnographie asiatique. *Revue Orientale et Americaine* 8:75–77.

King, R. 1844. Address to the Ethnological Society of London. *J. Ethn. Soc. London* 2:9–40.

Klemm, G. 1843–52. *Allgemeine cultur-geschichte der menscheit.* Leipzig.

———. 1858. *Die werkzeuge und waffen, ihre entstehung und ausbildung.* Sondershausen.

Laming-Emperaire, A. 1964. *Origines de l'archéologie préhistorique en France.* Paris.

Lubbock, J. 1865. *Prehistoric times as illustrated by ancient remains, and the manners and customs of modern savages.* London.

Miller, E. 1973. *That noble cabinet: A history of the British Museum.* London.

Mitford, N., ed. 1939. *The Stanleys of Alderley: Their letters between the years 1851–1862.* London.

Murray, D. 1904. *Museums: Their history and their use.* Glasgow.

Myres, J. 1944. A centenary of our work. *Man* 44:2–9.

Owen, R. 1853–55. *Descriptive catalogue of the osteological series contained in the museum of the Royal College of Surgeons.* London.

Penniman, T. 1946. General Pitt-Rivers. *Man* 46:70.

———. 1953. The Pitt-Rivers Museum. *Mus. J.* 52:243–46.

———. 1965. *A hundred years of anthropology.* London.

Petherick, J. 1860. On the arms of the Arabs and Negro tribes of Central Africa, bordering on the White Nile. *J. Roy. United Serv. Inst.* 4:171–77.

Pitt Rivers, A. H. L. F. [All entries through 1880 appeared under the name of A. H. Lane Fox.]

———. 1854. *The instruction of musketry.* Hythe.

———. 1858. The improvement of the rifle as a weapon for general use. *J. United Serv. Inst.* 2:453–88.

———. 1861. On a model illustrating the parabolic theory of projection of ranges in vacuo. *J. Roy. United Serv. Inst.* 5:497–501.

———. 1866. Roovesmore Fort. *Arch. J.* 23:149.

———. 1867a. Roovesmore Fort, and stones inscribed with oghams in the parish of Aglish, County Cork. *Arch. J.* 24:123–39.

———. 1867b. Primitive warfare. Part I. *J. Roy. United Serv. Inst.* 11:612–43.

———. 1868a. Primitive warfare. Part II. *J. Roy. United Serv. Inst.* 12: 399–439.

———. 1868b. Memoir on the hill forts of Sussex. *Procs. Soc. Antiqs. London* 4:71

———. 1869. Primitive warfare. Part III. *J. Roy. United Serv. Inst.* 13:509–39.

———. 1870. On the use of the New Zealand mere. *J. Ethn. Soc. London* 2:106–9.

———. 1874a. On the principles of classification adopted in the arrangement of his anthropological collection, now exhibited in the Bethnal Green Museum. *J. Roy. Anth. Inst.* 6:293–308.

———. 1874b. *Catalogue of the anthropological collection lent by Colonel Lane Fox for exhibition in the Bethnal Green Branch of the South Kensington Museum, June 1874, Parts I and II.* London.

———. 1875. On the evolution of culture. *Procs. Roy. Inst.* 7:496–520.

———. 1881. On the death of Professor Rolleston. *J. Roy. Anth. Inst.* 11:312–13.

———. 1881–98. *Excavations at Cranborne Chase.* 4 vols. Rushmore.

———. 1883a. On the Egyptian boomerang and its affinities. *J. Roy. Anth. Inst.* 12:454–63.

———. 1883b. *On the development and distribution of primitive locks and keys; illustrated by specimens in the Pitt Rivers Collection.* London.

———. 1887. Presidential address at the Salisbury meeting of the Royal Archaeological Institute. *Wilts. Arch. Mag.* 24:7–22.

———. 1888. Address as President of the anthropological section of the British Association, Bath, September 6, 1888. *Rep. Brit. Ass. Adv. Sci.* 825–35.

————. 1890. *King John's House, Tollard Royal, Wilts.* Rushmore.

————. 1891. Typological museums, as exemplified by the Pitt Rivers Museum at Oxford, and his provincial museum at Farnham, Dorset. *J. Soc. Arts* 40:115–22.

————. 1894. *A short guide to the Larmer Grounds, Rushmore, King John's House, Farnham Museum, and neighbourhood.* Rushmore.

————. 1906. The evolution of culture and other essays. Ed. J. L. Myres. Oxford.

Pitt-Rivers Museum. n.d. *From the islands of the south seas 1773–4: An exhibition of a collection made on captain Cook's second voyage of discovery by J.R. Forster.* Oxford.

PR. See under Pitt Rivers.

Prestwich, J. 1859. On the occurrence of flint implements, associated with the remains of extinct mammalia, in undisturbed beds of the late geological period. *Procs. Roy. Soc.* 10:50–59.

Rawlinson, G. 1898. *A memoir of Major-General Sir Henry Creswicke Rawlinson.* London.

RUSI (Royal United Service Institution). 1831. *Prospectus of the United Service Museum.* London.

————. 1851–69. *Annual Reports.*

Russell, B., & P. Russell. 1937. *The Amberley Papers: The letters and diaries of Bertrand Russell's parents.* New York.

Schasler, M. 1868. *Les Musées Royaux de Berlin.* Berlin.

Siebold, F. 1843. *Lettre sur l'utilité des musées ethnographiques.* Paris.

Snow, P. 1861. A few observations on the wild tribes of Tierra del Fuego from personal observations. *Trans. Ethn. Soc. London* 1:261–67.

Spottiswoode, W. 1862. Sketch of the tribes of northern Kurdistan. *Trans. Ethn. Soc. London* 2:244–48.

Stocking, G. 1971. What's in a name? The origins of the Royal Anthropological Institute. *Man* 6:369–90.

————. 1973. From chronology to ethnology. Introduction to J. C. Prichard, *Researches into the physical history of man.* Chicago.

Thompson, M. 1960. The first inspector of ancient monuments in the field. *J. Arch. Assn.* 3:103–24.

————. 1977. *General Pitt-Rivers: Evolution and archaeology in the nineteenth century.* Bradford-on-Avon.

————. 1979. *Catalogue of Pitt-Rivers papers in the Salisbury and South Wiltshire Museum.* Typescript.

Tylor, E. 1865. *Researches into the early history of mankind and the development of civilization.* London.

————. 1871. *Primitive culture: Researches into the development of mythology, philosophy, religion, art, and custom.* London.

————. 1917. Pitt-Rivers, Augustus Henry Lane Fox. *Dict. Natl. Biog.* 22:1140–42.

Wilde, W. 1857–1866. *A descriptive catalogue of the museum of antiquity of the Royal Irish Academy.* Dublin.

Wilkinson, H. 1841. *Engines of War: Or, historical and experimental observations on ancient and warlike machines and implements, . . .* London.

Wittlin, A. 1949. *The museum, its history and its tasks in education.* London.

Manuscript Sources

Although they are cited in the present essay only indirectly by reference to my doctoral dissertation (Chapman 1981), my research involved extensive consultation of manuscript records and papers, including those of the Anthropological Society of London (Royal Anthropological Institute), the Archaeological Institute, the British Association for the Advancement of Science, Henry Balfour (Pitt Rivers Museum), Christies of London, Henry Christy (British Library), the Ethnological Society of London (Royal Anthropological Institute), John Evans (Ashmolean Museum), the Geological Society of London, the Hebdomadal Council (Oxford University Archives), Thomas Huxley (Imperial College of Science), the Institute of Army Education, the Lane Fox Papers (Leeds City Archives), the Linnaean Society of London, John Lubbock (British Library), the Oxford University Archives, the Perceval Papers (British Library), the Pitt Rivers Museum Archives, the Pitt Rivers Papers (Salisbury and South Wiltshire Museum), the Pitt Rivers Estate (Dorset County Record Office), the Rolleston Papers (Ashmolean Museum), the Royal Anthropological Institute, the Royal Geographic Society, the Royal Institution, the Royal Irish Academy, the Royal Society, the Royal United Services Institution, the Society of Antiquaries, the Salisbury and South Wilts. Museum, the Sotheby Sales Catalogues (British Library), the University Museum (Oxford), the War Office Papers (Public Record Office), and the Way Papers (British Library).

FROM SHELL-HEAPS TO STELAE

Early Anthropology at the Peabody Museum

CURTIS M. HINSLEY

Just after the Civil War, George Peabody, a Salem, Massachusetts, boy who had made a fortune in England in dry goods and the transatlantic trade, made a philanthropic mission to his native land, with the intention of endowing science museums at Harvard and at Yale, and a large fund for education in the conquered Confederacy (Parker 1971:165). At Harvard, his plans were momentarily frustrated by Louis Agassiz, the renowned Swiss geologist who had emigrated to the United States in 1846 (Lurie 1974). Transplanted to New England, where he married into a wealthy Boston family and established himself at Harvard, Agassiz seemed the apotheosis of the Brahmin gentleman scholar: a comprehensive naturalist who was also a broadly educated, urbane humanist. With his great scientific reputation, his institutional entrepreneurship, and his ability to mobilize wealthy patrons in both Boston and New York, he had by the Civil War come to dominate natural science in New England from the precincts of the Museum of Comparative Zoology at Harvard. By the early 1860s, his assurance shaded into arrogance; in 1864, his excessive paternalism and staunch resistance to Darwinian evolution spurred a rebellion among a number of his student assistants, led by the young icthyologist Frederick Ward Putnam, who left Harvard to return to become superintendent of the Essex Institute in George Peabody's native Salem (Dexter 1965; Mark 1980:14–55). When Peabody came to Agassiz a year later with the offer of $150,000 endowment, contingent on the Museum's bearing his

Curtis M. Hinsley teaches American history at Colgate University, and is currently writing a book on the history of anthropology in Boston, 1860–1920, centering on the Peabody Museum of Archaeology and Ethnology. He is also co-curator of an exhibit on the history of photography in anthropology opening at the Peabody Museum early in 1986.

name, Agassiz refused—which may have been a factor in Peabody's subsequent decision to support Agassiz's erstwhile student, Putnam, by endowing the Peabody Academy of Science in Salem in 1867. By that time, however, Peabody had already succeeded also in attaching his name to a museum at Harvard. His nephew, the paleontologist O. C. Marsh, had proposed that it be devoted to American archeology—a science whose links to ethnology (the study of human races) the Darwinian revolution was making ever more salient. Out of this confluence of contingencies was born the first specifically anthropological museum in the United States: the Peabody Museum of American Archaeology and Ethnology (Brew 1968:15).

Archeology and ethnology were not disciplines that excited widespread support in the world of science and scholarship in this period. Ethnology, particularly, had been compromised by its implication in the debates over the unity or plurality of the human species during the 1850s—in which Agassiz had been involved on the polygenist side (Stanton 1960); and when the Smithsonian Institution made American archeology the subject of its first major publication, the reviewer in the *Scientific American* had wondered whether there was not a "better and more profitable way of expending James Smithson's funds" than "collecting broken earthen pots and Indian wallets 'made long before the Flood'" (Anon. 1848). True, by 1866, the newly asserted antiquity of man and the doctrine of his primate origins portended a greatly heightened scientific relevance for American archeology and ethnology. Nevertheless, Harvard's hesitation in accepting the Peabody bequest is evident in a letter President James Walker wrote to Robert C. Winthrop, the chairman of the new museum's board:

> I have always been of the opinion that when a generous man, like Mr. Peabody, proposes a great gift, we should accept it on his own terms, not on ours. Even if we could persuade him to change his plans, and endow some other branch of the University, he would never take the same interest in it, or regard it so much as his own. We had better take what he offers, and take it on his terms, and for the object which he evidently has at heart. The object may not impress the College or the community, at first sight, as one of the highest interest or importance. There may be, and will be, as you say, disappointments in some quarters. But the branch of Science, to which this endowment is devoted, is one to which many minds in Europe are now eagerly turning, and with which not a few of the philosophical inquiries and theories of the hour are intimately associated. It will grow in interest from year to year.
>
> (PMA: JW/RW 10/66)

As a matter of fact, for some decades after accepting Peabody's endowment, the University did relatively little to support either his Museum or its "branch of Science." The battle of museum anthropology for legitimacy and acceptance in nineteenth-century America was part of a major intellectual and cultural shift. For most of the scholarly world, the study of mankind was still a branch of classical, humanistic study, rather than part of the realm of natural science. The Peabody Museum emerged during the transition between the two views, and its first decades reflected the difficulties of institutional and conceptual reorientation. Founded in the shadow of Agassiz's powerful intellectual, social and financial presence in the Boston community, it was caught in the midst of heated local debates over Darwinian evolution. And it faced a strong predisposition in established Boston circles against the worthiness of "primitive" peoples and their artifacts for the moral education of civilized nations. The outcome of such conditions was to give the Museum a marked disadvantage in raising funds and to place its officers in the position of brokering between patrons and fieldworkers, addressing different audiences in distinct voices. The resultant tensions deeply marked museum anthropology in Cambridge.

Classical Civilization and Paleolithic Man: Old World Models for New World Archeology

Perhaps not surprisingly, in view of Peabody's origins, the Museum was marked in the beginning by a strong Salem and anti-Agassiz bias. The first board of trustees included two Peabody nephews—one of whom was soon replaced by Henry Wheatland, the scientific patron of the Essex Institute of Salem—as well as Asa Gray and Jeffries Wyman, the professors of botany and of comparative anatomy at Harvard, and both of them Darwinian opponents of Agassiz. Through *ex officio* members, the Museum was interlocked with the Massachusetts Historical Society, the Boston Society of Natural History, and the American Antiquarian Society in Worcester. But if these relationships brought early collections to the Peabody, its Salem connections somewhat limited its access to Boston finances. While Agassiz's museum had put down deep roots in local soil, the Peabody was from the beginning perceived and treated as an outside institution.

Circumventing Agassiz was at once an intellectual, personal, and financial issue. Peabody had instructed that his museum address "the great questions as to the order of development of the animal kingdom and of the human race, which have lately been so much discussed" (PML:I). In other words, the Museum was expected to enter the evolution debate, where Agassiz' conservatism was well known. Under the circumstances the trustees were anxious to achieve two goals for their enterprise: financial stability and scientific respectability. Judging correctly that they could expect little additional help, Winthrop and treasurer Stephen Salisbury set out to invest their limited funds prudently and spend the proceeds cautiously.

In these matters the choice of the aging, ailing Wyman as the Museum's first curator made a difference. By 1865 the strain of lecturing had become too great for him and he had effectively stopped teaching. By virtue of gifts from family friends, however, Wyman enjoyed an income for life. The museum thus enjoyed its first curator at a discount. On the other hand, while it saved money, the failure (until 1887) to establish a professorial chair in anthropology probably damaged the discipline's image in the Harvard community. The decision was a matter of circumstances, for only Wyman's infirmity, and his absences from Cambridge, prevented him from assuming such a professorship along with the curatorial position. While he did not think it "even probable" that he would become professor in the Museum, in fact the various applicants for the position—Daniel Brinton, Charles Rau, Albert Bickmore among them—were not taken seriously. Winthrop reminded Wyman in 1868 that "I consider [the professorship] *yours* when it is best for you to take it" (PMA: RCW/JW 8/8/68); but Wyman knew that he would never be strong enough to accept. Nevertheless, until his death in 1874 he provided, through his reputation as comparative anatomist and his ongoing shell-mounds archeology, what the Museum most required: a solid scientific foundation.

In contrast to the magnificent material presence of Agassiz, Jeffries Wyman seems almost ethereal, perched precariously on the edge of existence. Historically, indeed, Agassiz has grown larger than life, while Wyman has virtually disappeared. If Agassiz was robust, Wyman was ill and faded; as he migrated southward each winter there was no assurance that the fragile man would return for another spring. Agassiz possessed a massive ego; Wyman seemed to have been born totally without one. Agassiz fought fiercely for scientific status and priority, while Wyman gave away ideas and discoveries for others to use. Agassiz was panoramic in the sweep of his generalization and taxonomy; Wyman lovingly investigated the minute, the exceptional, the individual.

By the time of his death Agassiz had built a major institution; in the summer of 1874, just before his death, Wyman could still be found quietly dusting and ordering his private collections, which filled a single room in Boylston Hall (Wilder 1910:200). "In Dr. Wyman's [Museum] we have an example," wrote Asa Gray later that year, "of what one man may do unaided, with feeble health and feebler means, by persistent and well-directed industry, without éclat, and almost without observation. While we duly honor those who of their abundance cast their gifts into the treasury of science, let us not—now that he can not be pained by our praise—forget to honor one who in silence and penury cast in more than they all" (Gray 1874:15–16).

The contrasts in the careers and contemporary evaluations of Agassiz and Wyman suggest a dichotomy in attitudes toward science as both personal experience and as social institution in mid-century Boston. While both men were valued, the science of Wyman was clearly not the science of Agassiz. Wyman stimulated a flurry of disparate digging and unconnected observations on the kitchen-middens of the New World, most of it intended to demonstrate assumed parallels with an adopted European model of antiquity, and perhaps the existence of an even greater antiquity in the New World (Wyman 1876). In its first few years under Wyman, the Peabody Museum functioned within this paradigm. Buying collections in Europe and supporting modest explorations in North America, the trustees endeavored to establish a comparative program. While they spent thousands of dollars on the foundation materials—notably the Rose, Mortillet, and Clement collections—they saw these outlays as a necessary first step. Eduard Desor, archeologist and Peabody Museum agent in Switzerland, advised Wyman at the beginning of the Museum's first year of operations that the main focus must be on America:

> Do not allow yourself to be mislead [sic] by the consideration, that since the American antiquities are not connected with the classic ages as in Europe, they are therefore less interesting. By no means. The remains of humanity are always and everywhere interesting.
>
> (PMA: ED/JW 1/1/67)

Desor's wise words may have served to guide the early Peabody. After negotiating in Europe for the Wilmot Rose collection in 1868, Winthrop wrote home enthusiastically: "These Danish specimens, with the Mortillet & the Clement, will give us a grand European basis for comparison, & we shall be in a condition to defy all competitors on our own soil, & shall be equal to almost any collection abroad" (PMA: RW/JW 9/10/68). While the Peabody trustees acted decisively, however, they fully appreciated that scientific respectability could not be bought.

Indeed, there were important groups in the Boston intellectual and financial community that remained unimpressed with New World studies, despite Wyman's efforts and those of Putnam, who returned from Salem to Cambridge to succeed Wyman as curator in 1874. Consider, for example, a discussion that took place on May 15, 1880, at the second annual meeting of the Archaeological Institute of America, which already enjoyed a membership of more than 100 Boston gentlemen. Founder-president Charles Eliot Norton and the twenty-six members present listened intently as their guest for the afternoon, Major John Wesley Powell, himself recently the founder of the new Bureau of Ethnology in Washington, made the case for the study of North American archeology. When Powell had finished his account of the Bureau's current and planned work, however, one of Boston's prominent cultural figures, Charles C. Perkins, bluntly challenged the usefulness of such

Jeffries Wyman, taken by Oliver Wendell Holmes, August 11, 1865 (photograph number N31071, courtesy of Ann Wyman and the Peabody Museum, Harvard University).

efforts in America. A trustee of the Museum of Fine Arts, Perkins suggested that American materials would be readily available for some time to come; he urged instead that the Institute concentrate its resources on classical, Old World sites, so that, as he put it, "we may lay our hand upon something to be placed in our Museums."

Francis Parkman, Boston's elder statesman of historical letters, responded that the object of the Institute was to acquire knowledge rather than art objects, and this could best be accomplished in America. But F. E. Parker rose to support Perkins: If knowledge was the true aim of the Institute, "then this knowledge should be *useful* and not *simply curious;* and the knowledge which was useful to us was not that of barbarians but that of cultivated races which had preceded us." Even if we possessed "all the pottery ware, kitchen utensils and tomahawks" the Indians had ever made, "it would be no better for us." In contrast, classical collections would "improve the people and repay expenditure."

Parkman tried again. Mr. Parker, he replied, did not understand the "bearing" of ethnological work. Although "household utensils, pottery ware, etc., were interesting themselves," the study of tribes involved "questions of the greatest importance, the evolution of the human race, its civilization, and many questions of the greatest interest"—to which Parker simply responded that he saw "no reason for beginning the work of the Institute at a point where the civilization was inferior to our own instead of superior."

It was left to Putnam, as curator of the Peabody Museum, to summarize the positions he had heard: "The widest field for the study of Ethnology," he remarked, "is in America, where the study ought to begin; here we have everything of man dating back farther than anything in the old country; we must study the art of these races to find out about their migrations and distribution; if *Ethnology* is the aim of the Institute, then America is the proper field; if *art only* in its highest development" is the aim, then the other side of the ocean was the proper field of operation (AIAP: Minutes of General Meeting 5/15/80). For his part, Powell later commented caustically on encounters with such men when he observed that "our archaeologic institutes, our universities, and our scholars are threshing again the straw of the Orient for the stray grains that may be beaten out, while the sheaves of anthropology are stacked all over this continent; and they have no care for the grain which wastes while they journey beyond the seas." (Powell 1890:652).

As Putnam sensed, the debate between Old and New World enthusiasts in the new Boston institution was no mere choice of geography. It was a question of how best to build museums of mankind, and more generally, how to approach the study of archeology. On the one hand, there was Lewis Henry Morgan, the dean of American anthropologists, arguing in a letter to Charles Eliot Norton, that Grecian and Syrian relics should be left securely buried, while research was directed to "our more humble Indian antiquities" which, "lower in public estimation," were "perishing daily" (AIAP: LHM/CEN 10/25/79). On the other, there was Norton's own feeling that "what we might obtain from the old world is what will tend to increase the standard of our civilization and culture"; and that if "we are ever to have a collection of European Classical Antiquities in this country we must make it now"—since, as Perkins put it, "classic collections are limited in extent and there is a great run upon them" (AIAP: Minutes of General Meeting 5/15/80). The one approach implied building museums by encouraging active collecting by researchers in this country; the other, in the context of available resources of personnel, implied building collections by the purchases of agents abroad. More generally, though, the question was whether archeology was to go forward within the Great Tradition of humanistic scholarship as established since the Renaissance through the fields of linguistics, art, architecture, and archeological reconstruction, looking chiefly to the Mediterranean world. Or was the study of humanity to be more profitably pursued through the younger, vigorous tradition of the post-Darwinian natural sciences—through study of origins, development, and variation of mankind and human cultures over the face of the earth? Colin Renfrew has recently referred to this persistent difference in purpose and perspective as the "great divide" which still separates archeology as classics from archeology as science (Renfrew 1980). But in the Boston context, it was not only a question of research and institutional strategy; it also became a social index and a financial factor.

Culture and Commerce: Moral Education in the Gilded Age

Some of the social and personal factors involved were suggested in a letter written by Putnam to Morgan, telling him more about the man they had to deal with in the Archaeological Institute of America. After identifying Norton as the first professor of art history at Harvard, Putnam added that he was

> also a man of high social function and is rich, with a fine house and large grounds here in Cambridge. So far as I know he has not taken an active interest in American antiquities or ethnology, but he is well up in all that relates to classic art. To my knowledge he has never been inside of the Peabody Museum, and he has not the slightest idea of what I have done or am trying to do there. If you can get him interested in the exploration of the remains of the ancient peoples of America you will be doing a good thing, for he is a man of considerable influence in Cambridge and Boston and he would be well backed up. . . .

> (FWPP: FWP/LHM 1/31/80)

Against the traditional view of Boston cultural decline during the "Gilded Age," some scholars emphasize the efforts of men such as Norton to reassert moral guidance in an increasingly pluralist, democratic, and unmanageable city through "influence" rather than through politics. With such institutions as the museum, library, symphony, and university, Norton was able to avoid the fate of the mere aesthete who indulged in bemoaning the crass tendencies of his age (Green 1966; Harris 1962; cf. Horowitz 1976).

The decline of American gentility was a national phenomenon closely associated with urban growth, immigration, and startling changes in demographic and political balance (Persons 1973). Boston was only one of many variations, but a unique one where constant vigilance against social, financial, and moral slippage had continuously produced investment in art, science, and commerce for the public welfare. Boston began as a garrison of precarious souls; corruption and decline always seemed to threaten from beyond or within.

Since the days of the first Winthrops, New England cultural stability consisted in blending social and religious respectability, financial stability, and political leadership in certain persons and families. The elements were inseparable and presumably inherited. But the immigration, urbanization, and ward politics of the mid-nineteenth century shattered the correspondence of these cultural components, splitting off political power from social prominence. The result was an unhappy condition in which gentlemen were without political issue and men of politics were clearly not gentlemen. Understandably, gentlemen of the post–Civil War generation looked back with nostalgia even as they struggled for moral influence through other means.

The haunting fear was inconsequence—the decline to mere aestheticism, to talking in closed circles among good fellows who intuitively understood. And the danger was great because the temptation to turn away from a tawdry, grasping commercial society to the pleasant companionship of kindred spirits was alluring. To some, the fabric of New England culture seemed to be visibly unraveling, and only men of supreme courage and energy could prevent further shredding. In this effort to hold society together, education was absolutely crucial: the education of social leaders, at Harvard; and the education of the public through schools, museums, and so forth. Theodore Lyman expressed the need to his brother-in-law, Alexander Agassiz, in 1873:

> Just now there is a tidal stream of commercial life which sweeps into itself all the energy and talent of the United States—only here and there is it resisted by men of peculiar temperament or peculiar genius. The state of mind thus induced is so incompatible with that of scientific thought that, when men by success, or through exhaustion, leave commercial enterprise, they are incapable even of conceiving what science is and mistake it—when they try to understand it—for something that will lead to preserved beef, or patent washing fluids. . . . What we must keep trying to do—and what we *have* done very successfully—is to make Harvard College larger and as many sided as possible—that is, to present learning in as many forms as possible
> (AAP: TL/AA 5/4/73)

Lyman's concern for moral education was shared by the men who founded the Archaeological Institute, and who constituted the cultural elite of Boston: Norton, student of Dante and the standard-bearer of high culture; Charles Perkins; Martin Brimmer, wealthy philanthropist, president of the Museum of Fine Arts, world traveler and art collector. Others were Norton's cousin and president of Harvard, Charles W. Eliot; Augustus Lowell; and Henry P. Kidder. As Neil Harris has observed of the board of directors of the Museum of Fine Arts in this period, "this was not a group of idle aristocrats or newly rich entrepreneurs intent on raising their social status through a connection with the fine arts" (Harris 1962:551). To men of Norton's background and education the burden of public enlightenment was tangible and serious, a noblesse oblige that served at the same time, they believed, as the surest route to peaceful, gradual social improvement in community and nation.

The heart of education lay in the teacher as model and the subject matter as inspiration. Together, model and inspiration would elevate the student morally, inculcating a sense of religious awe, artistic appreciation, and manly responsibility—finally creating those elusive qualities of nineteenth century gentility: "character" and "taste." Understandably, in this vision of education as inspiration only the finest, perfect products of human genius had a legitimate place; not surprisingly, they tended to be identified narrowly and ethnocentrically. Why, after all, expose young men and women to the everyday, the mundane, the imperfect? Little use or profit could be gained from such experiences. As Theodore Lyman advised the Harvard president: "A young and learned man, who yet has . . . no belief that one thing is really *better* than another, is one of the most dismal spectacles conceivable." Such a generation would drift the country "Devilward" (CWEP: TL/CWE 6/8/71).

Thus, when Norton, Parker, Brimmer, and others talked of "knowledge" as opposed to "mere curiosity," they had in mind spiritual elevation, an ennobling influence that worked in mysterious ways, through the beholding of the best in human products and instilling similar aspirations in the beholder. "A man who would judge well of foreign people and profit by them, must first study and get his mind solid and muscular, and capable of seeing things as they are, and of comparing them" (CWEP: TL/CWE 6/8/71). It was not a question of science versus art, but a cultural style or approach toward natural and human products. Its scientific equivalent was a form of natural theology: the close, minute study of nature in order to reveal the divine plan and intricate foresight of the Creator. This was only an alternate route to the same goal: religious inspiration and moral improvement of the investigator.

Many American scientists of the nineteenth century voiced such sentiments. Jeffries Wyman made the connection between nature and art to Robert Winthrop in 1874: "I sometimes think that we should stand in the presence of the more attractive scenes of nature as well as works of art, give our whole souls to them, and pass on" (PMA: JW/RW 2/19/74). For Wyman, in fact, scientific and artistic landscapes became indistinguishable as divine poetry. In the culture of these men, science could be art, for they shared a vital characteristic: a pious stance toward the works of God and man. Order, permanence, and stability were the relevant principles. According to this vision, perfection in art and culture made sense. There were high and low points in art and in human history, to be sure, but these were understood as degrees of relative accomplishment toward a single standard.

Charles Darwin had rocked this world of assumptions with a frightening vision of a possibly purposeless universe of chance. If any order were to be found there, it would be statistical, not divine. But while clerics argued vigorously (and often beside the point) against what they perceived to be an atheistic cosmology, among Boston gentlemen the response was less religious than aesthetic; their complaint was against the ugliness of struggle and natural selection. Again, Jeffries Wyman spoke out of personal despair for a whole generation: "This struggle for existence everywhere is an *awful* spectacle—not one perfect form on earth, every individual, from crystal up to man, imperfect, warped, stunted in the fight" (Dupree 1953:245). Darwin, he added, had raised questions that "we had been brought up to consider out of the reach of discussion." On scientific grounds Wyman accepted Darwin's hypothesis as a satisfactory theory. But aesthetically and morally Wyman renounced such an appalling, unlovely vision. If history were nothing more than a process of constant adjustment, of ongoing imperfection, where could one turn for aesthetic criteria or moral standards?

Norton's vision of the cultural mission of education—and, indeed, of archeology—provided an answer:

> Deprived as we are of the high & constant source of cultivation found in the presence of the great works of past ages, there is the greater need that we should use every means in our power to make up for the loss of this influence upon our youth, and give to them so far as possible some knowledge of the place these works hold in history, and of the principles of life & character which they illustrate. We need to quicken the sense of connection between the present generation and the past; to develop the conviction that culture is but the name for that inheritance, alike material and moral, that we have received from our predecessors, and which we are to transmit, with such additions as we can make to it, to our successors.
>
> (CWEP: CEN/CWE 1/15/74)

Brahmin Funding for the Archeology of Indian Shell-Heaps

Although the matter was not posed that way, the problem facing the men of the Peabody Museum was to reconcile such a view of culture with the humbler but more embracive definition being articulated within evolutionary anthropology (Tylor 1871)—or, at a more practical level, to relate their own anthropological collecting to the categories of classical archeology and high art accepted by their potential patrons. It was a challenge to make a con-

vincing case for paleolithic or neolithic artifacts. On his first European buying trip for the Museum in 1868, Robert Winthrop consistently described his
purchases as good "investments" and "perfect" specimens—employing the
phrases of two familiar worlds: finance and art (PMA: RW/JR 8/8/68). But
even if, like Oliver Wendell Holmes, one gave the "ragpickers" of prehistoric
archeology a French disguise—"They delight me, these *Chiffonier* expeditions among the shell heaps of nations, almost as it would to dredge the
Tiber" (JWP: OWH/JW 10/21/68)—it was still difficult to equate the shell-
heaps of Maine, Florida, or even the Swiss Lakes with the ruins of Italy or
Greece. Daniel Brinton managed to remain optimistic that "American archaeology will in time rank equal with that of Egypt and the Orient" (JWP:
DB/JW 4/6/68), but he still expressed disappointment with the cultural status
of Florida shell-heaps.

In truth, North American archeology was a combination of backyard
scrabbling and high aspirations. George Peabody, nephew of the founder,
caught the tone well in starting a letter to Wyman: "My uncle tells me you
have been pitching into some clam heaps . . ." (JWP: GP/JW 5/27/67). And
S. Weir Mitchell left an engaging description of a summer's day spent "raking
over an Indian shell-heap" with Wyman: "bone needles, fragments of pottery
and odds and ends of nameless use went with a laugh or some ingenious
comment into his little basket" (Mitchell 1875:356).

Here lay the foundations of North American archeology. The rhetoric was
revealing. Whether one accepted Darwin entirely or in part, the museum
anthropology of the new Peabody issued a challenge: it was clearly to be a
science of humanity, not a history of art or an institution for the appreciation
of high art. The impact of evolutionary thought on museum anthropology
was precisely to give attention to the everyday, the mundane, and the imperfect. Focus increasingly turned to the many rather than the few, the common
rather than the exceptional, as the keys to cultural understanding. The bulk
of anthropological treasure is mundane; sober deflation of expectations prepared the way for new criteria of cultural evaluation (Hinsley 1981:103).

As essential as such artifacts are to anthropology, they did not in the nineteenth century produce enthusiasm or financial support from either private
sources or Harvard College. Beginning in 1875, Putnam gave countless "parlor talks" in Cambridge and Boston in an effort to raise funds for fieldwork in
New Jersey, Ohio, Tennessee, California, and elsewhere. Typical of Putnam's
perpetually harried state was the following note of 1883 to his Salem mentor,
Henry Wheatland:

> I am now working night and day on my Annual Museum Report and getting
> my collections of the past year in order and cataloguing them for the Report.
> We have never had so much material come in in a year before. I must show it
> off to advantage and speak on it, in order to get further aid for my

expl[orations] next year. I've given a parlor lecture at Mrs. Warren's which I
hope will turn well, as I interested a number of ladies in the work.
(HWP: FWP/HW 1/17/83)

But with the exception of his drive to save Ohio's Serpent Mound—which
had the selling points of romantic aura and largeness of scale—Putnam's
efforts were only moderately successful.

Nor was there much help from Harvard. Rather, the early years were
marked by squabbles over who would pay for heating and lighting (PMA:
CWE/Asa Gray 8/12/75). The Harvard Corporation held the Museum at
arm's length, as Winthrop reported to the trustees in 1885:

> At our last Annual Meeting, I made a statement to the Board in regard to the
> anomalous relation which this Institution seems to hold to the University . . .
> At any rate the President's Annual Report of this year, like that of several
> previous years, does not recognize the Peabody Museum in any form or shape.
> I cannot think such a condition of things just to the memory of Mr. Peabody
> or consistent with the character which the Institution sustains to the Univer-
> sity. I am perfectly sure that President Eliot has no unkind or disrespectful
> intention in this course of absolutely ignoring our Museum. But the result of
> such an omission from the Annual Reports of the President cannot fail to be
> injurious to our interests—as we are not recognized as a worthy department of
> the University, & not brought to the attention of the public as a subject of
> interest.
> (PMA: Minutes of Trustee Meeting 6/12/85)

Over time, Putnam had some success building a small financial base around
the Boston nexus on which Agassiz had so successfully drawn. Between 1881
and 1896, it has been estimated, 90 percent of Putnam's expedition money
came from donations (Casler 1976:7). Prior to 1890, however, Putnam was
unable to tap the established Brahmin sources that had nourished Agassiz's
institution. His trustees were not physically or socially vigorous individuals,
despite their respected names, and Putnam's status did not give him initial
entree to important circles. Origins counted in Boston, and like generations
of his ancestors, Putnam had grown up in Salem; furthermore, his neglect to
obtain even a Bachelor's degree during his years at Harvard with Jeffries Wyman and Louis Agassiz cast a shadow. The Museum trustees waited twenty
years—until 1885—to try to fill the Peabody professorship in anthropology,
and even then Agassiz's son Alexander was able to block Putnam's appointment for still another two years. "You know I don't believe in Putnam's capacity, but he is honest and industrious and an excellent *curator*," Agassiz
later explained to President Eliot—"I only objected to his being made professor" (CWEP: AA/CWE 8/8/94). In numerous ways Putnam showed the
scars of social and professional doubt; though he rarely stopped to rest, the

Museum he headed was by 1890 still only beginning to establish its operations on a firmer ground of local support.

Amateur Archeologists and the Antiquity of Man in America

The social and financial tenuousness of Putnam and his museum of anthropology during the first twenty-five years of the Peabody made a clear imprint on methods, theoretical statements and, especially, on field relationships. Afraid of a misstep, Putnam became a cautious man. Anxious to encourage fieldworkers, he developed at the same time a valuable reputation for insisting on precise, thorough excavation and notation. In 1886 Frank Hamilton Cushing sketched the emerging image of Putnam, and it was one of respectable conservatism:

> His work in the Ohio mounds must take rank as the first of its kind. It reminds one of the patient, detail-loving, even pedantic labors of the Danish, German and French Archaeologists in their shell-heaps, lake-villages and bone-caverns; yet it has more to recommend it than this! In it, there is no pottering over useless detail. While Professor Putnam leaves, literally, no stone—or clod of earth—unturned, unscanned, unfelt even,—he turns no stone or clod of earth uselessly. Above all his merits, however, I deem his absolute common sense the greatest,—always bridling and guiding his unflagging enthusiasm as it does. He has been for years, content to substitute scientific loyalty for sensationalism, and the only complaint made of him so far as I know,—his slowness to take advantage of his discoveries by rushing them into print—constitutes in my humble estimation his best praise.
>
> (FWPP: FHC/A. Hyatt 1/20/86)

But whatever his own reputation for methodological caution and theoretical conservatism, Putnam was at critical points at the mercy of the archeological amateurs who did so much of his fieldwork. In the case of Charles C. Abbott, this was to involve him in the most important disciplinary controversy of late nineteenth-century American archeology: the debate over the antiquity of man on the American continent (Meltzer 1983). For forty years Abbott maintained, in the face of withering ridicule—and with only timorous support from Putnam, whose training under Wyman predisposed him to the view—that he had discovered proof of paleolithic man on and around the Abbott family farm on the outskirts of Trenton, New Jersey.

After receiving an M.D. degree at the University of Pennsylvania in 1854, Abbott practiced medicine only two years before deciding to support his family by writing popular books and magazine articles on nature—a choice that was to mean a life of constant financial shortage. Abbott began sending ar-

Putnam digging in Foster's Earthwork, Warren County, Ohio, 1890. "This will be the standard for all time to come," he wrote of his methods for Ohio archeology to Charles Metz, November 11, 1882 (photograph number N1365, courtesy of the Peabody Museum, Harvard University).

tifacts to Putnam in 1870, when Putnam was still at Salem, and the two men
soon developed a close relationship based on mutual interest and need. Putnam came to view Abbott as his private New Jersey source, while Abbott saw
Putnam's institutional affiliations as a scientific road out of Trenton. When
Putnam moved to Cambridge in 1876, Abbott's loyalty went with him.

By that time, Abbott had already published "The Stone Age in New Jersey" (1872), which marked the beginning of public debate over paleolithic
man in America. Since many of his materials were surface or near-surface
finds, Abbott gave little heed to stratigraphy or geology. He modestly avoided
the issue of the identity of the early New Jersey peoples, content to have
demonstrated a development sequence parallel, he thought, to that of European prehistory. Thus Abbott's introduction to a national audience was re-
strained. Over the next five years, however, changes in both Abbott's ambitions and Putnam's standards, along with public criticism, began to strain
their friendship. Conscious of his new status as curator of the Peabody Museum in Cambridge, Putnam sensed correctly that he was to an extent on
trial. He soon became uneasy with the surface work and the purchased collections that Abbott continued to offer, and he urged his friend to undertake
careful digging. Putnam also became sensitive to Abbott's occasionally dis-
honest methods of obtaining materials, and he feared bad reflections on the
Museum. And as Putnam expanded his geographical scope, paying more attention to Tennessee and Ohio, Abbott's jealousy was aroused:

I thought you would be pleased with what I did the last six months, but as you
were somewhat disappointed, why I will try and do better, by going to "fresh
fields and pastures new." But you must remember that I am not the New Jersey
Indians and it isn't my fault that the cussed red-skins made prettier things in
Tennessee than they do here.
(PMP: CCA/FWP 7/27/78)

Abbott began, too, to feel the constraints of life as a mere collector from
Trenton. He longed to make more profound statements from a more prominent position. At the same time, though, thinking that he had established
New World antiquity, he felt bereft of ideas and purpose, as he confessed on
a dreary Sunday afternoon in the autumn of 1878:

But what of the future? Mere arrow-head gathering is impotent to suggest a
single new thought, and I seem like Othello, to be without an occupation.
Surely to go on digging in the gravel will not tell us anything new. . . . If in
the course of your thoughts from day to day, in archaeological matters, any
question arises, which you think it possible, I may be able to throw some light
upon, by some new style of field–work or otherwise, please let me know. . . .
Have pity on me, and send me an idea.
(PMP: CCA/FWP 10/78)

The views from Cambridge and Trenton steadily diverged. Abbott never dug as much or as carefully as Putnam desired, all the while absorbing hundreds of precious Museum dollars. At the same time Putnam grew more concerned with field method and supervision. When Abbott mistakenly purchased a fraudulent collection from "an ignorant shoemaker" in 1879, Putnam and the trustees cooled noticeably. Abbott begged for another chance, lest he be left "a ship without a rudder" (PMP: CCA/FWP 12/28/79).

The publication of *Primitive Industry* in 1881 buoyed Abbott once again. Abbott now proposed that the neolithic implements he had picked off the ground were the work of historic Indians, while the subsurface "paleoliths," which he claimed belonged to an older, glacial layer, were probably the handiwork of the autochthonous ancestors of the Eskimo. Subsequently he refined this theory to include an intermediate, "argillite" culture between the paleolithic peoples and the neolithic, jasper-using Indians. *Primitive Industry* was not a commercial success, however, and shortly after its appearance financial pressures intensified for Abbott. Despondently he vowed once again to quit science, and for a time he clerked in a Trenton bank. At this low point he appealed sadly to Putnam:

> Forced out of the ranks of scientific workers, of course you will all very soon forget me, but I have one request to make. Please do not erase my name from the lists of recipients of your Annual Reports. It will be a pleasure to me to yearly note your progress.
>
> (PMP: CCA/FWP 11/20/81)

But Abbott could not stay away, and within a short time he was inquiring again. Mixing wistfulness with threats to work for others, Abbott wondered aloud if there was "no hope among Boston's Millionaires; I suppose I should not hope for it. I've been snubbed by their Science always, although grown grey in loyal service" (PMP: CCA/FWP 6/3/83). "If your archaeological mightiness can find time," he reminded Putnam in 1883, Abbott was willing:

> The one great trouble of my life, that which embitters every day, is, that although I have studied very hard and in every way tried to prepare myself for scientific work, yet I must work alone, or not at all. Other men are gathered in and utilized, by schools, colleges, museums, etc. or down at Washington, but there has never been a place for me. . . . I never know a day when I do not wish I could be with you, and help with much of that museum work you mention. I know I have the necessary knowledge and skill, but the Fates laugh at me. . . .
>
> (PMP: CCA/FWP 9/12/83)

So it continued until the end of 1889, when Abbott got his long-awaited lucky break. With Putnam's blessing he became the first curator of archeology at University of Pennsylvania Museum in Philadelphia. "As you well know," Putnam reminded William Pepper, the University provost:

Dr. Abbott was for years placed in a very unpleasant position by the non-belief of many persons in the great discovery which he made showing that man existed in the Delaware Valley at a time preceding the deposition of the Trenton gravel. During those years it was my good fortune to be able to help him, and, through the Peabody Museum, to furnish the means for him to pursue his researches. Now that the scientific world gives him the full credit he so richly deserves, and he is offered an honorable position by the University of Pennsylvania, I am filled with happiness for his sake.

(FWP: FWP/WP 10/28/89)

Abbott's good fortune was short-lived. Soon after he began his curatorship in late 1889, he ran afoul of Daniel G. Brinton and Stewart Culin, the two prominent Philadelphia anthropologists (cf. Darnell 1970). Abbott had little notion of what a curatorship involved. He was largely dependent on Putnam for advice on accessioning and cataloguing, and he appears to have spent weeks doing nothing in his office. In October 1892 he was fired.

After his return to the Trenton farm in 1893, Abbott's relations with Putnam and the Peabody Museum entered a final, unhappy stage. After Abbott's departure for Philadelphia Putnam had hired another Trenton man, Ernest Volk, to continue his work. A humble, poorly educated, older bachelor devoted to his aging mother, Volk proved to be a malleable, conscientious, and worshipful disciple of Putnam—a great improvement over the irascible Abbott.

As government geologists and anthropologists in Washington stepped up their attacks on paleolithic man in the early nineties, Abbott, now exiled to his farm, screamed from the sidelines for Putnam to publish Volk's work. Though Putnam wavered, Abbott kept the faith:

Volk told me recently that you had told him that people had expressed the opinion that it was "absurd," "foolish" and "wasteful" to spend money in the Delaware Valley. . . . [I] still insist that here, in this river valley is the key that unlocks the problem of the antiquity of man in America. Explorations elsewhere will result and do result in captivating their eye; but the conditions in the Delaware Valley are now capturing the understanding. I look forward very soon to the utter confusion of the horde of back-biting doubters.

(PMP: CCA/FWP 7/16/97)

Putnam's hesitation was due in part to his respect for the unresolved questions about New Jersey geology. By 1897 he had apparently decided to let the geologists decide the disputed points. "As archeologists," he cautioned Abbott, "we have done our part when we say we have found the works of man in these special deposits. Now it is for the geologists to determine the age of these deposits" (FWP: FWP/CCA 6/26/97; cf. FWP/CCA 11/14/92). But caution only angered Abbott, who felt his whole scientific reputation at

Charles C. Abbott, photographed on his farm near Trenton, New Jersey (courtesy of Princeton University Library, Department of Rare Books and Special Collections).

stake. "Why I must stand by silent and be reduced by [William Henry] Holmes & Co. you do not make plain. . . . If Palaeolithic man is never acknowledged, it will be *your fault* and *inexcusably so*" (FWP: CCA/FWP 4/ 26/99). The relationship continued to sink. In 1900, having sold a piece of land for a trolley line, Abbott finally thumbed his nose at Putnam:

> Poor Abbott is fat, vigorous, full of work and very happy, and none the less so because a clique, of whom you are afraid, wag their heads solemnly when Trenton Archaeology is broached. Really, I think the tables are turned. It is not "Poor Abbott" but "Poor Putnam" now, and damned poor at that. The Anti-Antiquityites have been keeping you shaking in your shoes all these years and your boots are still shaking. . . .
>
> Ta-Ta,
> (FWP: CCA/FWP 12/12/00)

In 1911 the financial support of Charles Peabody permitted the history of Volk's work and his findings, along with geological studies of the Trenton deposits, to be published as part of the Peabody Museum Papers. Neither Volk nor Putnam cited Charles Abbott in their introductions to the volume (Volk 1911).

The historical landscape of American archeology is littered with traces of men who failed in their bids to become recognized scientists. In the patterns of his ambitions and his frustrating relation to the nineteenth-century Peabody Museum, Abbott was atypical only in the intensity of his reactions. To various degrees Putnam's fieldworkers—E. B. Andrews and Charles Metz in Ohio, E. O. Dunning and Edwin Curtis in Tennessee, Paul Schumacher and Edward Palmer in California and Utah—all exhibited the tensions of working for an institution that provided opportunity to contribute but could offer little hope for advancement.

Although Americans a century ago were inclined to see failure as a personal fault, "failure" in science was as much a result of structural limits as a question of personal competence. A critical need in many fields of American science in this period was the means of certifying the streams of investigators and contributors to the new disciplines. Professionalization was, from this perspective, a response to a social and structural problem—in effect, a human sorting process (Reingold 1976). In the various fields of anthropology this condition was worsened by a severe dearth of paid positions. Consequently an institution such as the Peabody Museum was restricted to narrow social groups for its workers. The choice came down, on the one hand, to adventurous naturalist-explorers who were willing to live on a pittance but who were poorly educated and difficult to discipline; or, on the other hand, to men of moderate leisure with small scientific ambition, satisfied to contribute without asking much in return. All had to be willing to work largely out of loyalty.

Michael Mulkay has argued that under conditions of "intellectual and social openness" it is difficult to assert the "intellectual control" required to
define problems and methods with precision; thus "consensus is achieved at
least partly by exclusion of nonconformists" (Mulkay 1972:16–17). Under
porous professional conditions men such as Abbott and Volk required above
all someone to vouch for their character, since they lacked academic creden-
tials or firm institutional positions. Thomas Wilson, curator of archeology at
the U.S. National Museum (and the lone defender of paleolithic man among
government workers) put his finger squarely on the issue in a letter to Putnam
in 1900. "Who is Volk, anyhow?" was the critical point, he reminded
Putnam:

> The argument in the whole affair depends largely upon his reputation and
> character for truth and honesty. While it was all well enough to compliment
> the men who furnished the money by which this discovery is made, I think it
> would have been wiser for us to have given expression to our belief in Volk's
> honesty and integrity, and thus our acceptance of his discovery as genuine.
>
> (FWP: TW/FWP 1/3/00)

In these words Wilson touched the sensitive heart of the matter for Putnam. As director of the Peabody Museum he addressed many audiences: fieldworkers, patrons, the public. Given his own social marginality, and the dubious stature of museum anthropology, Putnam found it more congenial to
praise the patrons of Peabody science than to commit himself publicly to men
like Abbott and Volk. Putnam made a career of cautious building; increasingly, he felt it necessary to keep a proper distance from questionable science.
However privileged he may have seemed to those on the periphery of science,
Putnam could never relax his scientific vigil, for fear that the whole structure
would collapse. A sense of the precariousness and the fragility of a career in
museum anthropology constantly shadowed him.

Mayan Civilization:
A Worthy Subject for the Professionally Worthy

Despite the formidable intellectual, social, and financial barriers that faced
Peabody Museum anthropology in its first twenty-five years, Putnam by 1891
could look back with some satisfaction. On the anniversary date of its founding, he took time from his duties as curator and now professor to write to
Henry Wheatland, the Museum trustee whom he had known since his own
early years at the Essex Institute in Salem:

I can't let the day pass without a few lines to you. The years have followed each other, until twenty-five years have passed since Mr. Peabody founded this museum Oct. 8, 1866. Well do I remember your telling of the gift he had made to Harvard and of our talking it over. Soon you became a trustee, and in 8 years the care and development of the Museum fell to me. Little did I think 25 years ago that I should be holding my present position, not only as head of the Museum then founded but also as head of a department of the University. How strange it all is! What grand results have come out of Mr. Peabody's gift! . . . Now [the Museum] stands foremost of its kind and so acknowledged[,] and is a place for study & research, a regular department of the University, & the boy you took in charge & led on in his early scientific studies is at the head.
(HWP: FWP/HW 10/8/91)

By the time Putnam wrote this, several of the major problems that had so long hindered the development of anthropology at the Peabody Museum were on their way to being overcome: on the one hand, finding a subject of inquiry that would seem worthy of support to groups within the Boston and New England social and cultural elite; on the other hand, training a group of investigators who would be deemed worthy of support in the more professional environment that was beginning to develop within the national anthropological community.

Although it was not explicitly seen this way by the actors, one can interpret Putnam's generation-long interest in "glacial man" on the American continent as a matter of making the best of Holmes' *chiffonier* archeology: if one were to study Indian shell-heaps rather than the monumental remains of classical civilizations, then to claim great antiquity for Trenton man was to claim, as it were, a paleolithic prize rather than to be a poor runner-up to European archeologists in the race of prehistory. Be that as it may, by 1890 it was long since evident that Abbott was no attraction to Brahmin backers, and he was becoming a bit of an embarrassment among anthropologists as well. Fortunately, a viable alternative research focus was by then emerging which was at once culturally and professionally more respectable: the study of ancient Mayan civilization.

In 1889, the Harvard Corporation appointed the first Visiting Committee to the Peabody Museum, headed by F. M. Weld, a prominent Bostonian with a longtime interest in the University. The support of the Weld family, as well as that of Charles P. Bowditch, proved an important stimulus: subscriptions to the Museum's publications rose substantially, and fellowships were provided for the newly recognized anthropology department (Casler 1976). Bowditch, who in the late eighties had become interested in Mayan culture while traveling in Central America, took up the cause of the Peabody Museum upon his return, in large part to pursue his own newly acquired interest in Central American archeology and ethnology (Hinsley 1984). In December 1891, the first of a series of Bowditch-sponsored expeditions to Copan, Honduras, departed under the leadership of John G. Owens, who the preceding fall had become Putnam's first graduate student in archeology.

With Bowditch's involvement, the Peabody Museum finally began to receive significant contributions from elite Bostonians. While this was no doubt in part due to Bowditch's own status, it was also surely due to the nature of the archeological prizes at stake in Central America. These were no longer the pickings of shell-heaps or Trenton gravels, whose claim to prehistoric primacy was vigorously disputed by scientific professionals in federal bureaus of geology and ethnology. Rather they were now the stelae and stepped pyramids of Copan, and later the gold and copal incense of Chichen Itza. If these were not in the direct lineage of European high culture, they were nonetheless clearly the products of the highest culture the New World had produced, as well as of a history steeped in romance. At last, Peabody

John G. Owens starting for the coast with moldings of sculpture from the hieroglyphic stairway at Copan, January 7, 1893 (photograph number N300, courtesy of the Peabody Museum, Harvard University).

archeology had found a subject that seemed comparable to that of the Mediterranean basin: a New World civilization worthy of a museum, worthy of investment, and worthy of study.

By 1891, Putnam had begun to offer a three-year research course based in the Museum and geared to the interests of graduate students; in 1894, his student George Dorsey received the first American Ph.D. in archeology. Once established as both the curator of the country's most important museum devoted solely to anthropology, and as the Professor of Anthropology at its most prestigious university, Putnam—who had also long served as permanent secretary of the American Association for the Advancement of Science—began to operate in a wider institutional arena. Chosen to take overall charge of the anthropology exhibits at the Chicago World's Fair, he went on to become a leading commuter-entrepreneur of American anthropology—heading the anthropology departments at both the American Museum of Natural History and the University of California, while continuing to maintain his position at Cambridge. At the Fair, in the American Museum, and again at Berkeley, he worked closely with Franz Boas, who was to succeed him as the leading figure of academic anthropology. By a de facto division of labor with Boas (and Boas' protégés), it was left to Putnam's Cambridge program to handle the training of the first generation of academic archeologists. While their numbers were until the first World War countable on the fingers of two hands, by that time the anthropological program generated out of the Peabody Museum had produced the first group of academically certified professionals in American archeology—most of whom served their apprenticeship in Mayan research (cf. Darnell 1969).

Acknowledgments

This paper is based on research supported in part by the National Science Foundation and the Colgate University Research Council.

References Cited

AAP. See under Manuscript Sources.
Abbott, C. C. 1872. The Stone Age in New Jersey. Am. Nat. 6:144–60, 199–229.
———. 1881. Primitive industry: Or illustrations of the handiwork in stone, bone and clay, of the native races of the North Atlantic seaboard of America. Salem.
AIAP. See under Manuscript Sources.
Anon. 1848. Editorial comment. Sci. Am. Feb. 5.
Brew, J. O., ed. 1968. One hundred years of anthropology. Cambridge.

Casler, J. C. 1976. Personalities, politics and patrons of the Peabody Museum of American Archaeology and Ethnology, 1866–1896. Unpublished bachelor's thesis, Harvard Univ.

CWEP. See under Manuscript Sources.

Darnell, R. 1969. The development of American anthropology, 1979–1920: From the Bureau of American Ethnology to Franz Boas. Unpublished doct. diss., Univ. Penn.

———. 1970. The emergence of academic anthropology at the University of Pennsylvania. J. Hist. Behav. Scis. 6:80–92.

Dexter, R. W. 1965. The 'Salem secession' of Agassiz zoologists. Essex Inst. Hist. Colls. 101:27–39.

Dupree, A. H. 1953. Jeffries Wyman's views on evolution. Isis 44:243–46.

Essex Institute. 1893. Letter from F. W. Putnam, 4/17/93. Hist. Colls. 30:186–89.

FWPP. See under Manuscript Sources.

Gray, A. 1874. Comments. In Jeffries Wyman: Memorial meeting of the Boston Society of Natural History. Boston.

Green, M. 1966. The problem of Boston: Some readings in cultural history. New York.

Harris, N. 1962. The Gilded Age revisited: Boston and the museum movement. Am. Quart. 14:546–66.

Hawkins, H. 1972. Between Harvard and America: The educational leadership of Charles W. Eliot. New York.

Hinsley, C. M. 1981. Savages and scientists: The Smithsonian Institution and the development of American anthropology, 1846–1910. Washington.

———. 1984. Wanted: one good man to discover Central American history. Harvard Mag. 87 (No. 2):64A–64H.

Horowitz, H. L. 1976. Culture and the city: Cultural philanthropy in Chicago from the 1880s to 1917. Lexington.

HWP. See under Manuscript Sources.

JWP. See under Manuscript Sources.

Lurie, E. 1974. Nature and the American mind: Louis Agassiz and the culture of science. New York.

Mark, J. 1980. Four anthropologists: An American science in its early years. New York.

Meltzer, D. J. 1983. The antiquity of man and the development of American archaeology. Advances Arch. Meth. & Theory 6:1–51.

Mitchell, S. W. 1875. The scientific life. Lippincott's Mag. 15:352–56.

Mulkay, M. J. 1972. The social process of innovation. London.

Parker, F. 1971. George Peabody: A biography. Nashville.

Persons, S. 1973. The decline of American gentility. New York.

PMA. See under Manuscript Sources.

PML. See under Manuscript Sources.

PMP. See under Manuscript Sources.

Powell, J. W. 1890. Problems of American archaeology. Forum 18:638–52.

Reingold, N. 1976. Definitions and speculations: The professionalization of science in the nineteenth century. In The pursuit of knowledge in the early American republic, ed. A. Oleson and S. C. Brown, 33–69. Baltimore.

Renfrew, C. 1980. The great tradition versus the great divide: Archaeology as anthropology? Am. J. of Arch. 84:287–98.

Stanton, W. *The leopard's spots: Scientific attitudes toward race in America, 1815–59.* Chicago.

Tylor, E. 1871. *Primitive culture: Researches into the development of mythology, philosophy, religion, language, art and custom.* 2 vols. London.

Volk, E. 1911. The archaeology of the Delaware River Valley. *Pap. Peabody Museum* 5.

Wilder, B. G. 1910. Jeffries Wyman, anatomist: 1814–1874. In *Leading men of science,* ed. D. S. Jordan. New York.

Wyman, J. 1876. Primitive man. *Am. Nat.* 10:278–82.

Manuscript Sources

In writing this paper I have drawn on research materials collected from the following manuscript sources, cited as abbreviated:

AAP   Alexander Agassiz Papers, Archives of the Museum of Comparative Zoology, Harvard University, Cambridge.

AIAP   Archaeological Institute of America Papers, Colgate University, Hamilton, New York.

CWEP   Charles W. Eliot Papers, Harvard University Archives, Cambridge.

FWPP   F. W. Putnam Papers, Harvard University Archives, Cambridge.

HWP   Henry Wheatland Papers, Essex Institute, Salem, Massachusetts.

JWP   Jeffries Wyman Papers, Countway Library, Harvard University Medical School, Boston.

PMA   Peabody Museum Archives, Peabody Museum of Archaeology and Ethnology, Harvard University, Cambridge.

PML   Peabody Museum Letterbooks, Peabody Museum of Archaeology and Ethnology, Harvard University, Cambridge.

PMP   Peabody Museum Papers, Harvard University Archives, Cambridge.

I wish to thank all the repositories and archivists for their assistance.

FRANZ BOAS AND EXHIBITS

On the Limitations of the Museum Method
of Anthropology

IRA JACKNIS

Franz Boas is remembered as the founder of professional anthropology in this country, and for more than sixty years, the professional anthropology he did so much to shape has found its primary institutional locus in a particular setting: the university department. But Boas himself entered anthropology in the midst of what is often called its "museum age"—1880–1920 (Sturtevant 1969:622). His first anthropological employment was in the recently founded Royal Ethnographic Museum of Berlin, where as an assistant under Adolf Bastian from mid-1885 to mid-1886, he spent much of his time preparing for exhibition the artifacts that had been brought back by Johan Adrian Jacobsen from the Northwest Coast of North America. Boas' attraction to the peoples who were henceforth to be the ethnographic focus of his professional life began with these objects, which embodied a "flight of imagination" sharply contrastive to the "severe sobriety" of the eastern Eskimo, whom he had studied while undertaking ethnogeographic researches in Baffinland in 1883–84 (1909:307). Given a chance to meet their creators when Jacobsen brought a troupe of Bella Coola to Berlin in January 1886, Boas quickly began developing plans for the fieldwork he was to undertake that fall—the collections from which were sold to the Berlin museum. Settling afterwards in the United States, Boas was unsuccessful in seeking a position at the American Museum of Natural History, and his first regular jobs in this country were as geographical editor for the journal *Science* and as docent in the Department

---

Ira Jacknis is Research Associate in the Department of African, Oceanic, and New World Cultures at The Brooklyn Museum. His doctoral dissertation in anthropology at the University of Chicago, "The Storage Box of Tradition," concerns the relationship between museums, anthropologists, and Kwakiutl art, 1881–1981. He is continuing his research on various aspects of Boasian anthropology.

of Psychology of Clark University. His links with the world of museum anthropology remained strong, however, and were reasserted in the aftermath
of his resignation from Clark, when the major regional anthropological figure, Frederic W. Putnam of Harvard's Peabody Museum, took upon himself
the role of Boas' institutional patron (cf. Stocking 1968, 1974).

Putnam was supervising the Department of Ethnology and Archaeology at
the World's Columbian Exposition in Chicago, and he chose Boas as his
second-in-command. Although Boas himself did no collecting for the Exposition, and much of his effort was devoted to organizing fieldwork in physical
anthropology, he did supervise a large team of local experts in gathering an
impressive array of Northwest Coast specimens. When the Exposition was
over Boas worked for nine months packing, moving, and setting up the collections in the new Field Columbian Museum, but the job he hoped would
be permanent was forestalled by the political machinations of government
anthropologists (cf. Hinsley & Holm 1976).

Throughout this period, Boas had been conducting fieldwork on the
Northwest Coast for the Bureau of American Ethnology and the British Association for the Advancement of Science, and in the fall of 1894 he carried
on a further fieldtrip funded jointly by the British Association, the U.S. National Museum, and the American Museum—hoping that out of this might
eventuate a permanent job. It was in response to the request of Otis T. Mason, of the National Museum, for a "pretty complete collection illustrating
the whole winter dance ceremonial of [the Northwest Coast] tribes" (FBP:
FB/OTM 5/20/94) that Boas, with the help of his Kwakiutl assistant George
Hunt, undertook the most intensive participant-observation work of his career. Upon his return, Boas worked for two months preparing a "life group,"
a dramatic tableau of costumed mannequins, which the National Museum
exhibited at the Cotton States Exposition in Atlanta in the fall of 1895.

Meanwhile Putnam, who had just accepted the direction of anthropology
at the American Museum, was negotiating with the Museum's president,
Morris K. Jesup, to commission Boas to make "as complete a collection as
possible of models illustrating the different tribes [of the Northwest Coast]
and dressed in the garments of the people, and arranged in groups so as to
illustrate the life history of each tribe represented" (FBP: FWP/FB 7/16/94).
Boas was later asked to return to the Museum to supervise the installation of
the material he had collected that fall. Putnam hoped that this would be the
opening wedge in his protégé's permanent appointment; and indeed, after
several months of work, in January 1896 Boas was appointed Assistant Curator of Ethnology and Somatology, about six months before Jesup and Putnam were able to negotiate for him a parallel appointment at Columbia University.

Boas' first regular museum position was also to be his last. Although he held the American Museum appointment during what was probably the critical decade in the establishment of his intellectual and institutional leadership in American anthropology, it was a decade marked by increasing conflict of purpose and personal tension between Boas and the Museum administration. By May 1905 he had resigned from the Museum, concluding on both pragmatic and theoretical grounds that the sort of anthropology he was interested in was better carried on in an academic milieu. By emphasizing this shift, some historians (e.g. Darnell 1972:8–9) have left the impression that Boas had a superficial interest in museums, or that he valued them only as sources of support for fieldwork and research. By focusing on his exhibits, a medium dedicated to the popular presentation of anthropology, this essay attempts to cast light upon an alternate path, once of great concern to Boas, which has become lost to us in the Boasian reorientation of American anthropology.

Tribal and Typological Arrangement, 1887–1895

To replace Boas' early anthropology in its museum context, we may note that his first major theoretical statement on specifically anthropological issues came in a discussion of museum classification. In an exchange of letters in 1887 in the journal *Science*, Boas, with barely a year of museum experience, took on two of the leaders of American anthropology, Otis T. Mason of the U.S. National Museum and John Wesley Powell of the Bureau of American Ethnology (B.A.E.). In studying the collections in the National Museum, Boas had been disappointed to find that the objects from the Northwest Coast were "scattered in different parts of the building, and . . . exhibited among those from other tribes" (1887a:62). Encouraged by Director George B. Goode, Mason had arranged all his material according to universal "inventions"—fire-making, transportation, the crafts of pottery or basketry, etc., so that specimens from diverse cultures had been placed together according to the putative evolution of a technological type.

Against Mason's typological evolutionary scheme, Boas posed his own nominalist *Geisteswissenschaftliche* viewpoint (cf. Stocking 1974:8–12). The attempt to classify ethnological phenomena as "biological specimens" that could be "divided into families, genera and species" was based on the assumption that "a connection of some kind exists between ethnological phenomena of people widely apart." But in the human sphere, where every invention was the product of a complex historical development, "unlike causes" could "produce like effects" (1887a:61). The outward appearance of two phenomena might be identical, "yet their immanent qualities may be altogether

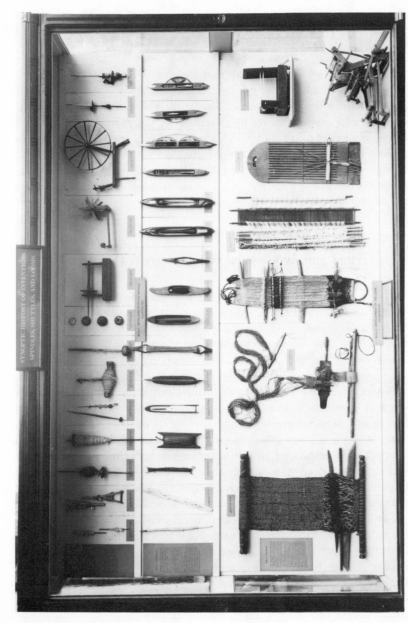

U.S. National Museum case, ca. 1890, showing the typological evolution of spindles, shuttles, and looms (negative number 21389, courtesy of the Smithsonian Institution).

different." Groupings based on a "deductive" approach to "analogies of outward appearance" were therefore bound to be "deceptive" (1887b:66). Because "in ethnology all is individuality" (ibid.), the object of study must not
be "abstractions from the individual under observation," but "the ethnological specimen in its history and in its medium" (1887a:62).

Mason's interest in the adaptive utilitarian function of different inventions
in serving various "human wants" led him to focus on the external *form* of
the artifact, which was directly accessible to the visual inspection of the
curator. In contrast, Boas was advocating a transfer of anthropological interest from the external form to an artifact's *meaning*, which was not easily
accessible to psychological interpretation in utilitarian terms, because the
same object might carry a number of different meanings:

> The rattle, for instance, is not merely the outcome of the idea of making noise,
> and of the technical methods applied to reach this end: it is, besides this, the
> outcome of the religious conceptions, as any noise may be applied to invoke or
> drive away spirits; or it may be the outcome of the pleasure children have in
> noise of any kind; and its form may be characteristic of the art of the people.
> (1887b:65)

Thus the same implement, judged from a formal point of view, might belong
in a number of different departments of a typologically organized museum.

In the long run, this shift from form/function to meaning was to have
indefinitely ramifying consequences for the future of American anthropology;
but in the context of the 1887 debate, the problem it raised was the alternative principle of museum arrangement. If one could not group specimens
by their surface characteristics, how would the curator know which rightfully
belonged together? The answer was based on the cultural holism Boas had
imbibed from the German intellectual tradition. Just as Boas had suggested
that "the art and characteristic style of a people can only be understood by
studying its productions as a whole" (1887a:62), so more generally the meaning of an ethnological specimen could not be understood "outside of its surroundings, outside of other inventions of the people to whom it belongs, and
outside of other phenomena affecting that people and its productions"
(ibid.). The solution to the problem of arrangement was thus "a collection
representing the life of one tribe." Boas' "ideal of an ethnological museum"
was one that would be organized by a "tribal arrangement of collections"
(1887b:66–67). Practically, Boas suggested the exhibition of "a full set of a
representative of an ethnical group" with tribal peculiarities shown in "small
special sets" (1887c). Boas insisted that such an arrangement was not a classification, but a grouping only "according to ethnic similarities."[1]

---

1. Boas' advocacy of the geographical order was not original. In fact, his 1887 debate was

In his response, Mason gave no ground. Calling Boas' suggestion that un-like causes could produce like effects "a very ingenious one," Mason claimed that "it has nothing to do with the case," and reasserted the importance of the biological method in ethnology (1887:534). Mason was willing to admit "geographical areas" as one of the "classific concepts" by which museums could be organized—others being material, race, social organization, envi-ronment, structure and function, and evolution or elaboration. But as he later maintained, "They are all good, each bringing out phases of truth over-looked in others and it is only by a comparison of results that the whole truth may be reached" (1890:515). In defending his exhibit scheme, Mason pointed to his audience. People with all sorts of specialized interests—sol-diers, potters, musicians, artists—"desire to see, in juxtaposition, the speci-mens which they would study" (1887:534). Therefore, "in any museum every thing should tend to enlist the sympathies and cooperation of the greatest diversity of mind." Boas had convinced no one in Washington, where it was established policy to place no object on exhibition "which is not of evident educational value and likely to interest and instruct a considerable percent-age of the persons visiting the Museum" (Goode 1882:1).

Yet, within less than a decade, the National Museum began to arrange its exhibits according to a regional plan. While some (Brown 1980) have inter-preted this as evidence of theoretical convergence between Boas and his Washington colleagues, it seems that true to Boas' dictum, appearances are deceiving, and unlike causes can produce like effects (cf. Hinsley 1981:112). For a short time Boas and Mason overlapped, using common terms and ap-pearing to arrange exhibits in similar patterns, but they differed fundamen-tally in the total conceptual system of which these terms and patterns were a part.

The stimulus for this convergence was Mason's preparation of the Smith-sonian's ethnology displays for the Chicago World's Fair. Setting out to select representatives of the major stocks as depicted in the B.A.E.'s 1891 map of American Indian language groups, Mason soon realized that the character of the artifacts clustered not according to language or race, but according to local environmental zones. Although his cases at the Fair were still arranged by language stock, the message communicated to the public, and subse-quently elaborated by Mason, was that "the arts of life . . . are in each cul-ture area indigenous," and "are materialized under the patronage and direc-torship of the region . . ." (1894:215).

Although Mason had begun arranging exhibits according to locality even

---

reminiscent of one conducted a half century earlier between the Dutchman Philip von Siebold, taking the regional position, and the Frenchman Edmé-François Jomard, proposing the cross-cultural system (cf. Frese 1960:38–42). Boas would have been familiar with a geographical sys-tem from the institutions of his museological mentors, Bastian in Berlin and Putnam in Cam-bridge.

as he was being challenged by Boas, he was constrained from using this principle more broadly for several practical reasons. Many of his specimens had "false location and insufficient data" (1889:90), and since "it is often begging the whole question to assign a specimen to a certain tribe," he felt that "no harm can possibly come from putting things that are alike in the same case or receptacle" (ibid.). Full tribal displays were also forestalled by the chronic lack of space (1895:126). But perhaps most important, it was only with the field research and collecting of B.A.E. ethnologists like James Mooney, stimulated by specific commissions for the Fair, that Mason was to have enough reasonably complete and well-documented collections to allow such a tribal presentation.

The Chicago Fair was also the scene for the introduction to America of the "life group," a form of ethnographic display seemingly more in tune with Boasian principles.[2] Although the Smithsonian had used single mannequins to display clothing as early as the 1876 Centennial Exposition, only in 1893 were groups of such costumed figures arranged in dramatic scenes from daily life and ritual. Mason himself had been impressed with the village encampments of tribal peoples at the 1889 Paris Fair; the life group would give permanence to such compelling pictures, which were a popular success at several turn-of-the-century world's fairs (cf. Holmes 1903:201). Like the culture area, the introduction of the life group was stimulated by the more intense fieldwork sponsored by the Bureau of American Ethnology. Though the attractive designs were worked out under the direction of the artist-turned-archeologist William H. Holmes, many of the groups were based on the direct advice of experienced collector/ethnographers like Frank H. Cushing, James Mooney, and Walter J. Hoffman.[3] Like the habitat group in biology (Parr

2. European museums had adopted the life group several decades before their American counterparts. Growing out of a long tradition of waxworks, the first life groups were part of commercial exhibitions, such as the Chinese Collection and the Oriental and Turkish Museum, both of London, opening in 1842 and 1854, respectively (Altick 1978:292–93, 496–97). One of the first museums to exhibit these tableaux was the Museum of Scandinavian Ethnography, opened in Stockholm in 1873. The vivid and innovative display techniques of curator-director Artur Hazelius became widely known after he exhibited life groups at the Paris World's Fair of 1878 (Alexander 1983:245–46), and during the next decade many museums, especially in Germany and Scandinavia, began to install them.

3. Mooney and Cushing agreed with Mason that life groups should be arranged on the basis of "geo-ethnic" units, but they clashed over the implementation of this goal. During the installation of the Smithsonian exhibit at the Chicago Fair, Cushing edited Mooney's labels and "ordered additional artifacts from other tribes to be included in the Navajo and Hopi exhibit," based on Mooney's collections (Colby 1977:283). While Cushing regarded the culture within a region as essentially homogeneous, at least for purposes of display, Mooney proposed selecting one representative tribe from a region and exhibiting artifacts only from that single tribe, adhering to stringent standards of accuracy and detail (Mooney 1894). This opposition between a regional and tribal approach surfaced again in 1907 when George A. Dorsey criticized the areal displays of the post-Boasian American Museum.

1959) and the period room in history and art (Alexander 1964), the contemporaneously introduced life group was anthropology's attempt to create a functional or contextual setting for its specimens. Artifacts were thus displayed in association with related specimens from specific cultures, as Boas had called for. But instead of communicating cultural integration by means of object juxtaposition and labels, to be synthesized in the viewer's mind, the life group was a presentational medium, allowing these cultural connections actually to be *seen*. Not surprisingly, the life groups were enormously popular with visitors, and within a year, Putnam and the American Museum were making plans for their own series of life groups.

In spite of the new features the National Museum began to introduce in the mid-nineties, Boas and his colleagues were still far apart. Mason and Holmes never gave up their evolutionary and typological schemes; they merely augmented them with tribal and regional arrangements. Even more fundamentally, they saw their exhibits in a different ideological perspective. Mason foresaw a time when by "the multiplication of wants" and "the refine-

Life-group exhibit of Kwakiutl hamatsa initiate and attendants at the U.S. National Museum, ca. 1896 (negative number 9539, courtesy of the National Anthropological Archives, Smithsonian Institution).

ment of taste" the whole world would become "an unique, comprehensive and undivided home for the whole race" (1894:215). But according to Boas, "the main object of ethnological collections should be the dissemination of the fact that civilization is not something absolute, but that it is relative, and that our ideas and conceptions are true only so far as our civilization goes" (1887b:66).

Nevertheless, the experience of Mason and Holmes reveals that there was more involved in museum display than the conceptual issues addressed by Boas. Theoretical conceptions could only be realized to the extent that available materials and media allowed, and their realization was constrained also by the goal of attracting large appreciative crowds. As we shall see, Mason's movement toward a more Boasian stance foreshadowed Boas' move—for equally pragmatic reasons—toward a more Masonian position. It is against this theoretical and practical context that Boas' exhibits at the American Museum must be seen. Having criticized the Washington establishment, Boas now had a chance to put into practice his ideals of museum anthropology.

Constraints of Power, Money, and Authority

The exhibits here attributed to Boas were not his alone, since a museum display is the product of collaborative labor performed within a particular social system. The museum is an institution with roles for patrons and trustees, administrators, curators, scientific assistants, preparators, custodians, and visitors. Boas' tasks as curator were largely defined by the expectations others had of his role and he of theirs. We must begin, therefore, with a consideration of the resources Boas was given and of the freedom with which he was allowed to use them.

Like everything else at the American Museum of Natural History, anthropological exhibits were funded through a combination of public and private sources. The Museum's 1869 charter had called for the City of New York to pay for the land, building, and maintenance. Unlike the National Museum, which was beholden to a general, national constituency, the American Museum was thus compelled to attract the city's masses if it wanted to be assured of financial support. But the collections were owned by the twenty-four trustees, who funded expeditions, exhibit installation, and other operating expenses. Drawn from the financial elite of the city—bankers, railroad presidents, manufacturers, merchants, and lawyers—the Museum's supporters were businessmen, not scientists. Moreover, they tended to be nouveau riche, with a desire to prove their worth and bring glory to their city. By and large they were sceptical of research; as one said, this was better left to the Germans (Kennedy 1968:122).

Boas therefore often found that in order to support his vast plans of collection, research, installation, and publication he had to go beyond the trustees to a circle of patrons more favorably disposed toward his work. Flattering letters to possible patrons were a distinct genre of Boasian correspondence (Stocking 1974:285). Boas was able to play on a number of "soft spots": Archer M. Huntington and the Duc de Loubat had serious anthropological interests; Jacob H. Schiff and Henry Villard were German-born; railroad owners like Villard and Collis P. Huntington were asked for funding for expeditions to regions through which their railroads ran, citing the anticipated increase in "interest of the public" which exhibitions might stimulate (AMAC: FB/C. F. Newcombe 5/20/01). But Boas' most generous patron was in fact the Museum's president, Morris K. Jesup, a retired banker who gave $250,000 for an expedition to the north Pacific coasts of Asia and America.

Then, as now, most wealthy patrons were more willing to donate magnificent collections than to pay for more mundane operating costs, despite the fact that the cost of collecting was "insignificant as compared with the expense of installation" (AMCA: FB/MKJ 12/11/97). In 1895 Boas estimated that it cost the museum $200 per life group figure, most of it due to the great amount of skilled labor necessary (FWPP: FB/FWP 12/5/95). Thus it tended to be the lot of the dedicated trustees to make up the deficits.

As the ultimate source of funds (directly, from their own pockets, or indirectly, through their political connections), the trustees were the ultimate authority in museum governance. The board, however, usually acquiesced in the decisions of the President. This was especially true during the term of Jesup, who served from 1881 to 1908, and was largely responsible for making the Museum a great center for research and exhibition. Until 1901, Jesup was both chief executive and operating officer; after that the zoologist Hermon C. Bumpus assumed responsibility for much of the day-to-day running of the institution, first as assistant to the President and then as Director.

During Boas' tenure the Department of Anthropology consistently listed the largest staff of curators—three when he arrived, four by the time he left. As in a university, curators were ranked by full, associate, and assistant level, and in anthropology, they were designated also by regional (Mexico and Central America) and subdisciplinary specialty (ethnology or anthropology). In addition to permanent curatorial staff, the Museum hired on contract a series of field researchers. After making their collections, men such as Alfred Kroeber, Waldemar Jochelson, and George Hunt often spent a period in residence writing up their research, preparing labels, and directing exhibit installation.

Each department also employed a set of "scientific assistants," or support personnel. In 1903 these included a secretary, a card cataloguer and label-writer, a general installer, a model maker, a figure maker, and a general assistant (AMDA: Departmental Report, Fall 1903). The number of such assistants varied, depending on the tasks at hand and support from the central administration. Craftsmen with special skills could also be hired on contract, and various workers were delegated from the office of the superintendent: carpenters, printers, and floor attendants.

For Boas the points of tension within this structure arose when he had to deal with the central administration. Within his own department he seems to have wielded complete control, with curators as well as assistants, assigning tasks as he saw fit. Extra-departmental relations, however, were a constant source of frustration. His own museum preparators were frequently called off departmental work to do other tasks, making it difficult to plan coordinated efforts. Necessary supplies and labor were often not forthcoming. One petty, but typical, complaint to Jesup illustrates the general problem:

> For the arrangement of one case in the north Hall . . . I need a number of wooden stands, which have been made and partially painted. Mr. Wallace [the superintendent] informs me that there is no appropriation for giving these stands the second coat of paint that they require. I beg to ask for authority to have these stands painted, since the case looks very bad in its present condition.
>
> (AMDA: FB/MKJ 1/19/99)

Much more serious, though, were Boas' relations with his superiors in the museum hierarchy. As chairman, Frederic Putnam was his immediate supervisor. When, for instance, Boas proposed the Jesup Expedition, the President insisted that Putnam direct the project, at least on paper (Mark 1980:39–41). But as Putnam was only at the Museum one week out of four, Boas was in effect free to direct the department's affairs. This very absence, however, led to severe strains between the two. By 1902 it appeared to Boas that their work was at cross-purposes, due to a lack of full communication (FBP: FB/FWP 4/6/02), and the following year Boas objected to Putnam's supervision on grounds that are obscure, but which seem to have stemmed from Boas' position as professor at Columbia (FBP: FWP/FB 2/6/03). The impasse was effectively resolved by Putnam's resignation from the Museum at the end of 1903 (cf. Mark 1980:43–46).

With the central administration, Boas insisted on a fairly autonomous position: "if an institution wants me, it does not want me merely to carry out orders, but also to lay plans for work" (FBP: FB/FWP 12/18/95). Accordingly, Boas requested that he be allowed to communicate directly with President Jesup. Throughout his tenure Boas continually called attention to his "inferior position," and threatened, on at least one occasion, to go elsewhere (AMDA: FB/FWP 12/1/98). Although Jesup seems generally to have approved of Boas' research, to the extent that he could understand it, Boas' exhibits continually dissatisfied him. He often complained that there were not enough labels (FBP: FWP/FB 7/2/96), and he once felt he had to direct Boas "to state that the Eskimo clothing is the real genuine article not manufactured" (FWPP: FB/FWP 2/11/97). After viewing an Alaskan display which displeased him, Jesup demanded the final say over installation (FWPP: FB/FWP 11/12/96). This divergence between Jesup and Boas over who was to have final authority for the displays was in fact the expression of underlying differences of attitude, philosophy, and purpose which were resolved only by Boas' resignation in 1905.

Constraints of Audience and Purpose

Boas defined three purposes for museums: entertainment, instruction, and research (1907:921)—each of which was correlated in a general way with three museum audiences: children and the great body of less educated adults; elementary teachers and a limited group of more educated adults; and advanced scholars (AMDA: FB/MKJ 5/28/98). For each group of visitors Boas offered a different kind of exhibition.

> Just as our school system requires, beside primary and grammar schools, high schools and universities, so a large museum should fulfil the function of a primary objective school for the general public, as well as serve those who strive for higher education and help to train the teacher. The educational methods of university, high school, grammar school, and primary school are different; and thus the methods of exhibition must differ, according to the public to which we appeal.
>
> (FBP: FB/MKJ 4/29/05)

Much of Boas' exhibit activity was predicated upon the belief that the majority of visitors—as much as 90 percent—"do not want anything beyond entertainment" (1907:922).

> The people who seek rest and recreation resent an attempt at systematic instruction while they are looking for some emotional excitement. They want to admire, to be impressed by something great and wonderful; and if the underlying idea of the exhibit can be brought out with sufficient clearness, some great truths may be impressed upon them without requiring at the moment any particular effort.
>
> (Ibid.)

To appeal to such audiences Boas tried to overlay education on a base of entertainment, by using a few striking displays such as life groups, arranged so that their main point was instantly perceptible.

Boas had more trouble with the second level, those seeking "systematic instruction" (1907:925), for he believed that their educational needs would in fact be best served by small museums, such as could be instituted in schools. A large museum could not be effectively arranged so that all didactic systems of interest were contained, and if only one such system were adopted, the collections would be artificially confined. Aside from separate branch museums, Boas recommended arranging for this second audience small synoptic series in each hall or gathered together in one hall.

It was in such a series of educational displays, proposed to President Jesup in the late nineties, that Boas came closest to Mason's approach. Boas suggested an exhibit that would show "how the most primitive tribes depend entirely upon the products of their home, and how with the progress of civilization wider and wider areas are made to contribute to the needs of man." Such exhibits "would become of great interest to the tradesman," Boas hoped, "showing the development of the trades of the carpenter, the blacksmith, the weaver, etc. in different cultural areas." (AMDA: FB/MKJ 5/28/98).

Building on his earlier training in an embracive tradition of geography, Boas often spoke of human history as an intimate part of the environment: "the description of a country as the theatre of historical events is the best basis for elementary teaching of Natural Sciences" (AMCA: FB/MKJ 3/2/97). Three proposed exhibits on New England at the arrival of the Pilgrims, the discovery and conquest of Central America, and Arctic whaling were to show "the nature of the country, its products, its inhabitants, the manner in which the natives utilized the products of nature and how the immigrants utilized them" (ibid.).

Although none of these was ever built, Boas' conception of them shows that he took very seriously the problem of finding suitable topics for different segments of the general audience of a large urban museum of natural history. As he worked on these proposals over 1897 and 1898, Boas consulted with school officials so that the exhibits would form "the strongest possible stimulus to the system of teaching in our Public Schools" (ibid.). Echoing the founders of many Gilded Age museums, Boas pointed to the "interests of manual and technical training" (AMDA: FB/MKJ 5/28/98), hoping, as they did, that manufactures would be improved by the exposure of craftsmen to the accumulated heritage of the world's cultures (cf. Goode 1889:72–73). But perhaps the most important component of this audience was the many newly arrived and poorly educated city dwellers. "No other portion of our people are in more urgent need of educational advancement, and the instruction of no other class will act more favorably upon the whole body politic" (AMCA: FB/MKJ 3/2/97). It was precisely for these nonprofessional patrons that the city supported the Museum, and Boas worked to meet their needs.

The scientists, however, the smallest sector of the museum audience, were

for Boas the most important part: "the essential justification for the maintenance of large museums lies wholly in their importance as necessary means
for the advancement of science" (1907:929). If research on material culture
were not done at the large museum it could be done nowhere, for it was "the
only means of bringing together and of preserving intact large series of material which for all time to come must form the basis of scientific inductions"
(ibid.). A prime example of such collection-based research was Boas' 1897
study of "The Decorative Art of the Indians of the North Pacific Coast."
Drawing only from American Museum collections, Boas was able to codify
for the first time the formal principles of this style.

For Boas, advanced research was intimately linked to advanced instruction, and he worked carefully to match the needs and opportunities of university and museum. By 1899, the year he was made a full professor and the
Columbia Department of Anthropology became autonomous, Boas felt that
the Museum's ethnological collections "are now well arranged, and can be
used to advantage for advanced instruction and for research" (AMCA: FB/
MKJ 12/31/98). That year he initiated ethnology courses taught at the Museum and illustrated them with specimens, and in 1902 even offered a successful course in museum administration.

At this point both university and museum needed one another. During the
summer graduate students "carried on field-work for the Museum, and have
thus enjoyed the advantage of field experience" (FBP: FB/N. M. Butler 11/
15/02), while the Museum gained well-documented collections. During the
academic year, the graduate students "based their researches largely on the
collections of the Museum" (ibid.). The students thus received professional
training, the results of which were embodied in the exhibits and publications
of the Museum. The program's success can be seen in the work of Columbia's
first Ph.D. in anthropology, Alfred L. Kroeber. Kroeber's expedition to Arapaho territory, funded by Mrs. Jesup, returned to the Museum with its first
collections from the American Plains. Kroeber then combined artifactual
and textual evidence for his thesis on Arapaho decorative symbolism (1901).

Scientists shared with the general public the need actually to *see* the collections in order fully to exploit them. In recounting how he had come to
write his famous article on Eskimo needle cases (1908), Boas remarked:

> With the problem of the influence of traditional styles upon invention before
> my mind, I went through the collections of the National Museum, and hap-
> pened to find in one case most of the needle-cases here discussed assembled.
> Without being able to see them, I am sure the point would never have come
> home to me.
>
> (FBP: FB/A. M. Huntington 4/13/09)

Accordingly, Boas recommended that because of "the multiplicity of the points of view from which the material can be viewed," as well as differences in "size, form, and material," anthropological material "can only be stored satisfactorily in such a way that each specimen can be seen" (1907:930–31). But if scientists needed to see specimens, they did not need elaborate exhibits, especially those with a high ratio of models and mannequins to actual artifacts.

The fieldtrips that generated both the study collections and the exhibits thus had quite different goals for Boas and the administration. Of the Jesup Expedition to the Northwest Coast, Boas wrote:

> The work which we are carrying on is by no means primarily collecting, but it is our object to carry on a thorough investigation of the area in which we are working. The specimens which we obtain are not collected by any means from the point of view of making an attractive exhibit, but primarily as material for a thorough study of the ethnology and archaeology of the region.
> (AMDA: FB/G. M. Dawson 5/2/99)

Director Bumpus thought otherwise. "Field expeditions of the Museum must not be carried on for scientific purposes, but only to fill gaps in the exhibitions: . . . if accidental scientific results can be had, they are acceptable, but . . . they must not be the object of field-work" (FBP: Memo, Interview with Jesup & Bumpus 5/17/05).

At the beginning of his tenure, however, Boas still felt that these diverse interests could be harmonized. Collections were to be divided into an "exhibition series" for the general public and a "study series" for the specialist. "All specimens that do not serve to illustrate certain facts or points of view must be excluded from the Exhibition Series and included in the Study Series" (FWPP: FB/FWP 11/7/96). Thus while the exhibition series was almost wholly dedicated to "Public Instruction," the study series served the advancement of science. Such a division, dating back at least to Louis Agassiz in 1860 (Meyer 1905:324–25), had become widely adopted by Boas' time, especially by American museums. Over the decade he remained at the Museum, Boas was to find that it was no easy thing to realize this dual ideal in practice.

Boas and the Practice of Museum Exhibition

What did Boas' exhibits look like, and why? In evaluating these exhibits it is necessary to consider to what extent the displays flowed directly from Boas' conscious intentions, and to what extent they failed to match these goals.

As a case study we will consider in detail the Hall of Northwest Coast Indians. This hall, from his major area of research and exceptionally well-
documented for a turn-of-the-century exhibit, received the most direct and
continuous attention from Boas, and thus best embodied his vision of exhibition.

In addition to his strongly held views on the theoretical implications of
museum exhibits, Boas approached his task with an implicit philosophy of
the exhibit process itself. For a man whose work reveals a certain aversion to
visual thinking (Jacknis 1984:43–52), Boas was quite sophisticated in his
understanding of how the average visitor experiences a museum exhibit.
With an approach evidently derived from his earlier doctoral research on
psychophysics as well as his own observations on visitor behavior, Boas strove
to gain the attention of the viewer, to concentrate it upon a single point,
and then guide it systematically to the next in a series of points. The constant
danger was the loss of attention, either through confusion due to the multiplicity of points, or boredom due to the repetition of effects. As we go
through Boas' exhibits we will see these principles applied again and again
on various levels.

The structure of our discussion will mirror that of the museum as the visitor
traces a route through a hierarchy of nested spaces—the permanent environment of the building, creating the halls, which enfold the temporary and
movable "museum furniture" (cases and mounts), and a range of nonspeci-
men components (mannequins, models, graphics, and labels), surrounding
the objects themselves (cf. Brawne 1982:9–37).

The Museum Building

Boas arrived at the Museum in a period of vast expansion (Wissler
1943:table 6). In 1896 parts of two halls were devoted to anthropology; by
the time he left there were eight (about two-thirds for ethnology, the rest for
archeology), most of them housed in a separate anthropology wing that
opened in 1900. But in spite of this generosity of space, Boas did not get the
kinds of spaces he wanted. Like most curators, he had little to say about the
planning, even for the wing built during his tenure, complaining later that
"a thorough reorganization of museum administration will not be possible
until the plan of operation of the museum is decided upon before the museum
building is erected" (1907:933).

Believing as he did that the major purpose of a large museum was to accumulate the artifactual base for scholarship, and that, on the other hand,
the exhibits were primarily for the general viewer, Boas thought that "the
line between the exhibition halls open to the general public and the study
collections open to students should be drawn much more sharply than is
generally done" (AMDA: FB/F. Hooper 6/13/03):

In planning a museum, I should be inclined to arrange a series of exhibition halls for the public on the ground floor. . . . Above these I should arrange a number of halls with lower ceilings for study collections, but accessible to the public. Here the cases can be placed close together; and systematic arrangement would be the prime object, not attractive exhibitions. These halls would be used by teachers, high-school scholars, students, etc. . . . Over these halls would be storage-rooms, workshops, offices, etc.

(Ibid.)

He in fact recommended a ratio of one unit of exhibition hall to two units of study collections to one unit of work-rooms.

For the thwarting of this plan Boas blamed the Museum's architecture.

Hall of the American Southwest and Mexico, American Museum of Natural History, ca. 1902 (negative number 488 [photograph by E. F. Keller], courtesy of the Department of Library Services, American Museum of Natural History).

"The whole museum . . . is laid out in large magnificent halls [and] the pro-portional amount of space available for storage in a building of this kind is so small that full use of the stored material for scientific purposes is entirely out of the question" (1907:932). At a time of such active collecting, even the construction flurry of the nineties could not keep pace, and the high-ceilinged halls robbed needed space from storage areas. Specimens had to be stored wherever there was room, often in the exhibition halls themselves (AMDA: FB/MKJ 3/25/99).

In a period when lighting was still largely natural, illumination was an-other structural feature over which the curator had little control. The North-west Coast Hall was part of the original museum building, and large glass windows had been generously donated by Theodore Roosevelt, Sr., a founder-trustee and owner of a plate-glass company. But with the glass com-ing down almost to the floor along both side walls, there was a terrible prob-lem of reflection in the cases, which was "particularly disturbing in ethno-logical collections on account of the smallness of the objects" (AMDA: FB/MKJ 1/11/97). Fading was also a problem: "the skylight destroys our speci-mens, and . . . attendants in the halls are required in order to regulate the light according to the position of the sun and clearness of the sky" (AMDA: FB/MKJ 6/13/99). Although by the turn of the century artificial illumination (a circle of bare bulbs ringing each column and a decorative fixture over each large case) helped brighten evenings and dark days, it did not yet allow the special effects of later museum dioramas.

Hall Arrangement

Much of the curator's art lay in the proper juxtaposition of objects, whether in cases or in halls. Boas had argued in 1887 that the particular grouping of specimens was a classificatory act, which, in turn, would com-municate to the visitor a particular theory of (material) culture, and despite some concessions, he was generally able to arrange his American Museum halls in accordance with these ideals.

The content of the halls was determined by provenance, subdiscipline, and size. By and large, all anthropology halls were contiguous, on each of four levels. Halls were apportioned on the basis of collection strengths, with an entire large hall each for Northwest Coast ethnology and Mexican archeol-ogy. In the case of relatively small collections such as South America or the American Southwest, archeology and ethnology were combined. Where pos-sible, neighboring halls were devoted to contiguous regions: the Eskimo were next to the Northwest Coast, Siberia adjacent to the Eskimo. A residual hall, the West Vestibule, held the oversized items such as totem poles, tipis, and petroglyph casts (cf. Hovey 1904 for a complete listing and description of the Museum's halls).

In arranging cases within a single hall, Boas strove to direct visitor attention along a structured path. Viewing order was suggested most directly by the sequence of numbers and letters over each vitrine, which also served as an index to descriptions in a guide leaflet. Boas tried to avoid a large central aisle flanked by rows of cases, because visitors would "wander from right to left without order and it is impossible to compel them to see the collections in such a manner that they will have the greatest possible benefit from a short visit" (AMDA: FB/MKJ 1/11/97). His preferred solution was to install a partition down the center, with the cases set up against it: "By dividing the Hall into two longitudinal halves . . . visitors are compelled to see the collections in their natural sequence, and even if they pass through only one half of the Hall will be more benefited than when seeing one alcove here, one there" (ibid.). A bonus in this plan was the potential use of the added wall space for maps, diagrams, large labels, murals, and the like.

From the evidence at hand, it seems that Boas never fully implemented this scheme, though he came close in his Northwest Coast Hall, where two parallel rows of low desk cases for archeological specimens stretched between a life group and a village model in large cases at either end. While it was possible to walk down a small central aisle between the two rows, most visitors walked along the outer sides, passing next to the large alcove cases holding the bulk of the collections. Within the latter, specimens were arranged according to two separate principles: "First, a general or synoptic collection of specimens obtained from the entire area, designed to illustrate the culture of the people as a whole; Second, several independent collections, each illustrating the peculiarities of the culture of a single tribe" (Hovey 1904:41).

The synoptic series, installed in the first five polygonal cases along one side, was grouped by cultural domains: the use of natural products, basic industries, house furnishings, dress and ornaments, trade and barter, hunting and fishing, travel and transportation, armor and weapons, musical instruments, decorative art, and clan organization. Following these, the cases in the tribal series snaked up one side of the hall and down the other, in order from north to south (of both the hall and the region): first the Tlingit, then Tsimshian, Haida, Bella Coola, Kwakiutl, Nootka, and Coast Salish, followed at the end by exhibits from the geographically neighboring but culturally distinct interior Plateau tribes. Boas included them in both the Jesup Expedition and the hall resulting from it in order to ascertain and then illustrate the limits of the culture area and the effects of local history and environment. Within each of these tribal units materials generally followed the sequence used in the synoptic series, with local omissions and additions.

Such a scheme served several functions at once. Prepared primarily for the general visitor (FBP: FB/MKJ 4/29/05), the briefer synoptic series was a kind of "condensed culture," presenting the main outlines of the culture area. The rest of the collections, arranged geographically, explored in greater depth more specialized topics. Given the shortage of usable storage space, this dual plan effected a compromise between heavily didactic displays open to all, and the closed storage areas open only to qualified researchers. Finally, the bulk of the geographically arranged collections would form the "indifferent background" necessary to set off the few striking displays. Boas seems consciously to have intended that a great part of the exhibits would be ignored by the general public (1907:923–25).

Installation

In a period of burgeoning collections and additions to the building, the order and arrangement of halls was constantly being changed; the Northwest Coast Hall was substantially altered in almost every year of Boas' tenure. The Northwest Coast collections filled only the east half of the Ethnology Hall when it opened on November 30, 1896, the other half being occupied by material from the Eskimo, northern Mexico, and Melanesia. Although they included Boas' Kwakiutl life group and a model of a Kwakiutl village, and the introductory synoptic series was already in place, many of the Northwest Coast materials were prior holdings, arranged simply according to who had collected them (FWPP: FWP/Report to MKJ 6/96). Upon completion of the new wing, the other specimens were moved out, leaving the entire hall for the rapidly accumulating specimens of the Jesup Expedition, and in 1901 the previous arrangement by collector was replaced by Boas' tribal scheme. Though the *Annual Report* for 1902 claimed the hall to be "completed in its main features," it saw several further changes before Boas left. Following the visit of George Hunt in the spring of 1903 the Kwakiutl collections were rearranged, and where necessary, recatalogued and relabeled. Later that year Salish and Sahaptin collections were rearranged, and in 1904 the Emmons Tlingit basket collection was added, along with new models of Kwakiutl fish traps and Kwakiutl case labels.

Although Boas worked, where possible, toward a permanent installation, he realized that for most of the halls it was "necessary to make the principle of arrangement somewhat elastic, allowing for the introduction of material that . . . will fill gaps in existing collections" (AMDA: FB/MKJ 11/14/97). While some of this flexibility was achieved by changing labels and moving cases, most came from leaving space within the case. Not appreciating Boas' motives, Jesup expressed his concern that "the collections were spread over great spaces, and it looked to me more as if the aim was to get [more] cases than the proper use of those we had" (AMCA: MKJ/FWP 8/2/02). But faced with the alternatives of closing the hall until the entire display was complete, or adding specimens haphazardly as they arrived, Boas chose to adhere to a structured scheme: "It would seem best to prepare first of all those exhibits which will make clear the idea of the whole arrangement and then add gradually the details as time and funds will permit" (FWPP: FB/FWP 11/7/96).

In the midst of this constant exhibit activity, Boas insisted that the Museum maintain the proper atmosphere for viewing the collections. Recalling
the "sanctuary" in the Dresden Museum, in which the Sistine Madonna was
exhibited, he insisted that

> everything in the hall should be calculated to increase the impression of dignity
> and of aloofness from every-day life. No dusting, no mopping, no trundling-
> about of boxes, should be permitted in a hall visited by the public, because it
> disturbs that state of mind that seems best adapted to bring home the ideas for
> which the museum stands.
>
> (1907:932)

Cases and their Contents

Unlike earlier private "cabinets," the major public museums of the late
nineteenth century employed a range of devices to clarify and explain the
import of the object at hand. Technological innovations were adopted as
rapidly as they were introduced. Accordingly, Boas' museological concerns
were forced to descend to the level of cases, mannequins, models, mounts,
graphics, and labels.

Cases served several functions. They stored and supported specimens, in
addition to protecting them against dust and the prying hands of visitors.
Boas was contantly berating the administration for sending him cases which
would not lock and for not giving him enough security guards. Although
many of the cases in the Northwest Coast Hall dated from the opening of
that part of the building in 1877, all new cases had to be custom made in the
Museum's shop, and artifacts could not be displayed until the requisitioned
cases were supplied.

Boas insisted that single mannequins be placed inside cases with the artifacts in order to demonstrate the correct disposition of costumes, ornaments,
and tools: "arranging ethnological specimens such as dress, ornaments, etc.
without them would be exactly the same as though Prof. Allen would hang
unmounted skins in his cases, or as though Prof. Osborn would leave his
specimens imbedded in rock and unmounted" (FWPP: FB/FWP 11/7/96).
Scattered around each hall there were plaster busts, depicting racial features
and the art of face painting (cf. Anon. 1906). Almost every hall also contained a detailed model of native habitations, although on a scale of 1:20—
since it was "impossible to show full size native habitations, because they take
such a vast amount of space without being thoroughly instructive" (FWPP:
FB/FWP 11/7/96). Diagrammatic models were used extensively to demonstrate special topics, like the different stitches used in basketry, or the iconography of Northwest Coast designs.

Hall of Plains Ethnology, American Museum of Natural History, ca. 1904 (negative number 42642 [photograph by I. I. C. Orchard], courtesy of the Department of Library Services, American Museum of Natural History).

Graphic material in the cases consisted of drawings and photographs. Especially in his displays of art, Boas employed explanatory drawings: "When I say for instance, this [design] is a beaver, I want to point out on a good sketch, what parts characterise the beaver" (FWPP: FB/FWP 11/16/95). Although enlarged photographs were used in the cases, Boas did not employ them as systematically as the National Museum. When it came to the supporting elements within the cases, Boas and Putnam both felt that "the only conspicuous thing we wish to have in the case is the object itself, and next to that the label; but [that] the mounting should be as inconspicuous as possible" (FBP: FWP/FB 11/18/95). Accordingly, the small metal stands used to support artifacts were painted the color of the shelves. Because he found that the standard bluish-white labels contrasted too much with the mostly dark specimens, "so that the whole case assumes an appearance of restlessness," Boas tried to "quiet down the appearance of the whole Hall" by using case labels matching the shelves and specimen labels approximating the specimen color (FWPP: FB/FWP 9/12/96).

Attention was again concentrated in the arrangement of the artifacts on the shelves: "I have selected from among the material all the typical specimens and have arranged them so that each case presents a certain point of view in Indian life" (FWPP: FB, as quoted in FWP report to MKJ 6/30/96). Furthermore,

> In arranging the collections I have, of course, not crammed the cases, but placed the material so that it can be seen to advantage. I do not believe that we can interest the public, if we do not give each specimen a chance to be seen individually and so that its label can be studied in connection with it.
>
> (FWPP: FB/FWP 9/12/96)

Although in contemporary photographs we see cases that appear quite crowded, it may be that Boas was forced to display more of the collection than he would have wished, because of a lack of storage space. Alternatively, our sense of what is crowded and what is spacious may have changed over the decades, as the general cultural shift from Victorian plenitude to Art Moderne spareness produced a re-evaluation of aesthetic sensibilities in museum display (cf. Harris 1978:159–68). Be that as it may, Boas' successor, Clark Wissler, in 1908 found plenty of specimens that could be profitably removed (AMNH Annual Report for 1908:36, cf. Dorsey 1907:585).

Life Groups

The life group mode of display would seem to be the perfect device to depict the kinds of local and contextual meanings and functions Boas was trying to get across, and at first, Boas' plans were extremely ambitious. After outlining eight groups, comprising twenty-eight figures, he estimated that he

Case of Bella Coola masks in the Northwest Hall, ca. 1905 (negative number 386 [photograph by R. Weber], courtesy of the Department of Library Services, American Museum of Natural History).

would need another twenty groups with about seventy additional figures (FWPP: FB/FWP 12/5/95). Yet by early 1900 only twenty-three figures had been completed, and many of these were used individually, not in groups (AMDA: FB/MKJ 2/24/00). Despite their popular appeal, the problems they presented in scientific and artistic veracity seem to have made them not worth the great effort they entailed.

Of all contemporary exhibit techniques the life group called for the greatest amount of materials, time, and skill. Several media were then available for modelling the figures, among them wax, papier-mâché, and plaster (cf. Goode 1895). Like the National Museum, the American Museum used plaster, which was relatively easy to work with and durable, and provided a good surface for paint. The life group preparator for the American Museum was

Caspar Mayer, whom Boas regarded as a sculptor of "great talent." "He is particularly well fitted to our work on account of the strong tendency to accuracy and realism," and as "an enthusiastic student [he] is really grasping the scientific aims of his work" (FWPP: FB/FWP 8/5/96).

The method developed by Mayer involved taking plaster life casts of the face and various body parts (FWPP: FB/FWP 10/1/96; Wissler 1943:222). These casts came from diverse sources: some were collected along with the artifacts in the field (as were the casts for Boas' two Kwakiutl groups), some from the visiting circus or the Carlisle Indian School, and some from occasional visits of natives to New York. Occasionally, when casts from life were unavailable, model makers worked from photographs and measurements. Boas himself demonstrated the poses for the National Museum figures (cf. Hinsley and Holm 1976:308–10), and had his field photographer record several poses for the American Museum cedar crafts group (cf. Jacknis 1984:33–36). Clay molds were made from the preliminary casts, and the parts of the body were joined with modelling clay. The whole was then reproduced in a

Franz Boas demonstrating a pose of the Kwakiutl hamatsa dancer for model makers at the U.S. National Museum, February, 1895 (negative number 8304, courtesy of the National Anthropological Archives, Smithsonian Institution).

final plaster cast, and the skin color painted on. The figures were then combined with artifacts, again, either collected specifically for the display (as for Boas' Kwakiutl groups) or drawn from existing collections. This entire process was guided, whenever possible, by the original field collector.

Most of the groups produced during Boas' tenure came from the Northwest Coast and Eskimo—regions strongly represented in the Museum's collections, where Boas' own expertise sped matters along. Although documentation is vague, apparently groups from northern Mexico, the American Plains, and Siberia were also completed before 1905. In their subject matter, Boas' groups were hardly distinguishable from those of Holmes and other contemporary museum anthropologists. Typically, each group showed "a family or several members of a tribe, dressed in their native costume and engaged in some characteristic work or art illustrative of their life and particular art or industry" (AMAC: FWP/MKJ 11/8/94). The groups frequently depicted the construction of artifacts as well as their use. Because Boas tried to represent both male and female subsistence activities, and children were usually included in larger scenes, a home scene was the perfect condensation of these characters and activities. In keeping with Boas' theme for the educational displays, most scenes demonstrated the relation of man to nature. The Kwakiutl cedar crafts group vividly illustrated the role of this plant in their life: "A woman is seen making a cedar-bark mat, rocking her infant, which is bedded in cedar-bark, the cradle being moved by means of a cedar-bark rope attached to her toe" (Boas 1900:3–4). The other figures included a woman shredding bark, a man painting a box, another man tending a fire with tongs, and a young woman drying fish over a fire.

For Boas, the primary purpose of the life group was to catch the visitor's attention and direct it to more specific exhibits (FWPP: FB/FWP 11/7/96). Speaking of the cedar crafts group, he wrote:

> I have taken notice that on Saturdays when the Public leave the Lecture Hall, they invariably look at the group and then turn to the adjoining case and I find by their remarks that I succeeded in reaching the end that I had in view in this arrangement. The visitors discuss the uses of the implements comparing them to those they see in the group and stop to read the labels.
>
> (Ibid.)

Given their role as glorified stop signs, Boas invariably tried to position life groups in a central aisle adjacent to the larger cases holding the primary collection.

Yet despite their evident success, life groups from the beginning had for Boas a series of drawbacks: the inherent limitations of realism; the distraction caused by impressive display techniques; and the dulling of effect through repetition. Although the life group strove in principle for realism, the circumstances of museum exhibition conspired to defeat that goal:

The Northwest Coast Hall from the south, ca. 1902 (negative number 351 [photograph by E. G. Keller], courtesy of the Department of Library Services, American Museum of Natural History).

It is an avowed object of a large group to transport the visitor into foreign surroundings. He is to see the whole village and the way the people live. But all attempts at such an undertaking that I have seen have failed, because the surroundings of a Museum are not favorable to an impression of this sort. The cases, the walls, the contents of other cases, the columns, the stairways, all remind us that we are *not* viewing an actual village and the contrast between the attempted realism of the group and the inappropriate surroundings spoils the whole effect.

(FWPP: FB/FWP 11/7/96)

The larger the group, felt Boas, the harder it was to achieve the illusion of reality, because more of the distracting background would be included in the vista, and because even with ample museum space the group would be crowded, compared to its natural state. Boas therefore recommended that only small, unified groups be constructed.

The limitations Boas faced become clearer when he described what would be necessary for a really successful illusion:

> In order to set off such a group to advantage it must be seen from one side only, the view must be through a kind of frame which shuts out the line where the scene ends, the visitor must be in a comparatively dark place while there must be a certain light on the objects and on the background. The only place where such an effect can be had is in a Panorama Building where plastic art and painting are made to blend into each other and where everything not germane to the subject is removed from view. It cannot be carried out in a Museum Hall.
>
> (Ibid.)

In fact, however, all the life groups constructed by Boas or the National Museum were meant to be viewed from all sides, without the illusionistic painted backgrounds and lighting effects of the diorama—which were popularized only after 1910 by Clark Wissler at the American Museum (1915), and Samuel Barrett at the Milwaukee Public Museum (1918).

Realistic effects were equally elusive in the case of mannequins, especially when they were viewed at close range.

> No figure, however well it may have been gotten up, will look like man himself. If nothing else, the lack of motion will show at once that there is an attempt at copying nature, not nature itself. When the figure is absolutely lifelike the lack of motion causes a ghastly impression such as we notice in wax-figures. For this reason the artistic effect will be better when we bear in mind this fact and do not attempt too close an approach to nature; that is to say, since there is a line of demarcation between nature and plastic art, it is better to draw the line consciously than to try to hide it.
>
> (FWPP: FB/FWP 11/7/96)

In order to stylize the figure Boas recommended three methods: figures should be shown in a moment of rest, not at the height of action; skin color and texture should be an approximation only; and the hair should be represented by paint or modelling, not by actual hair. Although wigs of real hair were in fact used, otherwise the groups under Boas' direction do follow these strictures.

Boas was also concerned lest "the element of impressiveness" that life groups possessed might "overshadow the scientific aim which they serve" (ibid.). He was also critical of museums in which "the group is arranged for effect, not in order to elucidate certain leading ideas" (ibid.). In a later essay Boas gave an example from the American Museum habitat dioramas. Visitors marveled at a case of gulls hovering with no apparent support over ocean waves. Rather than studying the bird and surroundings, they came away instead with "admiration of the technical skill exhibited in the installation" (1907:923).

In this context, more was not better. For with the "undue multiplication of groups of the same type," the "impressiveness of each is decreased by the excessive application of the same device" (1907:925). Again Boas offered evidence from his own experience: "Any one who will observe the visitors of the United States National Museum strolling through the Catlin Hall, which contains the Indian groups, will readily see how the first group seems very interesting, and how quickly the others appear of less and less interest and importance" (ibid.). Familiar with the psychophysical principle that the repetition of a stimulus led to habituation, Boas felt that such large displays should be used sparingly and set off against an "indifferent background." Thus, although Boas believed life groups to be a necessary display technique, especially for the general visitor, they forced to his attention the compromises he had to make in the attempt to popularize anthropology.

Labels and Texts

By its nature the museum display communicates primarily through the medium of tangible objects. The extent to which words—in the form of labels, pamphlets, or monographs—were able to complement, supplement, or supplant the object became for Boas the ultimate limitation to the possibility of a museum anthropology.

Labels were quite important to Boas. The departmental secretary acted as label-writer, whenever possible basing the copy on the monographs prepared by the original field collectors. Labels were arranged hierarchically: each case contained a large, summary label such as "Nootka" or "Northern Plains Tribes"; smaller labels announced smaller units such as "Ceremonials" or "Games"; near each specimen was a tag with basic identifications. Similarly, the import of the life groups was spelled out with a set of labels, each commenting on a different aspect of the scene.

For such popular halls as the Northwest Coast and Mexico, brief pamphlets were prepared, "easily read as one passes from case to case" (Gregory 1900:63). Boas' guide to the Northwest Coast Hall, printed in November 1900, proved to be so popular that all five thousand copies had been given out within seven months (FWPP: FWP/MKJ Report for 1901). For those wishing further detail, copies of the monographs prepared by Museum scientists were chained to the appropriate cases. Collections were in fact installed as nearly as possible in the order of the treatment in the monograph, so that each publication was "a full description of the contents of a case or of several cases (AMDA: FB/H. C. Bumpus 8/21/02). By 1902, however, some of the monographs were getting too heavy to attach to cases, and thereafter visitors wishing to consult them were directed to the Museum's library (AMDA: FB/

H. A. Andrews 9/16/02). From labels for the general visitor to monographs for the advanced scholar, each visitor was thus offered verbal information at the level he or she desired. Here again we see how Boas attempted to harmonize diverse interests by a system of overlay and juxtaposition.

But from the very beginning, Boas felt that the exhibited artifacts were ultimately subordinate to the monographic interpretation of the scientist. Upon hearing that the Chicago Fair administration would not pay for the publication of scientific reports. Boas complained to Putnam that

> The specimens are only illustrations of certain scientific facts. . . . The specimens from the North Pacific Coast are interesting, but their vital interest lies in their interpretation. . . . The collections will remain dead letters until this interpretation which is indicated on the labels is substantiated in a report.
>
> (FWPP: FB/FWP 12/11/93)

When Mason and Goode commissioned Boas to prepare an annotated description of the Northwest Coast artifacts in the National Museum, they intended to use this catalog as a basis for exhibit labels. Goode stressed to

The Northwest Coast Hall, northern end, American Museum of Natural History, ca. 1902 (negative number 12633, courtesy of the Department of Library Services, American Museum of Natural History).

Boas that it would be inappropriate for them to publish the manuscript Boas intended to submit, which consisted largely of social and linguistic data. "The work of the Museum is limited," Goode maintained, "to the administration of the collections under its charge"—the main object was "to bring under control the *collections* which we now have" (FBP: GBG/FB 2/5/95). Yet by this time Boas had largely completed the manuscript, and although "The Social Organization and the Secret Societies of the Kwakiutl Indians" did discuss the cultural context of artifacts, using National Museum specimens as illustrations, it was hardly an annotated catalog.

During Boas' American Museum tenure, his policy of delaying labeling until the corresponding monographs had been completed was a continuing bone of contention. Although Jesup had instructed that any collection placed on exhibition "should be a complete thing labeled and defined," he had been "surprised" after a visit to the halls, to find "how little I knew or could find out about them" (AMCA: MKJ/FB 8/2/02). In reply Boas simply asserted that "publication, installation, and labelling go hand in hand": "Every contribution to the publications of the Museum in this section is a contribution to our labelling" (AMDA: FB/H. C. Bumpus 8/21/02).

From there the disagreement rapidly spread to the relation of fieldwork and research, and to its communication in exhibition. Bumpus admonished Boas, "I cannot help feeling that I may have made a fundamental mistake in yielding to the urgent appeals for purchases and continued field work and the general enlargement of our collections, rather than to have first cared for the proper installation of the material actually on hand" (AMCA: H. C. Bumpus/FB 12/18/03). Denying that fieldwork interfered with the work of installation, Boas argued that the "fragmentary state of most of our collections" in fact necessitated more fieldwork for proper installation. "In the three halls in which our fieldwork has been most systematic, the labelling is most complete and satisfactory" (AMDA: FB/H. C. Bumpus 8/21/02). Thus did a disagreement over labeling—a matter of exhibit installation—escalate to a challenge to Boas' basic conception of a professional anthropology. Such strains could not go long unresolved.

Boas' Resignation from the American Museum

Having come to feel that these frustrations and constraints were not accidental, but the expressions of inherent limitations in museum anthropology, Boas began in the fall of 1904 the final train of events that led to his resignation. That October he informed the administration that "the work in the Museum did not seem to me profitable, and I preferred to be relieved of administrative duties . . . but that I would like to continue the scientific work in which I am particularly interested" (FBP: FB/H. F. Osborn 5/6/05). Bumpus, however, instead asked Boas to take on an added responsibility when the Departments of Ethnology and Archaeology were recombined after having been separated in 1903. Realizing that a suitable replacement could not be found, Boas acceded to a unified chair, but only under strict conditions: more money was to be pledged for fieldwork, and Boas was to have complete and total control over the new department. After five weeks of review of departmental activities, Boas submitted a report to Bumpus. This report, and Bumpus' fierce attack upon it, proved to be Boas' final undoing at the Museum.

Boas made a series of appeals to President Jesup, which led to a May 17 meeting with the Director and the President. When Jesup sided with Bumpus, Boas decided his position was untenable, and by the end of the week had submitted his letter of resignation, citing "fundamental differences of opinion relating to administration between the director and myself" (FBP: FB/MKJ 5/23/05). An agreement with the Museum called for his functional separation as of July 1, 1905, but for his continued supervision for one more year of the scientific work of the department—essentially the editing of the Jesup Expedition reports.

The divergence of the two sides came out clearly in the prime grievances cited by each. For Boas, authority was the stumbling block. He refused to allow the Director to appoint someone not under his own direct control to carry out installation work, and he objected violently to Bumpus countermanding orders he had issued for such work. He was "absolutely unwilling to be curator and as such responsible for the department, and to have no other function than to carry out the instructions of the director" (FBP: FB/H. F. Osborn 5/6/05). As far as Jesup and Bumpus were concerned, the main problem had to do with Boas' exhibits. Thus, Bumpus directed Clark Wissler to redo the Blackfoot Indian display so that it would then be "intelligible, instructive, orderly, and attractive" (FBP: HCB/FB 4/28/05), and he found the Mexican Hall "entirely unworthy" in either "scientific or educational" terms (ibid.)—noting specifically the lack of systematic order and comprehensible labels. But, in the end, the two problems of authority and exhibit style were one, for what bothered the administration was not so much Boas' research, but his exhibit work, and it is in this arena that they attempted to intervene. Although his ultimate interests lay elsewhere, Boas would not yield responsibility for public displays in his department.

A microcosm of these divergent positions and a precipitating cause for Boas' resignation was the installation of the Peruvian collection. According to Jesup, this collection, which had been "gotten together at large expense," had remained in the Museum "for a long time without any approach to adequate classification, instructive labeling, or creditable exhibition" (FBP: MKJ/FB 4/28/05). Instead of waiting for Boas, Jesup directed Bumpus and Adolphe Bandelier, the collector, to arrange the exhibit. In keeping with systematic arrangements elsewhere in the Museum, the team devised a scheme of fixed categories, either by function (house life, industries, personal adornments) or by material (stone, wood, clay). To someone who had advocated the position that "in ethnology all is individuality" in a debate almost two decades earlier, the Bumpus-Bandelier scheme must have been especially frustrating; and to have such a typological exhibit imposed in his own department from without only compounded the problem. As for the delay in arranging the collection since entering the museum, Putnam had responded to this issue when it had first arisen in 1897: "It is often necessary to spend days upon a specimen which is afterward put on exhibition in a few minutes, and only the final result, the simple exhibition of the object, is noticeable" (FWPP: FWP/MKJ 5/10/97).

But there were probably also more profound ideological differences at issue. Echoing the optimistic evolutionism so widespread in his age, Jesup had called for "a series illustrating the advance of mankind from the most primitive form to the most complex forms of life" (FBP: Notes of interview with MKJ & HCB, 5/17/05). Echoing his earlier remarks that "civilization is not something absolute . . . and that our ideas and conceptions are true only so far as our civilization goes" (1887b:66), Boas, in one of his final pleas to Jesup, talked of his desire to impress upon the general public "the fact that our people are not the only carriers of civilization, but that the human mind has been creative everywhere" (FBP: FB/MKJ 4/29/05).

The clash between Boas and Jesup was inevitable, given their fundamentally opposed opinions about the Museum's audience and purpose. Jesup, himself not a trained scientist, wrote: "In my experience, I find that any one who is capable of interesting children or youth in *any* subject will always get and retain the interest and attention of older people" (FBP: MKJ/FB 5/2/05). Although Boas recognized the two levels of a general and advanced audience, he refused to reduce the displays to the lowest level: "By adapting every exhibit to the level of the needs of the uneducated, we frustrate our object of adding to the knowledge of the educated who come here in search of more special information" (FBP: FB/MKJ 4/29/05).

Attacking the facile popularizers of science, Boas later warned of the danger when "intelligibility is too often obtained by slurring over unknown and obscure points which tend to make the public believe that without any effort, by listening for a brief hour or less to the exposition of a problem, they have mastered it" (1907:922). Boas wanted his exhibits to "bring out the sublimity of truth and the earnest efforts that are needed to acquire it" (1907:923). He had long believed that the needs of various audiences could be reconciled, even within a single exhibit, but if he was forced to choose, he felt that specialized interests came first.

Two years after his resignation Boas summarized his experience in a general essay on the "Principles of Museum Administration." Although he still held out hope for the proper scientific use of museums, the essay represented his museological swan song. Over time, Boas' confrontation with "the limitations of the museum method of anthropology" began to resonate, theoretically and institutionally, throughout American anthropology. By 1907 he had concluded that "the psychological as well as the historical relations of cultures, which are the only objects of anthropological inquiry, can not be expressed by any arrangement based on so small a portion of the manifestion of ethnic life as is presented by specimens" (1907:928). This theoretical reorientation took some time to establish itself. Boas' own attempt to move anthropology from an artifact-based utilitarianism to a more contextual, relative, and psychological stance was to find its major methodology in the creation of native texts, which in many ways still possessed an object-ive character. A more observational and behavioral kind of anthropology had to await the work of his students in the twenties (cf. Stocking 1976:13–23).

As far as the institutional base of anthropology was concerned, Boas by 1905 had come to question his earlier position that "university instruction" and the "general educational aims of the Museum" were both "very easily harmonized" (FBP: FB/Zelia Nuttall 5/16/01). Nor were his experiences unique. Of the early joint university-museum programs, which existed at Harvard, Pennsylvania, Berkeley, and Chicago, as well as at Columbia, only the one at Harvard continued to thrive as such; and because it concentrated almost solely on archeology, it was the exception which proved the rule (cf. Darnell 1969:140–264). At all the others the same kinds of constraints, though in different combinations and emphases, worked to divide the interests of the museum and those of the university. Although museums continued until 1930 to be a major locus for anthropology, especially for research (cf. Stocking 1976:9–13), the end of the "museum era" had long since been foreshadowed in the end of Boas' own museum connection.

Acknowledgments

This is a revised version of two earlier papers, completed in 1975 and 1979. For helpful comments on preceding drafts, I would like to single out George Stocking, and thank also John Adams, Douglas Cole, Raymond Fogelson, and Curtis Hinsley. For the opportunity to present portions of this material in lecture I thank the Newberry Library, Chicago; the Field Museum of Natural History, Chicago; Public Broadcasting Associates, Boston; and the Los Angeles County Museum of Natural History. I also acknowledge the permission of the various repositories to consult and to cite documents, and to publish photographs—which, at the Editor's suggestion, have in several instances been cropped.

References Cited

Alexander, E. P. 1964. Artistic and historical period rooms. *Curator* 7:263–81.

———. 1983. Artur Hazelius and Skansen: The open air museum. In *Museum masters: Their museums and their influence*, 239–75. Nashville.

Altick, R. D. 1978. *The shows of London: A panoramic history of exhibitions, 1600–1862.* Cambridge, Mass.

AMAC. See under Manuscript Sources.

AMCA. See under Manuscript Sources.

AMDA. See under Manuscript Sources.

Anonymous. 1906. The series of ethnographical busts. *Am. Museum J.* 6:4–6.

Barrett, S. A. 1918. Photographic and panoramic backgrounds: Anthropological groups. *Museum Work* 1:75–78.

Boas, F. 1887a. The occurrence of similar inventions in areas widely apart. In Stocking 1974:61–63.

———. 1887b. Museums of ethnology and their classification. In Stocking 1975:63–67.

———. 1887c. Reply to Powell. *Science* 9:614.

———. 1897a. The decorative art of the Indians of the North Pacific Coast. *Bul. Am. Museum Nat. Hist.* 9:123–76.

———. 1897b. The social organization and the secret societies of the Kwakiutl Indians. *Rept. U.S. Natl. Museum, 1895*:311–738.

———. 1900. *Ethnological collections from the North Pacific Coast of America: Being a guide to Hall 105.* Am. Museum Nat. Hist. New York.

———. 1907. Some principles of museum administration. *Science* 25:921–33.

———. 1908. Decorative designs of Alaskan needlecases: A study in the history of conventional designs, based on specimens in the U.S. National Museum. *Procs. U.S. Natl. Museum* 34:321–44.

———. 1909. The Kwakiutl of Vancouver Island. *Mem. Am. Museum Nat. Hist.* 8:301–522.

Brawne, M. 1982. *The museum interior.* New York.

Brown, T. M. 1980. Cultural evolutionists, Boasians, and anthropological exhibits: A new look at American anthropology, 1887–1905. Unpublished master's thesis, Johns Hopkins Univ.

Colby, W. M. 1977. Routes to Rainy Mountain: A biography of James Mooney, ethnologist. Unpublished doct. diss., Univ. Wisc.–Madison.

Darnell, R. D. 1969. The development of American anthropology 1879–1920: From the Bureau of American Ethnology to Franz Boas. Unpublished doct. diss., Univ. Penn.

———. 1972. The professionalization of American anthropology: A case study in the sociology of knowledge. *Soc. Sci. Inform.* 10:83–103.

Dorsey, G. A. 1907. The anthropological exhibits of the American Museum of Natural History. *Science* 25:584–89.

FBP. See under Manuscript Sources.

FWPP. See under Manuscript Sources.

Frese, H. H. 1960. Anthropology and the public: The role of museums. *Mededelingen van het Rijksmuseum voor Volkenkunde* 14.

Goode, G. B. 1882. Plans for the installation of collections. *Procs. U.S. Natl. Museum, 1881.* Appendix 16.

———. 1889. Museum history and museums of history. *Papers Am. Hist. Assn.* 3:252–75. In *Smithsonian Inst. Ann. Rept., 1897.* Part 2:63–81 (1901).

———. 1895. Recent advances in museum methods. *Ann. Rept. U.S. Natl. Museum, 1893:23–58.*

Gregory, W. K. 1900. Guide to Northwest Coast Hall. *Am. Museum J.* 1:63.

Harris, N. 1978. Museums, merchandising, and popular taste: The struggle for influence. In *Material culture and the study of American life,* ed. I. M. G. Quimby, 140–74. New York.

Hinsley, C. M., Jr. 1981. *Savages and scientists: The Smithsonian Institution and the development of American anthropology, 1846–1910.* Washington.

Hinsley, C. M., Jr., & B. Holm. 1976. A cannibal in the National Museum: The early career of Franz Boas in America. *Am. Anth.* 78:306–16.

Holmes, W. H. 1903. The exhibit of the Department of Anthropology, Report on the exhibits of the U.S. National Museum at the Pan-American Exposition, Buffalo, New York, 1901. *Ann. Rept. U.S. Natl. Museum, 1901:200–18.*

Hovey, E. O., ed. 1904. A general guide to the American Museum of Natural History. *Guide Leaflet* No. 13.

Jacknis, I. 1984. Franz Boas and photography. *Studies Visual Commun.* 10:2–60.

Kennedy, J. M. 1968. Philanthropy and science in New York: The American Museum of Natural History, 1868–1969. Unpublished doct. diss., Yale Univ.

Kroeber, A. L. 1901. Decorative symbolism of the Arapaho. *Am. Anth.* 3:308–36.

Mark, J. 1980. *Four anthropologists: An American science in its early years.* New York.

Mason, O. T. 1887. The occurrence of similar inventions in areas widely apart. *Science* 9:534–35.

———. 1889. Report upon the work in the Department of Ethnology in the U.S. National Museum for the year ending June 30, 1886. *Ann. Rept. U.S. Natl. Museum, 1886:87–91.*

———. 1890. The educational aspect of the U.S. National Museum. *Johns Hopkins Univ. Studies Hist. & Pol. Sci.* 8:504–19.

———. 1894. Ethnological exhibit of the Smithsonian Institution at the World's Columbian Exposition. In *Mem. Int. Cong. Anth.,* ed. C. S. Wake, 208–16. Chicago.

———. 1895. Department of Ethnology. *Ann. Rept. U.S. Natl. Museum, 1893:125–32.*

Meyer, A. B. 1905. Studies of the museums and kindred institutions of New York City, Albany, Buffalo, and Chicago, with notes on some European institutions. *Ann. Rept. U.S. Natl. Museum,* 1903:311–608.

Mooney, J. A. 1894. Outline plan for ethnologic museum collection. National Anthropological Archives. Typescript.

Parr, A. E. 1959. The habitat group. *Curator* 2:107–28.

Stocking, G. W., Jr. 1968. From physics to ethnology. In *Race, culture and evolution,* 135–60. New York.

———. 1976. Ideas and institutions in American anthropology: Toward a history of the interwar period. In *Selected Papers from the American Anthropologist, 1921–1945,* 1–44. Washington.

Stocking, G. W., Jr., ed. 1974. *The shaping of American anthropology, 1883–1911: A Franz Boas reader.* New York.

Sturtevant, W. C. 1969. Does anthropology need museums? *Procs. Biol. Soc. Washington* 82:619–50.

Wissler, C. 1915. In the home of the Hopi Indians. *Am. Museum J.* 15:343–47.

———. 1943. Survey of the American Museum of Natural History. Central Archives. Am. Museum Nat. Hist. Typescript.

Manuscript Sources

In writing this paper, I have drawn on research materials collected from the following archives, cited as abbreviated.

AMAC.   American Museum of Natural History, Department of Anthropology, Accessions 1894–95 and 1901–36. New York.

AMCA.   American Museum of Natural History, Central Archives, Department of Library Services. New York.

AMDA.   American Museum of Natural History, Department of Anthropology, Departmental Correspondence. New York.

FBP.   Franz Boas Papers, Professional Correspondence. American Philosophical Society. Philadelphia.

FWPP.   Frederic Ward Putnam Papers. Correspondence. Harvard University Archives. Cambridge, Mass.

PHILANTHROPOIDS AND VANISHING CULTURES

Rockefeller Funding and the End of the Museum Era in Anglo-American Anthropology

GEORGE W. STOCKING, JR.

The Commodity Economy of Evolutionary Anthropology

Despite its implicit nominal assertion of generalized human relevance, anthropology through most of its history has been primarily a discourse of the culturally or racially despised. The marginality of its human subject matter has not for the most part strengthened anthropology's claim on the limited resources society makes available to support the pursuit of nonutilitarian humanistic knowledge. And while anthropologists have attempted in various ways to argue the social utility of a knowledge of "Others," such claims have only occasionally been honored. As a result, the resources that sustain and constrain the creation of anthropological knowledge have been limited. They have also often been indirect and mediated, in the sense that anthropological activities have been incidentally or adventitiously supported by funds intended for some other purpose, channelled usually through institutions not specifically anthropological. Characteristically, this mediation has involved a complex negotiation of not-fully-comprehended cross purposes.

This often implicit mediation is variously evident in the late nineteenth and early twentieth centuries, when the discipline had barely got a foothold in universities—whose presidents and trustees were in any case little able (or

---

George W. Stocking, Jr., is Professor of Anthropology and Director of the Morris Fishbein Center for the History of Science and Medicine at the University of Chicago. He has just completed a year as John Simon Guggenheim Memorial Foundation Fellow, during which he finished *Victorian Anthropology*, a book on British social evolutionism.

112

inclined) to support research in the human disciplines. Although Lewis Henry Morgan devoted $25,000 of his own funds to the single-minded pursuit of data on kinship systems (Resek 1960:106), and General Pitt Rivers was able to hire crews of workmen to dig barrows on his own estate (Chapman 1981), in general those who wished to carry on more-than-avocational anthropological research had to rely on resources other than those solely under their personal control. In the United States, government support proved to be a possibility. John Wesley Powell's success in 1879 in convincing Congress that anthropology would be useful in getting Indians peacefully allocated to reservations made it possible for the Bureau of Ethnology to underwrite a large amount of research on topics somewhat tenuously related to that end (Hinsley 1981). So also, Franz Boas in 1908 managed to fund environmentalist physical anthropological research under the umbrella of a congressional commission devoted to the restriction of the immigration of "racial" groups presumed to be genetically inferior (Stocking 1968:175). But in Great Britain (Van Keuren 1982), government was much less forthcoming; and in both countries the golden age of government funding still lay far in the future.

In this context, anthropologists had to turn to wealthy individual benefactors, and to a particular cultural institution—the museum—which was in turn supported largely by their benefaction (cf. Kusmer 1979). Here, again, the mediation of cross purposes was often in evidence. Support for the establishment of anthropological work at the University of California may be seen as a well-intentioned subversion of Mrs. Hearst's instinct of aesthetic accumulation from the artifacts of classical culture to the languages of digger Indians (Thoresen 1975). So also, in seeking support for Far Eastern research in the aftermath of the Spanish American War, Franz Boas appealed to the commercial interests of the entrepreneurs of transcontinental railroads; but he also justified his request to these archetypes of the American way in terms of a relativizing appreciation of the achievements of distinctive civilizations (Stocking 1974:294–97). Such attempts to build bridges of enlightened self-interest were always problematic; try as he might, Boas could not raise money from Andrew Carnegie and others for a museum of Afro-American culture (316–18).

Insofar as support was forthcoming, it was facilitated by the fact that material objects served as both commodity and medium of exchange within the restricted political economy of anthropological research. From the perspective of donors whose beneficence was sustained by success in the world of commodity production, palpable and visible objects could be seen as a return on investment, even if their aesthetic or utilitarian value was minimal by conventional cultural standards. From the perspective of anthropologists, the collection of objects for sale to museums was an important if somewhat tenuous means of capitalizing research on less marketable topics. Between them, at the center of the political economy of anthropological research, stood the museums, institutions premised on the collection and display of objects. Although not often devoted solely to anthropology, they were prior to the first World War the most important single institutional employers of anthropologists, and channelled into anthropological research an amount of support that has yet to be calculated—the return for which was most quickly evident in the boxes and bundles of cultural objects sent back for warehousing and display (cf. Darnell 1969:140–235).

Quite aside from the nature of its political economy, a number of intellectual factors also conspired to sustain an object orientation in anthropological research. To a much greater extent than today, knowledge itself was thought of as embodied in objects; William Rainey Harper took it for granted that a museum was as essential as a library to the creation of a great university (Stocking 1979:11). As a discipline organized around the principle of change in time, and devoted primarily to groups that had left no written records, anthropology had a strong internal intellectual push toward the collection and study of material objects permanently embodying moments of past cultural or racial development. Within an evolutionist framework, human physical remains, archeological finds, and contemporary material culture were the most ready means of graphically illustrating the development of mankind; and though they were not convenient for public display, even the texts collected by linguists had rather an "object" character (Stocking 1977). Indeed, it might be argued that the existence of an object orientation within each of its major subdisciplines was one of the strongest factors sustaining their somewhat problematic presumptive unity in a general "anthropology."

While Boas might have questioned whether the tendency is inherent in museum display per se, it seems likely that in an ideological milieu befogged by evolutionary racialist assumption, such an object orientation often contributed to a degrading and distancing objectification of the "Others" who had made the objects, and who were themselves literally objectified in museum displays. Be that as it may, there seems to have been some tendency for the more object- and museum-oriented anthropologists to be more closely identified with the dominant groups in American culture, and with the cultural ideology that justified their dominance (Stocking 1968:270–307).

Already before the outbreak of the first World War, however, the evolutionary viewpoint had been brought seriously into question, first in American and then in British anthropology. The historically oriented diffusionisms that immediately succeeded it still to some extent sustained an object orientation insofar as they conceived culture as a collection of easily transportable thing-like "elements." But even within the "historical school" certain leading figures in both countries had already begun to move away from an object-oriented museum-based anthropology. By 1905, when he severed his connection to the American Museum of Natural History, Franz Boas had clearly decided that the psychological issues that had always been central to his concern could not be effectively pursued in a museum context (cf. Jacknis, this volume). In England, the emerging social anthropological orientation of Radcliffe-Brown and Malinowski strained not only against the object-oriented museum tradition, but against historical anthropology itself (Stocking 1984). In Boas' case, this movement was associated with a more general critique of racialism; in the British case, it reflected at least a more positive valuation of the culture of "savages." While "Others" themselves might still in a metaphoric sense be objectified by the scientizing orientation that long survived the demise of evolutionary anthropology, in both countries "objects" as such were soon no longer to provide a focus for the unity of anthropology.

But if there was an endogenous intellectual movement within anthropology away from objects and museums, it was by no means evident to all at the time that this trend was to become dominant in the Anglo-American tradition. On the contrary, the immediate postwar period was one of considerable ferment and even disarray. In the United States, there was a brief reaction against the newly dominant anti-evolutionary cultural anthropology of Boas and his students, many of whom shared his immigrant background and anti-war sentiments. Taking advantage of Boas' attack on several museum-oriented anthropologists who had carried on espionage work for the United States government, a group of Waspish "patriots" attempted a coup in the American Anthropological Association in 1919, and were momentarily successful in ousting Boas from leadership. Some among them sought to redefine anthropology in "hard" scientific racialist terms, and to reorient it away from the historical study of the American Indians toward important arenas of contemporary domestic and foreign concern—the problems of immigration restriction and the peoples of the Pacific (Stocking 1968:270–307; cf. 1976).

In Britain, where the movement away from evolutionism had been later and less cohesive, the groupings within the discipline were more diverse. Although an elder generation of museum-oriented anthropologists still dominated the Royal Anthropological Institute, a strongly diffusionary school had emerged under the leadership of the neurological anatomist-cum-Egyptologist Grafton Elliot Smith, who sought to derive all human culture from a group of seafaring, sun-worshipping builders of megalithic monuments. Somewhere in between were the ethnographically oriented anthropologists who occupied the important positions at Oxford, Cambridge, and the London School of Economics—several of whose students were turning away from historical questions toward the present-day "functioning" of the groups they studied in the field (Langham 1981; Stocking 1984).

In this situation of lively intellectual competition, the commitments made by a major new funding alternative—the private foundation—could be a powerful selective influence. And indeed Rockefeller philanthropy, which did so much to reshape the whole range of human science in this period, was also to play a major role in determining the outcome of the post-evolutionary reorientation of Anglo–American anthropology.

From Human Biology to Cultural Determinism

By 1920, the vast bulk of the $450,000,000 which the ambiguous dynamic of robber barony and protestant ethic had set aside for "the well-being of mankind" had already been received by the four institutionalized Rockefeller philanthropies—the Rockefeller Institute for Medical Research, the General Education Board, the Rockefeller Foundation, and the Laura Spelman Rockefeller Memorial (Fosdick 1952:ix). Their organization and administration, however, would not reach mature form until 1928, and the early 1920s were a period of redefinition of philanthropic priorities and of transition in administrative style. Prior to this time, the dominant role in the definition of philanthropic policy had been played by Frederick T. Gates, the Baptist minister who long served as the elder Rockefeller's philanthropic aide-de-camp, and whose primary interest lay in the field of medicine and public health. When John D., Jr., decided in 1910 to devote himself almost full time to philanthropy, his somewhat broader vision of social welfare tended to meet Gates's resistance (Fosdick 1956:138–42). Although early initiatives in the social sciences ran aground upon the conflict of corporate and philanthropic interest in the aftermath of the "Ludlow Massacre" in 1914 (Grossman 1982), the elder Rockefeller's creation of the Laura Spelman Rockefeller Memorial in 1918 to further his late wife's social reform interests reopened the possibility of social scientific research (Bulmer 1981). After 1920, in the context of a broadening of Rockefeller philanthropic activity overseas and an increasing focus on the support of institutions of higher learning, there was a general shift towards the encouragement of research as the best means of promoting human welfare (Fosdick 1952:135–45; Karl & Katz 1981; Kohler 1978; Bulmer 1981).

The movement toward academic research reflected the greater prominence within Rockefeller (and other) philanthropies of a group of academically trained foundation bureaucrats who came to play a very influential role in the determination of policy (Kohler 1978; Bulmer & Bulmer 1981:358–59). In relation to anthropology, the key figures were Beardsley Ruml (who had received a Ph.D. in psychology at Chicago under James Angell), Edwin R. Embree (who had studied philosophy and served in administrative posts at Yale), and Edmund Day (who had been professor of economics at Harvard and Michigan). As the intellectually free-wheeling director of the Spelman Memorial, Ruml was instrumental in convincing its trustees in 1922 that practical social welfare must be grounded first on a firm foundation of social scientific research. When the Foundation proper established a Division of Studies in 1924, Embree played a key role in organizing a program of research into "Human Biology." Day was subsequently to become Director of the Division of Social Sciences when all the research activities of the various Rockefeller philanthropies were consolidated within the reorganized Rockefeller Foundation in 1928. All three men shared Ruml's orientation toward the social sciences: that practical social welfare depended on developing first a more rigorously "scientific" and empirical social science, based on first-hand observation of living human beings rather than on historical materials, classificatory systems, or general theoretical speculation—a social science that would produce "a body of substantiated and widely accepted generalisations as to human capacities and motives, and as to the behavior of human beings as individuals and groups" (quoted in Bulmer & Bulmer 1981:362).

For Ruml, biology was one of the social sciences, and as Embree's program title suggests, a generalized "psychobiological" orientation was very influential in Rockefeller philanthropic circles in the early 1920s. Heavily influenced by racialist and evolutionist assumption still widely prevalent in the natural and social sciences—and momentarily resurgent in anthropology—it implied a kind of theoretical unity underlying a number of issues of practical social concern, ranging from immigration and crime to public health and mental hygiene to fertility and child development. Insofar as it expressed a generalized concern with the composition, quality, and control of the population of a complex industrial society, this postwar distillation of the progressive impulse may easily be interpreted as an ideological expression of the class interests of leading groups within a maturing corporate capitalist system (cf. Haraway 1977). To a considerable extent, however, the story of Rockefeller anthropology in the interwar period is that of the redirection of the interest in "human biology" toward the study of human sociocultural differences.

Although it was in Day's division that a program in cultural anthropology was eventually to develop, the earliest Rockefeller involvement in anthropology developed willy-nilly out of the research of Davidson Black, a Canadian army surgeon who took the chair in embryology and neurology at the Foundation's Peking Union Medical College in 1918 (Hood 1964). Black had become interested in human paleontology while studying comparative anatomy in 1914 with Elliot Smith, who was then working on the "remains" of Piltdown Man. Despite the fears of Foundation officials that Black's anthropology would distract him from teaching (RAC: R. M. Pearce/DB 4/4/21), he was able to carry on the work that led to the discovery of Peking Man in 1926, and over the next decade the Foundation's previously limited support

reached a total of almost $300,000 to Black and his successor Franz Weiden-
reich.[1] In 1920, Elliot Smith himself was a principal beneficiary of some
$5,000,000 the Foundation gave to support medical research at University
College, London (Fosdick 1952:109; cf. Fisher 1978)—and which incidentally sustained the institutional base from which Smith and his disciple William Perry propagated their controversial diffusionist notions. In this context,
Smith for a while seems to have been cast in what was to become an infor-
mally recognized role in the Rockefeller philanthropies: that of "expert anthropological advisor."

Davidson Black's work, like the China interest generally, had a somewhat
special status within Rockefeller philanthropy. With the development of the
psychobiological research orientation of the early 1920s, however, several
interdisciplinary proposals put forward by scholars in the United States were
to lead towards a more systematic program in anthropology. The first two of
these came to the Spelman Memorial, and their fate reflects the influence of
Ruml's personal, institutional, and intellectual affiliations in academic psychology. Ruml's own psychological research had been in mental testing, and
during the first World War he had worked on the large-scale psychological
testing program carried on for the U.S. Army (Bulmer 1981:354). One of
the leaders of that program, Robert Yerkes, went on to take a leading position
with the National Research Council [N.R.C.], which was heavily funded by
the Foundation; and when Yerkes approached the Memorial in 1923 for
money to support the N.R.C.'s new Committee on Scientific Problems of
Human Migration, Ruml was immediately receptive (RAC: RMY/BR 2/26/
23). Although the Committee began as a de facto research arm of the immigration restriction movement, the $132,000 contributed by the Memorial
over the next four years in fact helped to undermine traditional restrictionist
assumptions. The work of the Committee was heavily influenced by Clark
Wissler, whose own mildly nativist leanings enabled him to mediate between
the racialism of the hard-science establishment and the cultural determinism
of the Boasian school, with which in general he identified. In this context,
Rockefeller support for the N.R.C. (which included a major fellowship program in the biological sciences), had by the early 1930s sustained a considerable amount of Boasian anthropological research, including Mead's work
in Samoa, Herskovits' physical anthropological studies of the Negro, and
Klineberg's studies of the intelligence of Negro migrants—each of which

1. Although there is no single overall summary of dollar figures for Rockefeller support of
anthropology, an internal office document (Program and Policy, folder 910), initialed NST and
dated 3/31/33, lists "Anthropology appropriations made by LSRM and RF" to that date, by
institution (or in some cases, individuals). In arriving at overall totals for the period, I have
supplemented these figures with later appropriations, as indicated in particular institutional files,
or in the *Annual Reports* of the Rockefeller Foundation, 1934–38.

were major building blocks of the emerging anti-racialist scientific consensus (Stocking 1968:299–300; cf. Coben 1976).

Later on in 1923, Ruml received a second psychobiological initiative that was to lead toward cultural studies. His mentor Angell, who became the president of Yale in 1921, proposed the establishment of a "Psycho-Biology Institute" that would study psychic life from a comparative point of view with emphasis on man and the higher primates (RAC: JNA/BR 5/4/23; cf. Haraway 1977). The plan fitted well with Ruml's policy of developing a few major social scientific research centers, and by the following June, when Angell had succeeded in attracting both Yerkes and Wissler to Yale, the Spelman Memorial voted $200,000 to support the Institute of Psychology over a five-year period (RAC: BR/JNA 6/27/24). Reorganized in 1929 as the Institute of Human Relations, the Yale project was ultimately to receive many millions from the various Rockefeller foundations. Although the major anthropological item was $550,000 for Yerkes' primate researches, there was a small but significant flow of support to more culturally oriented studies under Wissler, and over the long run the Institute was heavily influenced by the increasingly dominant environmental and cultural orientation within the social sciences generally (May 1971).

A third psychobiological initiative in 1923 led, in an even more dramatic transformation of motive, to the first major Rockefeller programs in cultural anthropology per se. In December of that year, the racial polemicist Madison Grant forwarded to the Rockefeller Foundation a proposal from the eugenicist Galton Society for a study of the effects of natural selection among Australian Aboriginals as "the best approach to a proper understanding of the artificial conditions of selection now operating in civilized communities" (RAC: MG/R. B. Fosdick 12/29/23). When the proposal was referred to Embree in the newly organized Division of Studies, he followed up already established anthropological connections within the Foundation by writing for advice to both Davidson Black and Elliot Smith, who had just been invited to lecture at the University of California in 1924 (RAC: ERE/DB 3/19/24; ERE/GES 3/19/24). En route, Smith stopped off to consult with Embree, Wissler, and C. B. Davenport, another leading Galton Society racialist (RAC: ERE/CBD 4/10/24). Somewhat to the consternation of the Society, which felt control of the project slipping away, Embree sent Smith on to Australia to investigate the local anthropological situation—following a general Rockefeller Foundation policy that its own initiatives must always be linked to some local commitment of resources and personnel (RAC: ERE/GES 5/7, 5/8/24).

The Australian scene was at that point in some confusion. A plan to found a university chair in Sydney in anthropology, which was developed at the second Pan-Pacific Science Congress in Sydney in 1923, had been undercut when a British colonial officer sent out to advise the government on the administration of its island mandates told them that "special training in anthropology was not advisable" for colonial administration (RAC: GES/ERE 5/19/, 5/21/24). Encouraged by Rockefeller support, however, the Prime Minister agreed to reconsider his opposition, and within the next several months Elliot Smith was able to report that two of the state governments had voted financial support (RAC: GES/ERE 9/30, 11/5/24). In the meantime, the sudden death of the Sydney professor of anatomy, and the refusal of Davidson Black to leave Peking to replace him, undermined the biological aspect of the scheme, which the Australian National Research Council had in any case from the beginning conceived in social anthropological terms (RAC: GES/ERE 6/17/25). Late in November 1925, the Foundation received news that Elliot Smith, A. C. Haddon, and a third elector had chosen for the chair A. R. Radcliffe-Brown, one of the two leading exponents of "functionalist" social anthropology, over the historical diffusionist A. M. Hocart (RAC: Office Memo, 11/28/25). Although Radcliffe-Brown was completely unknown to the Rockefeller people, they invited him to tour American anthropological institutions on his way to Australia (RAC: G. Vincent/ARB 1/7/26).

By this time, the Australian scheme had become linked with other research initiatives that had developed in the Pacific in the postwar period. In 1919, the N.R.C. had established a Committee on Pacific Exploration (later, Investigations), which took the lead in organizing the first Pan-Pacific Science Congress; and about the same time Yale University and the American Museum of Natural History had joined in a cooperative scheme designed to revitalize the Bernice P. Bishop Museum of Honolulu. H. E. Gregory, the Yale geologist who became chairman of the N.R.C. Committee, was appointed Director of the Bishop Museum, fellowships were established for Yale graduate students, and $40,000 given to Yale was channelled through the Museum to support four anthropological field parties of the Bayard Dominick Expedition to Polynesia. Wissler, a member of the N.R.C. Pacific Committee, became "Consulting Ethnologist," and a physical anthropologist was sent from the American Museum to round out an anthropological staff that had jumped from one to seven (Stocking 1968:297–98). By the time the Rockefeller Foundation became interested in Australian anthropology, Gregory was looking for further sources of support for the Bishop Museum program (RAC: ERE/HEG 5/29/25).

Almost simultaneously, the Foundation received another initiative from Hawaii, when the president of the University there forwarded a memo on the study of racial differences written by S. B. Porteus, an Australian-born educational researcher who had just come from the Vineland, N.J., Training School for mental defectives—another stronghold of the eugenics movement (RAC: ERE/A. L. Dean 1/5/25; Porteus 1969). Faced with all these possibilities in the Pacific, Embree came out himself to investigate, traveling first to

Australia with Wissler, and then returning to Honolulu, where they were joined by E. G. Conklin, a leading biologist associated with the Galton Society (RAC: ERE/A. L. Dean 5/29/25; ERE/Vice Chancellor, Univ. of Sydney 7/1/25; ERE/HEG 7/1/25). Despite the turn away from biology, Embree sent back a favorable report on the Australian plans (RAC: ERE/G. Vincent 12/20/25); and while the Wissler and Conklin reports from Hawaii were oriented toward human biology and racial psychology, they also emphasized the need for institutional cooperation, in line with Rockefeller policy of developing regional research centers (RAC: "Rept. on Res. in Biol. in Hawaii" 3/26).

In this context, the Foundation voted in May 1926 to make five-year grants to support all three Pacific research proposals. The smallest ($50,000 on a matching basis, later supplemented by $14,000 more) was for the Bishop Museum's continuing research program, which had been primarily cultural from the beginning—although its traditional ethnological focus on Polynesian migration could be interpreted in racial terms (BPBM 1926:25). In contrast, the support given to the University of Hawaii, totalling $215,000 over the next ten years, at first supported researches like those on racial temperament by Porteus and the anatomist Frederick Wood Jones. But when Jones left in 1930, the biological researches carried on by H. L. Shapiro were thoroughly in the Boasian tradition, and a series of visiting Chicago sociologists gave the whole program a decidedly culturalist turn (RAC: "Appraisal, U. of Hawaii, Racial Res." 8/38). In Australia, the money funnelled through the Australian N.R.C. did support some physiological researches, as well as field work by Porteus on the intelligence of Australian Aboriginals. But the bulk of the almost $250,000 granted by 1936 went for social anthropological field work there and in the nearby Southwestern Pacific (cf. RAC: ARB, "Rept. on Anthro. Work in Aust." 6/28/30).

The general pattern was clear enough: a number of "psychobiological" research proposals, several of them initiated by people with close ties to racialist doctrine, immigration restriction, or the eugenics movement, were favorably received by the new generation of administrator/academics, who were interested in furthering empirical social scientific research into human capacities, motives, and behavior. In almost every case, however, these initiatives were partially or totally transformed, as Rockefeller administrators accommodated to the rising current of sociocultural and environmental determinism within anthropology and the surrounding social sciences.

The Turn to British Functionalism

Although there were to be several later grants in support of research in human biology, these occurred within the framework of the cultural orientation that increasingly characterized Rockefeller anthropological activities in the later 1920s. Their somewhat tentative and ad hoc growth may be illuminated by considering the development of several more specifically anthropological initiatives within Ruml's social science program at the Spelman Memorial. In the United States, the earliest of these was an appropriation of $13,500 to the University of Chicago in 1926 to cover the first three years salary of Edward Sapir, the brilliant linguistic anthropologist (RAC: A. Woods/J. H. Tufts 5/19/25). When Sapir joined his colleague Fay-Cooper Cole in forwarding a program for field research (RAC:FCC/L. K. Frank 3/5/26; JHT/BR 3/29/26), however, the matter was sidestepped, despite favorable evaluations from Wissler and two Memorial staff members (RAC: L. Outhwaite, Memo. 4/9/26). Ruml apparently preferred at this point to work within the interdisciplinary regional social science centers the Memorial was already funding. Since these were given discretionary power over block-grant funds, anthropological work received support within the limits of the local definition of purpose and balance of disciplinary power. Thus when the Sapir-Cole request was channelled to the University of Chicago's Committee on Local Community Research, its mandate was stretched to cover Cole's archeological work in Illinois (RAC: L. C. Marshall/BR 5/31/26; cf. Bulmer 1980). Similarly, at Columbia, where Boas carried weight in the Committee for Research in the Social Sciences, anthropology was the indirect beneficiary of significant Spelman Memorial support (RAC: A. Woods/N. M. Butler 5/28/26).

In the meantime, a spinoff of the Cole-Sapir initiative was to lead toward further Rockefeller involvement in anthropology. The archeological training program Cole ran in the summer of 1926 stimulated more general interest among anthropologists in the N.R.C. in an "intercollegiate field-school" in the Southwest, where, coincidentally, local archeological interests had made a direct personal appeal to the younger Rockefeller during a visit he made there in 1926. Successfully co-opting or overriding the local interests, the nationally oriented anthropologists were instrumental in establishing a Laboratory of Anthropology modeled on the Marine Biological Laboratory at Woods Hole, Massachusetts. Over and above Rockefeller's large personal gift for physical plant, the Museum and Laboratory of Anthropology in Santa Fe received a total of $92,500 in Memorial and Foundation support during the next ten years, the great bulk of which went to support summer field work parties sent out from established university departments of anthropology (Stocking 1982).

Although more than half of the Laboratory's field work was to be in ethnology and linguistics, the impetus that led to it had come from anthropologists whose orientation was still rather traditionally "historical." Developments during this period in England, however, were to lead to Rockefeller involvement in a more "functional" anthropology. As part of Ruml's policy of supporting regional social science centers on a worldwide basis, the Memorial gave substantial support to the London School of Economics [L.S.E.], where investigations into the human and environmental bases of economics and politics fitted well with the psychobiological orientation then prevailing among Rockefeller officials (Bulmer 1981). Indirectly, this support helped to further work in cultural anthropology, which had been augmented in 1923 by the appointment of Bronislaw Malinowski, protégé of Charles Seligman, the School's Professor of Ethnology—an appointment which, paradoxically, had been designed to counter the development of Elliot Smith's rival (and also Rockefeller-funded) school of anthropology at University College.

Although Malinowski was the beneficiary of Rockefeller-funded research assistants, large-scale direct support to anthropology in Britain developed outside the School in relation to attempts to apply anthropology to practical problems of colonial administration (cf. Kuklick 1978). British anthropologists were quite active at this time in trying to counter unfriendly official attitudes like those evidenced in the matter of the Australian chair. Emphasizing the importance of racial psychological studies in colonial administration, Seligman and others sought to reform the rather stodgy Royal Anthropological Institute so that it might take on the more utilitarian functions of an imperial Central Bureau of Anthropology modeled after the U.S. Bureau of American Ethnology (RAC: C. G. Seligman/W. Beveridge 3/13/24). Although an appeal for funds to Ruml in May 1924 elicited no immediate action (RAC: J. Shotwell/BR 5/6/24), the Australian matter kept the issue of applied anthropology before the attention of Rockefeller officials. Early in 1925, Elliot Smith sent Embree clippings from the London *Times* in which he and others argued the importance of anthropology for empire (RAC: GES/ERE 1/20/25). In the meantime, men more directly involved in colonial affairs were also interested in furthering research initiatives.

At a conference in September 1924, a group of world missionary leaders and others critical of native policy in Africa advanced the idea of a "Bureau of African Languages and Literatures" to further native education through "the medium of their own forms of thought" (Smith 1934:1). Among them was Dr. J. H. Oldham, who had close relations with several American philanthropies interested in promoting the ideas of the Tuskegee Institute as a model for African education, and also with highly placed British colonial officials who shared his view that research into "the human factor" was the key to preventing the "impending racial conflicts" threatening Africa (Bennett 1960). Early in 1925 Oldham went to New York to drum up financial support, and when he subsequently forwarded more detailed plans to the Rockefeller people, they were favorably received (RAC: JHO/A. Woods 6/9/25). At a conference that September, the planners of the African Bureau broadened their project to include the study of African social institutions, "with a view to their protection and use as instruments of education" (Smith

1934:2). Returning to New York for further discussions with Ruml, Oldham argued that a nation with so many of the "African race" within its own borders could not afford to remain indifferent to the economic and social problems created by the rapid movement of capital into the African continent (RAC: JHO/BR 11/9/25). At the same meeting in which it appropriated $17,500 for the Royal Anthropological Institute over the next five years, the Spelman Memorial also voted support "in principle" for Oldham's scheme (RAC: BR/JHO 11/725), although it was not until a year later that it actually allocated $25,000 over a similar period to what had by then become the International Institute of African Languages and Cultures (RAC: BR/JHO 10/26/26).

Having made this commitment to British anthropology, Rockefeller officials apparently decided to establish closer contact with its prospective leaders—the Memorial inviting Malinowski for an anthropological tour of the United States which overlapped Radcliffe-Brown's similar tour for the Foundation (RAC: BR/BM 11/12/25). Although neither venture led to the mass conversion of the American "historical school" to "functionalism," Malinowski's, especially, was viewed as a great success. Crisscrossing the continent, he met leading "gentlemen of colour" in the South, visited Indian reservations in the Southwest, taught summer school at Berkeley (where he had earlier left a "meteoric trail"), and gave joint seminars with Radcliffe-Brown to Boas' students at Columbia. Everywhere he went, Malinowski urged the behavioral study of "the cultural process" in the ongoing present, insisting that it was "high time" anthropology took up earnestly "the economic problems and legal aspects of the present blending of human strains and cultures" (RAC: BM, "Rept. of American Tour" n.d.). The climax of his tour came when Malinowski joined Wissler in discussing the present state of anthropology at the Hanover Conference of the Rockefeller-funded Social Science Research Council. After Wissler opened the conference by predicting a "revolt" within the discipline in favor of "what my friend Malinowski calls functional anthropology," Malinowski went on to discuss the method of the new anthropology, its relation to the other social sciences, and its relevance for contemporary social problems (SSRC 1926: I, 26, 42–54). The assembled social scientists and foundation officials were very impressed (54–71). As Charles Merriam had earlier suggested to Ruml, Malinowski was the first anthropologist he had met who wanted to bring the old antiquarian discipline in close relation to "living social interests" (RAC: CEM/BR 4/24/26).

Even so, the Rockefeller philanthropies made no further commitment to British anthropology at this time, apparently because of "internecine strife" centering around the personality and theories of Elliot Smith (RAC: J. Van Sickle, diary 10/6/30)—who by this time was losing his earlier position of influence with the Foundation, which in 1927 rejected a proposal to support cultural anthropology at University College (RAC: GES/ERE 6/18/27). Indeed, after the opening of 1925–26, there seems to have been a momentary drawback from anthropology within the Rockefeller philanthropies. Aside from a small grant to the International Congress of Americanists in 1928, the only further direct support prior to the reorganization of 1928 was to the Institute for Comparative Research in Human Culture at Olso, which received support totalling $45,000 by 1934. Nonetheless, it was clear that when major anthropological funding was resumed, "functional" anthropology would have an inside track.

Malinowski, Oldham, and the Prevention of Race Wars in Africa

With the reorganization of the Foundation accomplished at the end of 1928, the advancement of knowledge was now defined as its central function. Although it was still assumed that research should eventuate in practical reform, the Trustees had accepted the position that "the margin between what men know and what they use" was "much too thin" (Fosdick 1952:140). The new divisional structure was oriented toward the major areas of human knowledge, with the humanities and the natural sciences each for the first time given independent recognition, and E. E. Day as director of the Division of the Social Sciences. Day's first grants were carried out without much ado along already established lines. In May 1929 the Foundation made a five-year grant of $75,000 to the Chicago Department of Anthropology (RAC: N. S. Thompson/F. C. Woodward 5/27/29); the following fall it voted $125,000 over the same term to the German association of scientific workers, which the now-defunct Spelman Memorial had supported on several occasions. Although the latter grant was in fact for a eugenically oriented study of the German people (RAC: F. Schmidt-Ott/EED 9/5/29), and the Foundation subsequently gave a small grant to support research on twins by the physical anthropologist Eugen Fischer (RAC: R. A. Lambert/A. Gregg 5/13/32), Day's primary interest was clearly cultural, and over the next several years he moved toward a unified program in this area.

The first major input came from Malinowski, whose performance at the Hanover Conference Day had witnessed in 1926. Although he had established a cooperative relation with Radcliffe-Brown at Sydney, Malinowski was not inclined to rest satisfied with only indirect access to field work support. Since the Southwest Pacific was in Radcliffe-Brown's hands, Malinowski moved toward Africa, where little professional field work had been done apart from the surveys of his colleague Seligman. By the end of 1928, he had joined forces with Oldham in a campaign to win major Foundation support (cf. Stocking 1984).

The opening salvo was Malinowski's plea for a "Practical Anthropology" that would study the pressing problems of land tenure and labor as they affected the "changing Native" and the colonial administrator fearful of "what might be called 'black bolshevism'" (Malinowski 1929:28). When Day came to London in June 1929, Malinowski pursued similar themes in both conversation and a memorandum on "The State of Anthropology . . . in England" (BMP:n.d.; EED/C. G. Seligman 6/24/29). Although functional anthropology offered "a special technique" of "rapid research" to solve such problems as how much labor must be kept in a tribe to maintain its economic base, the British universities (save L.S.E.) lacked an effective field work orientation. The critical problem was therefore to provide field work money, and the most likely channel was the African Institute, which had already inspired favorable interest from the Colonial Office. At the same time, Malinowski forwarded to Oldham a confidential "Report on the Conditions in the Rocke-feller Interests" by an unnamed "American Observer" suggesting that they would be receptive to a large-scale appeal stressing "the mutual unification of knowledge by practical interests and vice-versa"—especially if it had to do with "problems of contact between black and white and the sociology of white settlement" (BMP: n.d.). Fearful that the Royal Anthropological Institute and Elliot Smith at University College might be developing competing plans that would sacrifice "sound" anthropology for the study of fossil man and the diffusion of Egyptian cultural influences to Nigeria, Malinowski urged Oldham to "play any trump cards" he held "with a clear conscience" (BMP: BM/JHO 6/11/29). His concern, however, was needless. Previously briefed by Ruml, Day already felt that Malinowskian functionalism was the coming thing in British anthropology, although he cautioned the Rockefeller European representative not to let Malinowski know of "our favorable prejudice" (RAC: EED/J. Van Sickle 11/16/29).

The first fruit of that prejudice was an arrangement whereby anthropological field work was supported under the existing Rockefeller scheme of international postdoctoral fellowships (RAC: BM/EED 8/3/29; JVS/EED 12/23/29). In the meantime, Malinowski and Oldham worked to develop a "million dollar interlocking scheme for African research"—interlocking, because a parallel initiative on behalf of the new Rhodes House at Oxford was supported by men so powerful politically that the Institute felt forced to coordinate planning (RAC: H. A. L. Fisher et al./Pres., RF 3/28/30). In their private communications to Rockefeller officials, however, Malinowski and Oldham made it clear that their own plans took priority (RAC: BM/EED 3/

26/30). These were developed largely by Malinowski, who had begun to get an indirect practical familiarity with the African scene through a series of informal "Group Meetings" beginning in December 1929, in which missionaries, interested colonial officials and anthropologists—sometimes confronting each other from separate sofas—discussed the problems created by culture contact (BMP: BM/JHO 2/9/30). At the end of March 1930, a printed appeal was forwarded to the Foundation in separate letters from Malinowski and Lord Lugard, the retired colonial proconsul and ideologist of "Indirect Rule" who presided over the African Institute (BMP: BM/EED 3/26/30). In order to meet the dangers threatening "to defeat the task of Western Civilization" in Africa and to protect the "interests of the native population" in a period when world economic conditions foreshadowed "rapidly increasing exploitation," it was essential to carry on systematic field research along the lines of Audrey Richards' ongoing study of the tribal context of native mining labor in Rhodesia. Toward this end, and toward the training of administrators and missionaries in a more enlightened understanding of African cultural values, the Institute was requesting £100,000 over the next ten years (BMP: Mem. Presented to RF 3/30/30).

Despite opposition from biological scientists in the Foundation and the threat of competing initiatives in Britain, Malinowski and Oldham were successful in gaining Rockefeller support. After entertaining one of the European representatives at his Italian alpine villa, Malinowski told Oldham that the key was to win over Selskar Gunn, a biologist in charge of all the Foundation's activities in Europe (BMP: BM/JHO 9/17/30). Warning Gunn of the "possibility of racial wars of considerable magnitude," Oldham recounted Malinowski's "enthusiastic" reception by a group of colonial governors at a meeting in London (RAC: SMG, Diary 9/25/30). With the biological opposition thus effectively neutralized, the Foundation voted the following April to allocate $250,000 in matching funds to the Institute over a five-year period. At the same meeting it rejected the Rhodes House plan on the grounds that the Institute was more international, less compromised by political considerations, and therefore more likely to secure additional matching funding (RAC: RF minutes 4/15/31).

Although there were later to be small grants to the Institut für Völkerkunde in Vienna and the Institut d'Ethnologie in Paris, and a somewhat reluctant renewal of the earlier small grant to the Royal Anthropological Institute (RAC: JVS/EED 5/29/31), the Foundation seemed clearly to have committed itself to Malinowskian functionalism, at least as far as the British sphere was concerned. But at the very moment when his influence was firmly established, Malinowski began to feel it threatened by the man whom he had been inclined to regard as his collaborator in the functionalist movement.

"The Biggest Anthropological Pie Ever Concocted"

When the impending termination of the original five-year grant and the rapidly deteriorating financial situation of the Australian state and federal governments threatened the continuation of the Sydney program in 1930 (RAC:
A. Gibson/EED 3/3/31), Radcliffe-Brown approached Rockefeller officials
with an omnibus plan that would combine an extension of the Australian
grant and a proposal of his own for South African research with the Rhodes
House and African Institute proposals then under consideration (RAC:
ARB/EED 9/17/30; ARB/M. Mason 11/17/30). Suggesting that the time was
ripe for more general consideration of Rockefeller anthropological policy,
Radcliffe-Brown argued that no other science was faced with so dire a threat
as that involved in the rapid disappearance of "the lower forms of culture,"
which might well vanish entirely "within the next generation." Fortunately,
in the few years left, the "newer anthropology" based on the "functional
study" of cultures as "integrated systems" might still formulate "general laws
of social life and social development." Focusing on the present and future
rather than the past, it might even approximate an "experimental science"
that would be of "immediate service to those who are concerned with the
administration and education of native peoples." What was needed was "the
establishment of a number of research institutions around the world" to undertake cooperative investigation of the surviving native peoples "area by area
and tribe by tribe" (RAC: ARB, "Memo. on Anth. Res." 11/17/30). Radcliffe-Brown, who was leaving Sydney to take up an appointment at the University of Chicago, proposed to make his visit to London for the centenary
meeting of the British Association in September 1931 the occasion for a
concerted effort toward this goal (Radcliffe-Brown 1931).

Although Radcliffe-Brown had asked for Malinowski's aid in pushing his
"vanishing cultures" plan (BMP: RB/BM 9/17/30), Malinowski seems to have
viewed his return from the antipodes as a threat to his own planning(cf.
Stocking 1984). Vacationing in France, he received reports that Radcliffe-
Brown was offering Oldham advice on how to implement the Institute's "five-
year plan," and that Oldham was taking seriously Radcliffe-Brown's argument
that studies focusing on economic life in terms of "social cohesion" were
preferable to more comprehensive ethnographic inquiries (BMP: A. Rich-
ards/BM n.d.; JHO/BM 9/9/31). Equally disturbing was Radcliffe-Brown's
suggestion that the School of Oriental Studies, which at this point also had
an application before the Foundation for massive aid, was a more logical
institutional center than the L.S.E. for anthropological research throughout
the Empire—a center that Radcliffe-Brown indicated his willingness to head
(BMP: RB/BM 9/27/31, 1/30/32, 5/25/32). Nonetheless, Malinowski was influential in getting the School of Oriental Studies grant scaled down to

$36,000 and redefined in complementary rather than competitive terms (RAC: S. M. Gunn, interview with BM 3/4/31; SMG/EED 12/7/31, 2/1/32), and Radcliffe-Brown settled in Chicago for the next six years. Once broached, however, the idea of comprehensive reevaluation of its work in anthropology was pursued within the Foundation itself.

By 1931, the Foundation's commitments in this area were fairly numerous. In addition to the program in Britain, those in Hawaii and Australia then being renewed, and the ongoing support to the Chicago department, the Foundation was in the process of making grants to two other American departments: Harvard, where support for anthropology complemented a major commitment to Elton Mayo's researches in industrial psychology at the Business School (RAC: A. W. Tozzer/EED 11/22/30); and Tulane, where the personal intervention of an elder statesman of the General Education Board, Abraham Flexner, won a somewhat reluctant support for a bibliographic project in Middle American research (RAC: E. Capps, "Memo. on Proposed Inst." 6/9/30).

Faced with these rather disparate activities, Day was quite receptive when Radcliffe-Brown pushed the case for cooperative systematic research while he was teaching at Columbia in the summer of 1931. At a staff meeting late in July, Day argued that Radcliffe-Brown's memorandum established "a strong presumptive case" for a more unified program in cultural anthropology, which would provide comparative data for a contemplated Division in Behavior and Personality that Day hoped might be funded at $300,000 a year over the next fifteen years (RAC: EED, "Foundation's Interest in Cult. Anth." 7/30/31). In this context, the Foundation formally recognized cultural anthropology as "a special field of interest, the development of which presents an element of urgency" (RAC: RF Rept. 1931:249). After extended discussion at another staff conference the following January (RAC: "Staff Conf." 1/21/32), the Foundation's officers decided to undertake a full-scale survey of anthropological activities throughout the world (RAC: EED/S. M. Gunn 1/25/32).

Although Day considered asking Radcliffe-Brown himself to take charge of the survey (RAC: EED/SMG 1/25/32), it was decided instead to hire Leonard Outhwaite, a currently unemployed former staff member of the Spelman Memorial who had studied anthropology at the University of California. Over the next few months, Outhwaite traveled throughout the United States and Europe, interviewing over two hundred anthropologists at fifty-one different institutions. Although he made it a point to start with a blank slate—spending time in the beginning attempting to define the word "primitive" (RAC: LO/EED 4/19/32)—Outhwaite's ties to the Boasian tradition inevitably gave the survey a different character than it might otherwise have had. He found Radcliffe-Brown "challenging" but "extreme" (RAC: LO/EED 4/19/32); and while he thought Malinowski was "reasonable," he was disturbed by his tendency to act as the "Tsar" of anthropology (RAC: LO/EED 6/10/32). Outh-waite could see no essential distinction between the two, and concluded that their differences were "not strictly scientific" (RAC: LO, "Anthro. in Europe"). The clearly evident theoretical differences between British function-alists and American historicists he saw as reflections of the differing cultures they had studied—and was therefore inclined to favor an essentially atheo-retical approach to field work. He was opposed to the functionalists' "narrow-ing" of anthropology, and while he accepted their notion of the systemic integrity of cultures, he insisted that this, too, must be understood as an historical phenomenon. In the end, he associated himself with the "best and most conservative workers in each country"—among whom he included Cole, Kroeber, Lowie, Wissler, Haddon, Seligman, and the Viennese diffu-sionists (RAC: LO, "Condensed Rept." 23).

In the meantime, the American Anthropological Association, apparently at Day's urging, had established a Research Committee to develop its own plans for the study of vanishing cultures. The preliminary draft circulated by the Association's Secretary, John Cooper, prior to the Committee's first infor-mal meeting gave major priority to a trait-oriented study of the North Amer-ican continent (UCBA: JMC/A. L.Kroeber 4/21/32). As the proposal was refined at Committee meetings, however, the initial Americanist bias was dropped for a cooperative worldwide orientation and a "catholicity of eth-nographic approach" which even envisioned studies of the same tribe by func-tionalist and historical ethnographers (UCBA: JWC/ALK, n.d.). The scant evidence of the Committee's proceedings (AAAP) suggests that the modifi-cation was engineered by Radcliffe-Brown and Alfred Kroeber—the former walking with deliberate caution and the latter by nature a compromiser. The final version was delegated to a subcommittee of five, in which Edward Sapir and Alfred Tozzer were aligned against Radcliffe-Brown and Wissler, and a major input in fact came from Boas, who later on was to side with Radcliffe-Brown against his Americanist colleagues on the relative importance of field work and "source study" (UCDA: JMC/F. C. Cole 1/25/33).

On June 24, 1932, the Committee forwarded to the Foundation a twelve-year research proposal, including field work on three hundred tribes through-out the world, at a total cost of $5,000,000 (UCBA: [JMC]/RF; [JMC]/EED). The Foundation, however, delayed consideration pending the completion of Outhwaite's survey (UCBA: JMC/Res. Comm. 7/1/32). Comparing his own with the Association's scheme, Outhwaite noted that their "general conclu-sions" as to the scientific urgency of a global salvage program and their overall methodological approach were essentially the same, although his own was smaller in scope. Accepting Wissler's view that major field work in North America could be completed in five years, Outhwaite estimated total expenses averaging only $250,000 annually over a fifteen-year period. Outside the North American area, Outhwaite felt that the less professionalized and relatively "poverty-stricken" state of European anthropology necessitated a gradual "strategic" approach, beginning with surveys of the major cultural areas to define specific research programs. Although emphasizing the importance of individual field work by "general anthropologists" with "all-round" training, he was critical of the traditional one man/one monograph approach, urging also the possibility of interdisciplinary, regional and comparative studies. The major difference, however, was one of governance. Internal and international jealousies made Outhwaite dubious of the Association's plan to have the program supervised by an executive committee dominated by Americans. Although he was optimistic that theoretical rivalries need not "in practice" be a serious problem, he favored centralized control by an internationally oriented nonpartisan body—namely, the Social Science Division of the Rockefeller Foundation. In this context he recommended that the Association's proposal be turned down, at least in "its present form," while the Foundation pursued its own planning (RAC: LO/EED 10/12/32; UCBA: JMC/Res. Comm. 11/28/21).

At Outhwaite's suggestion, however, the Association committee was asked to develop plans for the American Indian field that might be incorporated into subsequent Rockefeller planning (UCDA: JMC/M. Mason 3/6/33). After several months of discussions, the Committee reached an impasse over the relative importance of further field work as opposed to the systematization and publication of existing North American data. When the president of the Foundation notified the Committee on April 26, 1933, that no support was feasible at that time, Cooper suggested that his letter seemed "to settle the tie vote" (UCBA: JMC/Res. Comm. 4/28/33; M. Mason/JMC 4/26/33). By this time, the Foundation had in fact decided not to pursue a major program in anthropology.

The anthropologists were somewhat at a loss to understand what had happened. One contemporary nonparticipant suggested that there had been a "series of undercover battles" between Malinowski and Radcliffe-Brown, and between each of them and the Americans (RAC: W. L. Warner/EED 9/15/33). While we have seen some evidence of this, there is also evidence of a spirit of compromise in the Association Committee; and towards the end Malinowski and Radcliffe-Brown also seem to have joined forces in the attempt to win "the biggest anthropological pie ever concocted" (BMP: BM/ W. Beveridge 11/19/32). By that time, however, the decision was already being made, on larger grounds than the internecine bickerings of anthropologists.

The essential context was the world economic crisis of the early 1930s, which not only presented the Foundation with an overriding immediate problem of human welfare, but also drastically reduced the income from its endowment. When the Trustees met in the fall of 1932 to review the program in the social sciences, Day proposed a concentration on certain major practical problems of social engineering, and especially on economic stabilization (RAC: "Verbatim Notes, Princeton Conf." 10/29/32). Although Day himself was still inclined to support cultural anthropology, the Trustees were moving toward a major policy reorientation in which anthropology would find little place. The early months of 1933 in fact marked the nadir of depression in the United States, and by the time they met again in April, the decision had already been made to shelve Outhwaite's report (RAC: S. H. Walker/J. Van Sickle 4/4/33). For the next year, while the Trustees carried on a ponderous reappraisal of the whole Foundation program, Day somewhat reluctantly declared a "moratorium in the field of cultural anthropology" (RAC: EED/ D. H. Stevens 11/24/33; EED/A. Gregg 12/19/34). Early in 1934, the decision was made to terminate it entirely, as far as the Social Science Division was concerned, and let the director of the Humanities Division "pick up any part he wants to salvage" (RAC: Staff Conf. 3/8/34).

As it happened, the Humanities Division did not pick up very much. Prior to that time, its orientation had been quite traditional, emphasizing the preservation of source material. Its only support to anthropology was to linguistics—directly by the grant to the School of Oriental Studies, and indirectly through the American Council of Learned Societies, which in the ten years after 1927 funnelled $80,000 to the Committee on Research in Native American Languages (Flannery 1946). But the Humanities Division was also affected by the policy reorientation of 1933–34, moving away from the "aristocratic tradition of humanistic scholarship" toward the problems of mass communication, international cultural relations, and cultural self-interpretation in a democratic society—in which anthropology, as then conceived, was felt to have little place (RAC: D. H. Stevens "Humanities Program . . . : A Review" 1939). The discipline continued to receive Foundation support through general fellowship programs, through grants for interdisciplinary social science programs, and through a renewed program in "psychobiology" in the Division of Natural Sciences (cf. Kohler 1978). And for some time there were traces in the annual *Reports* of the "former program" in cultural anthropology, as payments continued to be made to a few major institutional recipients under tapering terminal grants. But by 1938 these had all ended. Two years later, the discipline reentered the Foundation through the side door, when the National Institute of Anthropology and History in Mexico City was funded by the Humanities Division under its program of Latin American cultural exchange (RAC: D. H. Stevens/R. Redfield 12/5/ 40); but this belongs to the postwar phase of Rockefeller Foundation history.

Social Scientific Knowledge and Corporate Self-Interest

Having traced in some detail the development of Rockefeller anthropological activities in the interwar years, it remains to consider more generally the forces influencing them, and their influence on the history of anthropology. In many other areas of Rockefeller activity, radical historical critics have found patterns of research reflecting the dominant ideology of corporate capitalist society or the class self-interest of its leading groups. Yerkes' primate studies have been treated as "Monkey Business, or Monkies and Monopoly Capital" (Haraway 1977); Rockefeller medicine as a conscious "strategy for developing a medical system to meet the needs of capitalist society" (E. Brown 1979:4); Rockefeller social science as a "way of distributing surplus wealth, which might otherwise go to the state in taxes," to produce "knowledge that would help preserve the economic structure of Western society" (Fisher 1980:258). Especially in view of recent concern with the "colonial formation" of anthropology (Asad 1973), the question therefore arises as to what extent and in what ways the anthropological research agenda may have been shaped by the self-interest or ideology of "the Rockefellers" as representatives of corporate capitalism or western colonialism. Given the limitations of the present source material,[2] and a reluctance to structure it in terms of a priori interpretive metaphor, it will not be possible to answer such questions in a fully satisfying manner. But having narrowed the angle and sharpened the focus of the historical lens, we may suggest some of the complexities of the historical processes by which anthropological research priorities seem to have been negotiated.

It will help to begin by formulating a criterion of scale. In appraising activities in the social sciences in 1934, a Trustees' committee estimated that of the $298,000,000 disbursed by the Foundation's constituent bodies, $26,225,000 had gone to support social science research (RAC: Rept., Comm. Appraisal & Plan); when direct support to anthropology was completed four years later, the total allocation approximated $2,400,000 disbursed among some two dozen institutions (cf. Ft. 1). Given what is known of Rockefeller decision-making processes in this period, it seems likely that the effective decision was in the hands of key staff members, within the framework of an overall philanthropic strategy. This is not to say that Trustees

2. Among the relevant limitations are: the fact that records of declined grants were not preserved by the Rockefeller Foundation; that the present research was restricted largely to Rockefeller files relating to particular anthropological activities and staff and trustee records immediately relevant to them, as they were available in 1977; and that it included only a portion of the potentially relevant personal and institutional manuscript collections elsewhere—as well as the fact that only a small fraction of oral communications is reflected in the documentary record.

limited themselves to approving staff decisions. Outsiders sometimes initiated proposals by direct appeal to the younger Rockefeller or close personal associates such as Raymond Fosdick, Abraham Flexner, or Colonel Arthur Woods; and their initialed comments on such correspondence carried great weight—as in the instance of Mayan bibliography at Tulane. But for the most part, key staff members had the major input, not only at a grant-to-grant level, but also in defining programs in particular areas. When the Trustees reevaluated the overall program in 1934, the social science program was clearly identified with Day personally, just as it had previously been with Ruml, and the human biology program had been with Embree.

Except at moments of general reevaluation, then, the forces most directly influencing program in anthropology seem primarily to have been those affecting the thinking of a rather small group of reform-minded academically oriented foundation bureaucrats, whom some in foundation circles jokingly referred to as "philanthropoids" (RAC: G. E. Vincent, Off. Diary 1/10/28), and the succession of anthropologists who advised them. No doubt their general ideological orientation was not radically antithetical to those of the Rockefeller Trustees, and their receptivity to specific anthropological initiatives was not unaffected by more general economic, social, and political considerations. But it was perhaps even more strongly influenced by their vision of social science, and by their response to the play of influences endogenous to the discipline itself, in the context of certain Rockefeller administrative policies (the reliance on local academic institutions, on block grants, on surveys of current work, and on expert scientific advisors).

It was in such a context that a number of "psychobiological" and even racialist initiatives became vehicles for cultural determinist research. While the control of the Boasians was briefly threatened in the immediate postwar period, they still represented, both intellectually and institutionally, the dominant force within American anthropology. Given the Rockefeller policy of relying on professionally acknowledged disciplinary expertise, then the shift away from racialist psychobiology, mediated through the role of Clark Wissler as expert advisor, followed from the fact of Boasian disciplinary dominance—even though Boas himself was never especially favored by Rockefeller philanthropoids, who were inclined to look instead to younger anthropologists with a more present-oriented, functionalist approach. This is not to suggest that Rockefeller support could not be an important selective factor in a situation where there was a more balanced competition of disciplinary trends. Ruml's and Day's "prejudice" in favor of Malinowski surely contributed to his rise at the expense of the diffusionists at University College. Neither is it to suggest that an anti-psychobiological thrust is to be found in all areas of Rockefeller activity. Quite the contrary, the present analysis assumes that in areas where the internal intellectual thrust of a discipline was less clearly marked, or the role of an established scientific advisor exerted a strongly countervailing force, then the outcome might be different—as the continued support of Yerkes, and the reassertion of psychobiological interests in the natural science division under Warren Weaver suggests (Kohler 1978). Nevertheless, it seems that within the social sciences the dominant thrust ran generally parallel to that in cultural anthropology, away from hereditarian viewpoints toward cultural determinism. It is of course possible to interpret the shift from instinct to culture itself in terms of changing ideologies of domination (Haraway 1977), but insofar as such arguments imply a conscious shaping of research agendas in the interest of some group outside the discipline, they do not seem to be substantiated by the present chronicle of Rockefeller anthropology.

The issue of the "colonial formation" of anthropology has been posed most sharply in relation to the Rockefeller role in supporting British social anthropology in Africa (Asad 1973). Again, it seems quite likely that the philanthropoids and anthropologists whose interaction largely determined research priorities shared a general orientation on issues of colonial policy. Whatever their personal feelings about its legitimacy or desirability, they accepted the post-Versailles colonial system as historically "given." The danger was that unenlightened exploitation, without regard to the welfare of the native populations, might lead to "racial wars." In this context, colonial anthropological research was indeed promoted as a means of making the system "work" more effectively, from the point of view of capitalist development and administrative efficiency, as well as native welfare: "The anthropologist's task is to convince the government officials and capitalists themselves that their long-run interests are in harmony with the findings of anthropology" (RAC: BM, in Van Sickle diary 11/29/29).

The present materials do not cast direct light on the extent to which Rockefeller Trustees might have been influenced by ulterior corporate or class interest in reacting to such appeals. But they do give a hint of ulterior disciplinary self-interest among the anthropologists making them. As Malinowski noted privately in 1931 anthropology was the least able of all academic disciplines to support itself. Academic anthropologists spent their time breeding young anthropologists "for the sake of anthropology and so that they in turn may breed new anthropologists." Yet there was "no practical basis to our science, and there are no funds forthcoming to remunerate it for what it produces." The Rockefeller money of the last several years had made field work possible; what must now be done was to capitalize on this "almost surreptitious deviation" and establish the discipline as a special branch of Rockefeller endowment (BMP: draft memo, "Res. Needs in Soc. & Cult. Anth."). Similarly, the proposed research centers of Radcliffe-Brown's vanishing cultures scheme were intended to provide "assurance that there will be openings" for the students who were to be trained for field work research (RAC: ARB, "Memo. on Anth. Res.").

Sustaining such a "surreptitious deviation" was not easy in a situation where colonial authorities were by no means wholly convinced of the utility of anthropological research, and often more than a little worried that it would somehow contribute to native unrest (cf. Kuklick 1978). In the fall of 1931, Oldham wrote to Malinowski suggesting that Paul Kirchoff, who had previously done research in Latin America under Boas, should be given an African Institute fellowship for field work in Rhodesia, with a view to convincing the Colonial Office of the practical value of anthropology in relation to Rhodesian mining developments (BMP: JHO/BM 11/19/31). Shortly before Kirchoff's planned departure, the Colonial Office suddenly refused him entrance to any British colony, letting it be known that he was suspected of being a communist agitator (BMP: JHO/BM 1/22, 2/16/32). Although Malinowski momentarily contemplated resignation from the African Institute rather than accept the Colonial Office's "bald veto" (BMP: BM/JHO 2/5/32), he was rather quickly swayed by Oldham's argument that "the large interests of anthropology and African research" should not be sacrificed in a "forlorn" crusade (BMP: JHO/BM 2/18/32). Convinced that the whole matter was a misunderstanding, and that Kirchoff was at most guilty of youthful indiscretion, Malinowski tried to send him to New Guinea, where he felt that even "the most intensive communistic doctrines" would present "no great danger" (BMP: BM/R. Firth 9/26/32). But this plan, too, was forestalled at the last minute by the Australian National Research Council on the basis of confidential information from British governmental officials (BMP: D. O. Masson/BM 9/26/32).

Although the actual substance of Kirchoff's research does not seem to have been at issue, and the Foundation, at Malinowski's urging, did give him a small grant to write up his earlier Latin American research, the constraining influence of this incident should not be minimized. At the time, the major participants concluded that in the future there must be a "very careful scrutiny of the past records and personality" of all candidates (RAC: T. B. Kittredge, Memo, talk with JHO & BM 10/24/32); and while Malinowski seems to have retained a tolerant attitude toward youthful political "indiscretion," oral testimony from this period suggests that he was not alone in warning aspiring young anthropologists that they must choose between radical politics and scientific anthropology.[3]

3. The oral testimony includes interviews with several senior anthropologists. Letters in the Malinowski papers indicate that Malinowski did not feel that Meyer Fortes's avowed radicalism was a bar to Rockefeller support (BMP: BM/JHO 2/5/32). Within the Rockefeller records proper, the only political reference of this sort that I noted related to Radcliffe-Brown: reporting on a conversation about anthropological matters, Van Sickle (somewhat out of immediate context)

To some extent, then, shared historical vision and disciplinary self-interest may have conspired to shape portions of the Rockefeller anthropological agenda to the "needs" of the colonial system; and at least one incident of active constraint—which may well have had archetypal, "once-burned, twice-shy" implications—helped to discourage research (or rather, a researcher) the British Colonial Office felt threatening to it. But if one considers the overall pattern of Rockefeller anthropological research, colonial considerations do not seem to have played a major determining role. During the period when the Trustees accepted the view that human welfare could best be achieved by the advancement of knowledge, the interaction of philanthropoids and anthropologists won the discipline a place within the Rockefeller social science program, giving it brief recognition as a special field of concentration, and for a moment even offering the prospect of sustained long run support. Once it had been dissociated from the charge of antiquarianism, its very exoticism enhanced its appeal: by the unique methodology of field work investigation, it offered an otherwise inaccessible knowledge of the generic impulses underlying human behavior. Day, who felt that anthropology had a more "scientific" technique than sociology, was clearly won over by its promise of an esoteric social scientific wisdom (RAC: "Verbatim Notes, Princeton Conf." 11/29/32). So long as the foundation had a program "in the field of human behavior," he felt that there were "values in the comparative data in ethnology that cannot wisely be ignored" (RAC: EED/A. Gregg 12/19/34). By 1933, however, the Trustees had begun to wonder about a social science program that spent more than ninety-five percent of its funds collecting facts and less than five percent determining "whether these facts could with any degree of effectiveness be applied to contemporary problems" (RAC: Rept. Comm. on Appraisal & Plan): "Is Day's social science program really getting anywhere? Is it too academic—too little related to practical needs?" (RAC: R. B. Fosdick/W. Stewart 7/10/34). When they then reversed (albeit temporarily) the priorities of the 1920s and turned to the "immediate problems of the today," anthropology was among the nonutilitarian programs that fell by the wayside. What had sold the discipline to philanthropoids like Day was not so much its alleged practical colonial utility as its promise of esoteric scientific knowledge; when the Trustees decided that serious practical concerns must be paramount, anthropology lost its place on the Rockefeller

---

noted that "R-B thinks that our present capitalistic system bears within itself the germs of its own destruction" (RAC: "Conversations with A. R.-B. 9/7–8/31). There is evidence, however, that Foundation officials were concerned that Boas gave too much field work money to women, who were felt unlikely to pursue professional careers (RAC: EED/FB 6/14/32; FB/EED 7/26/32); and that the candidacy of Godfrey Wilson was seen (in part) as a counterbalance to the high proportion of Jews and women among Malinowski's students (RAC: JVS "Training Fellows in Cult. Anth." 6/8/32).

agenda. Whether things would have happened differently if the prior "colonial formation" of anthropology had been more conscious, more consistent, more systematic and more thoroughgoing is perhaps a moot point.[4]

Rockefeller Funding and Museum Anthropology

To question oversimple notions of the exogenous determination of research agendas in anthropology is not, however, to deny the impact of Rockefeller funding on the development of the discipline in the interwar period. To weigh this impact, it may help to consider the scale of Rockefeller involvement from a different point of view. For if their appropriations in anthropology seem relatively small from the perspective of overall Rockefeller philanthropic policy, they loom somewhat larger when one considers their impact on the history of a rather small disciplinary community. Because the history of the political economy of anthropology is a virtually untouched field, no figures are available on its overall funding at different points in time. It may help, however, to keep in mind the budgets of two field work enterprises interwar anthropologists took as exemplars. The Bureau of American Ethnology, which British anthropologists sometimes looked to as a model of enlightened policy, had in its heyday a budget of between $30,000 and $40,000 a year, only a minor portion of which went for field work expenses (Hinsley 1981:276). The Jesup North Pacific Expedition of the American Museum of Natural History, which the American Anthropological Association Research Committee used as benchmark, had a budget totalling $100,000 over about a dozen years (UCBA: [JMC]/EED, n.d.). In this context, five million dollars would indeed have been a very large anthropological pie, and the two-plus million that Rockefeller philanthropy did provide was welcome nourishment in a period when institutional beltlines were tight.

Basing themselves on ten recent expeditions to such places as Samoa, Manus, Dobu, and Tikopia, the Research Committee estimated the average cost of extended overseas field work among still-functioning tribal cultures at $5,500; for tribes "on the point of extinction in North America from which information can be obtained only by questioning," $1,500 for a single summer's work would serve (ibid.). In using these figures to make a rough esti-

4. Or, one might add, if the alleged utility had been more effectively demonstrated: reacting to one paper by a Foundation fellow who had worked in Assam—as characteristic of the work of "most anthropologists"—one Foundation official commented in 1937: "Somehow such work seems of only slight importance to colonial administration, or the practical problems and the responsibilities for making the connections seem to rest on someone other than the anthropologist" (RAC: S. H. Walker/T. B. Kittredge 12/1/37).

mate of the total Rockefeller contribution to anthropological fieldwork, one is hampered by the difficulty of weighing such factors as the allocation between subdisciplines, or between the two styles of fieldwork, or the proportion for general institutional expenses—which in Australia apparently included the embezzlement of £30,000 by administrative personnel (RAC:A. Gibson/RF, cable, 5/31/34). But even if one assumes that only a quarter of the total Rockefeller support went to field work, the Foundation's anthropological grants supported the equivalent of one hundred summers of informant field work among American Indians and eighty periods of extended field work overseas—a figure not including anthropological field work done under the general Rockefeller fellowship program, or funded indirectly through the Social Science Research Council. Nor does it reflect support for field work through general institutional grants in the social sciences (such as the Institute of Human Relations at Yale), or through specific grants for other social science projects (such as the contribution Elton Mayo's program in industrial psychology made to Lloyd Warner's field work in Newburyport, Massachusetts). Neither does it allow for the stimulus of the "matching" provision that was frequently attached to Rockefeller institutional grants in anthropology. Considering that the total academic anthropological community in the Anglo-American sphere at the end of the interwar period numbered somewhere around 400, as measured by doctorates in *all* subdisciplines, then the Rockefeller contribution looms very large indeed. One has only to glance at the biographical information in the *Register of Members* of the Association of Social Anthropologists of the Commonwealth, or at the final summary of the activities of the Laboratory of Anthropology in Santa Fe (cf. Stocking 1982), to realize that Rockefeller money played a major role in underwriting the field work experience of a large majority of the anthropologists trained in the interwar period.

That money was not readily available from other sources. In the British sphere, there was a relatively small amount of research money available from the South African and several other colonial governments. In general, however, the British colonial establishment seems to have been swayed by arguments for the utility of anthropological research only to the extent that someone else was willing to pay for it. Until the late 1930s, as the British colonial reformer Lord Hailey observed with a certain patriotic regret, American money provided the main support for anthropological research in Africa (R. Brown 1973:184). Although certain other agencies (notably the Rhodes-Livingston Institute) picked up some of the slack when the Rockefeller Foundation withdrew, it was not until after the second World War that the British government began to support research on a large scale. In the United States, the major alternative support came from the Carnegie Institution, which was

heavily oriented to physical anthropology and archeology; such general ethnographic work as it sustained was an outgrowth of its interest in Mayan
archeology (CIW *Yearbooks*; cf. Woodbury 1973:64; Reingold 1979).

In contrast, Rockefeller money supported ethnographic work on a much
broader geographic scale, playing a major role in opening up two areas (Africa and Oceania) where the disintegrative impact of culture contact had not
gone so far as in much of North America. To the extent that the intellectual
movement of the discipline is a reflection of its empirical base, it seems likely
that this sustained the more behavioral, functional, and holistic currents
emerging in the 1920s and 30s (Stocking 1976). Insofar as that movement
reflects an institutional dynamic, the Foundation's particular institutional
commitments contributed to a similar end. Despite its antiquarian orientation in the humanities, the Rockefeller orientation in the social sciences,
both in its psychobiological and its cultural determinist phase, was consistently behavioralist. And although in the case of anthropology the Foundation did make grants to specific departments, the more general policy was to
work through interdisciplinary social scientific channels, all of which sustained those tendencies in anthropology that were moving away from the
traditional historical orientations. The pattern of Rockefeller institutional
support reflected this: the London School of Economics was supported at the
expense of Elliot Smith's University College; Chicago, Harvard, and Yale got
much more money than the more traditionally Boasian Berkeley and Columbia.

Although the prior institutional structure differed somewhat in the two
countries, the general institutional impact may be illuminated by the American case, where, as we have seen, the funding of anthropological research
was before the first World War channelled largely to (or through) museum
collections. Even the researches of the Bureau of American Ethnology were
strongly conditioned by its relation to the U.S. National Museum; and every
early major university department developed in direct relation to a museum,
either within the university itself, or preexisting in the same city. It was
clearly expected, both by university administrators and anthropologists, that
research would be sustained by this connection. As the names of major expeditions testify, money for anthropological research was frequently raised on
an ad hoc basis from individual philanthropists, who—like the younger
Rockefeller, in his personal philanthropy—tended to be more interested in
archeology than in other anthropological subdisciplines. In this context, getting money for nonarcheological research was always a problem. As we have
seen, this institutional framework reinforced a certain intellectual orientation: anthropology tended to be conceived as a study of the human past as it
was embodied in collectible physical objects, rather than an observational
study of human behavior in the present; its important relationships were to

the biological sciences represented in museums of natural history, rather than to the social sciences.

In this context, the impact of the Rockefeller program was considerable. For the first time relatively large amounts of money became available to anthropology through channels that were primarily controlled, not by private philanthropists or museum-men oriented toward the collection of physical objects, but by men oriented to social scientific research, for whom the past as embodied in the object was no longer a privileged form of data, and for whom the university was in general the favored locus of research. True, at least one-third of total Rockefeller support to anthropology went to physical anthropological work, and archeology continued to get a share of many institutional allocations. But in the negotiation of competing interests and conflicting cross purposes, the anthropological object no longer had the advantage of being a common denominator of intellectual interest or a primary medium of exchange in the political economy of anthropological research. Despite their support of ethnographic research through the Bishop Museum, Foundation officials made it clear at several points that they were not interested in museum work of the traditional sort, but in the various factors affecting human behavior in the present (RAC: EED/J. Van Sickle 7/1/31). In the context of a general contraction of museum budgets in the depression years, Rockefeller support thus encouraged an ongoing intellectual reorientation within the discipline toward the other social sciences and a more behaviorally oriented field research. In the British sphere, the impact of Rockefeller financing was very much the same. The relative neglect of the museum-oriented Royal Anthropological Institute, the central role of the London School of Economics, which had no museum connections, and the general posture of Malinowski and Radcliffe-Brown all contributed to the weakening of the historical tradition, and the strengthening of social scientifically oriented academic research.

A further consequence was the weakening of the unity of subdisciplines within a general "anthropology." True, the traditional hybrid character of the discipline in the Anglo-American tradition remained strongly in evidence in the American Anthropological Association and the Royal Anthropological Institute. But the interwar period saw a considerable heightening of subdisciplinary specialization; there were fewer "general anthropologists"; interdisciplinary interests were increasingly likely to carry cultural or social anthropologists toward the social sciences rather than towards the other traditional anthropological subdisciplines. Furthermore, the balance of subdisciplinary relations within anthropology had changed. "Ethnology"—the subdiscipline in which the others had been presumed to find, at least in principle, a retrospective historical unity—was being transformed or displaced. In the British sphere, "social anthropology" (whose opposition to "ethnology" had been proclaimed by Radcliffe-Brown in 1923) had by the end of the second World War established itself as a well-defined and institutionalized inquiry whose practitioners were in most contexts disinclined to march under a general anthropological umbrella. In the more pluralist institutional and theoretical atmosphere of the United States, there was no analogue to the Association of Social Anthropologists founded at Oxford in 1946. But although an historical "ethnology" remained a viable form of anthropological inquiry, its use as the name for the dominant anthropological subdiscipline was passing in favor of "cultural anthropology"—a category which, like its British analogue, was oriented toward the study of human behavior in the present (cf. Stocking 1976; 1984). Its practitioners were, for the most part, interested in objects primarily as personal keepsakes of transcultural experience, brought back to decorate the walls of their homes, or to distinguish their offices from those of other social scientists down the hall.

It is of course impossible to weigh the independent contribution of Rockefeller activities to the transformation we have been describing, if only because the Rockefeller program was defined in interaction between foundation officials and leading representatives of change within the discipline. But there can be no doubt that it played a critical role in a major disciplinary transformation. Significant numbers of anthropologists continued to be employed in museums, which continued to support important anthropological research; but the museum era of anthropology had come to an end—at least for the remainder of the century.

Acknowledgments

This paper was first drafted in 1977 when I was a fellow at the Center for Advanced Study in the Behavioral Sciences, revised following its presentation to the Chicago Group in the History of the Social [Human] Sciences in 1979, and recast in its present form in 1984 when I was a fellow of the John Simon Guggenheim Memorial Foundation. In addition to the two fellowship sponsors and the members of the CGHHS, I would like to thank Len Berk, Ronald Cohen, Barry Karl, Michael Schudsen, and Edward Shils, who commented on the manuscript, as well as the archivists of the various repositories in which I consulted manuscripts—particularly J. William Hess of the Rockefeller Archive Center. Insofar as it draws on other published and unpublished research I have done on the history of twentieth-century anthropology, there are other less immediate debts that I hereby anonymously reacknowledge.

References Cited

AAAP. See under Manuscript Sources.

Asad, T., ed. 1973. *Anthropology and the colonial encounter.* London.

Bennett, G. 1960. From paramountcy to partnership: J. H. Oldham and Africa. *Africa* 32:356–60.

BMP. See under Manuscript Sources.

BPBM. [Bernice P. Bishop Museum] 1926. *Report of the director.* Honolulu.

Brown, E. R. 1979. *Rockefeller medicine men: Medicine and capitalism in America.* Berkeley.

Brown, R. 1973. Anthropology and colonial rule: Godfrey Wilson and the Rhodes-Livingstone Institute, Northern Nigeria. In Asad, ed. 1973:173–98.

Bulmer, M. 1980. The early institutional establishment of social science research: The Local Community Research Committee at the University of Chicago, 1923–30. *Minerva* 18:51–110.

Bulmer, M. & J. 1981. Philanthropy and social science in the 1920s: Beardsley Ruml and the Laura Spelman Rockefeller Memorial, 1922–29. *Minerva* 19:347–407.

Chapman, W. R. 1981. Ethnology in the museum: A. H. L. F. Pitt Rivers (1827–1900) and the institutional foundations of British anthropology. Unpublished doc. diss., Oxford Univ.

CIW. [Carnegie Institution of Washington] 1929–40 *Yearbook.* Washington.

Coben, S. 1976. Foundation officials and fellowships: Innovation in the patronage of science. *Minerva* 14:225–40.

Collier, P., & D. Horowitz. 1976. *The Rockefellers: An American dynasty.* New York.

Darnell, R. D. 1969. The development of American anthropology, 1879–1920: From the Bureau of American Ethnology of Franz Boas. Unpublished doc. diss., Univ. Penn.

Fisher, D. 1978. The Rockefeller Foundation and the development of scientific medicine in Britain. *Minerva* 16:20–41.

———. 1980. American philanthropy and the social sciences: The reproduction of conservative ideology. In *Philanthropy and cultural imperialism: The foundations at home and abroad,* ed. R. F. Arnove, 233–69. New York.

Flannery, R. 1946. The ACLS and anthropology. *Am. Anth.* 48:686–89.

Fosdick, R. F. 1952. *The story of the Rockefeller Foundation.* New York.

———. 1956. *John D. Rockefeller, Jr.: A Portrait.* New York.

Grossman, D. 1982. American foundations and the support of economic research. 1923–29. *Minerva* 20:59–75.

Haraway, D. 1977. A political physiology of the primate family: Monkeys and apes in the twentieth-century rationalization of sex. Conference on "Historical perspectives on the scientific study of fertility in the United States," Am. Acad. Arts & Scis., December 8. Boston.

Hinsley, C. M. 1981. *Savages and scientists: The Smithsonian Institution and the development of American anthropology, 1846–1910.* Washington.

Hood, D. 1964. *Davidson Black: A biography.* Toronto.

Karl, B., & S. N. Katz. 1981. The American private philanthropic foundation and the public sphere, 1890–1930. *Minerva* 19:236–70.

Kohler, R. F. 1976. The management of science: The experience of Warren Weaver and the Rockefeller Foundation programme in molecular biology. *Minerva* 14:279–306.

———. 1978. A policy for the advancement of science: The Rockefeller Foundation, 1924–29. *Minerva* 16:480–515.

Kuklick, H. 1978. 'The sins of the fathers': British anthropology and colonial administration. *Res. Soc. Knowl. Scis. Art* 1:93–119.

Kusmer, K. L. 1979. The social history of cultural institutions: the upper-class connection. *J. Interdiscip. Hist.* 10:137–46.

Langham, I. 1981. *The building of British social anthropology: W. H. R. Rivers and his Cambridge disciples in the development of kinship studies, 1898–1931.* Dordrecht.

Malinowski, B. 1929. Practical anthropology. *Africa* 2:23–39.

May, M. A. 1971. A retrospective view of the Institute of Human Relations at Yale. *Behav. Scis. Notes* 6:141–72.

Porteus, S. D. 1969. *A psychologist of sorts: The autobiography and publications of the inventor of the Porteus Maze Tests.* Palo Alto.

RAC. See under Manuscript Sources.

Radcliffe-Brown, A. R. 1923. The methods of ethnology and social anthropology. In *Method in social anthropology*, ed. M. N. Srinivas, 3–38. Chicago (1958).

———. 1930. Applied anthropology. *Rept. 20th Meet.*, Aust. & N. Z. Assn. Adv. Sci., 267–80. Brisbane.

———. 1931. The present position of anthropological studies. In *Method in social anthropology*, ed. M. N. Srinivas, 42–95. Chicago (1958).

Reingold, N. 1979. National science policy in a private foundation: The Carnegie Institution of Washington. In *The organization of knowledge in modern America, 1860–1920*, ed. A. Oleson & J. Voss, 313–34. Baltimore.

Resek, C. 1960. *Lewis Henry Morgan: American scholar.* Chicago.

RF. [Rockefeller Foundation] 1924–37 *Annual Report.* New York.

Smith, E. W. 1934. The story of the Institute: The first seven years. *Africa* 7:1–27.

SSRC. [Social Science Research Council] 1926. The Hanover conference, Aug. 23–Sept 2. Mimeographed, 2 vols. New York.

Stocking, G. W., Jr. 1968. *Race, culture and evolution: Essays in the history of anthropology.* New York.

———. 1974. *The shaping of American anthropology, 1883–1911: A Franz Boas reader.* New York.

———. 1976. Ideas and institutions in American anthropology: Thoughts toward a history of the interwar years. In *Selected Papers from the American Anthropologist*, 1–53. Washington, D.C.

———. 1977. The aims of Boasian ethnography: Creating the materials for traditional humanistic scholarship. *Hist. Anth. Newsl.* 4(2):4–5.

———. 1979. *Anthropology at Chicago: Tradition, discipline, department.* Regenstein Library, Chicago.

———. 1982. The Santa Fe style in American anthropology: Regional interest, academic initiative, and philanthropic policy in the first two decades of the Laboratory of Anthropology, Inc. *J. Hist. Behav. Scis.* 18:3–19.

―――. 1983. The ethnographer's magic: Fieldwork in British anthropology from Tylor to Malinowski. *Hist. Anth.* 1:50–120.

―――. 1984. Radcliffe-Brown and British social anthropology. *Hist. Anth.* 2:131–91.

Thoresen, T. H. 1975. Paying the piper and calling the tune: The beginnings of academic anthropology in California. *J. Hist. Behav. Scis.* 11:257–75.

Van Keuren, D. A. 1982. Human science in Victorian Britain: Anthropology in institutional and disciplinary formation, 1863–1908. Unpublished doc. diss., Univ. Penn.

Woodbury, R. B. 1973. *Alfred V. Kidder.* New York.

Manuscript Sources

This paper is based primarily on research in the Rockefeller Archive Center, North Tarryton, N.Y. (cited herein as RAC). I have also drawn on manuscript materials in other archives, including the American Anthropological Association Papers (cited AAAP), in the National Anthropological Archives of the Smithsonian Institution; the Bronislaw Malinowski Papers (cited BMP), in the British Library of Political and Economic Science, London School of Economics; the archives of the Department of Anthropology of the University of Chicago (cited UCDA), in the Special Collections Department of the Regenstein Library, University of Chicago; and the archives of the Department of Anthropology of the University of California, Berkeley (cited UCBA), in the Bancroft Library.

ART AND ARTIFACT AT THE TROCADERO

Ars Americana *and the Primitivist Revolution*

ELIZABETH A. WILLIAMS

In 1928 an exhibition of pre-Columbian art was held in the Louvre's Pavillon du Marsan. Including almost a thousand objects, mostly from Central and South America, it was the first such exhibit to accent the aesthetic rather than ethnographic interest of such pieces. A catalog (*Les arts anciens de l'Amérique*) was prepared by the exhibit's organizers, the "Americanist" scholar Alfred Métraux and Georges-Henri Rivière, who on the strength of the show was soon to be hired as curator at the Musée d'Ethnographie du Trocadéro. An introduction by Raoul d'Harcourt, coauthor of an acclaimed work on Peruvian ceramics (1924), praised the exhibit's managers, the authorities who had sponsored it, and the high quality of the pieces shown. Although the catalog elsewhere averred that the exhibit's sole purpose was to illuminate artistic developments, d'Harcourt himself displayed a certain uneasiness:

> It will be objected in certain quarters that by reason of the frequently ritualistic or purely utilitarian character of the chosen pieces, this exposition falls into the domain of ethnography, and this will be true. But, aside from the fact that from a broad perspective aesthetics belongs to that science, where indeed it occupies a favored position, nothing would appear to be more legitimate than to group objects from the special point of view of their artistic form and *décor*, taking into account . . . the idea of beauty which is at work in and incorpo-

---

Elizabeth A. Williams, currently Instructor in the Department of History at the University of Georgia in Athens, is the author of "Institutional Stalemate: French Anthropology in the Nineteenth Century," *Isis* (1985). Her current research, funded by a National Science Foundation Scholar's Award, explores further the history of French anthropological theory and institutions in the nineteenth century.

rated in them. Such a procedure renders more directly visible the style of an epoch or a region and makes comprehensible the play of neighboring influences.

(Arts anciens, x)

That d'Harcourt was so hesitant to affirm the aesthetic interest of pre-Columbian works in 1928 occasions some surprise. Europe's awakening to the beauties of art primitif is generally traced to a much earlier date, either to the changed sensibility in the work of Van Gogh or Gauguin or to the "discovery" of primitive sculpture by Picasso and other avant-garde artists in 1906–7 (Laude 1968; Curtis 1975; Rubin 1984). Moreover, it has recently been argued that in Paris after the first World War there emerged among ethnographers and modernist aesthetes a distinct vision (captured in the construct "ethnographic surrealism") that "destabilized" such traditional categories of high culture as the opposition between art and artifact (Clifford 1981). If so, we might interpret d'Harcourt's hesitation as a late reflection of traditional prejudices against the "primitive arts," or perhaps as an indicator of generational and cultural fissures in French ethnographical circles ("traditionalists" versus "modernists"). But there can be no doubt that he echoed ambivalences long expressed among ethnographers trying to determine the place of ethnographic artifacts in traditional classifications of artistic production.

In the nineteenth-century museum, unlike its predecessor the eighteenth-century cabinet de curiosité, exhibits were expected to reflect some clear rationale: museums of natural history presented instructive exhibits; museums of art presented things of beauty. But the place of ethnographical displays in this scheme of things was not wholly clear. Some ethnographers argued that their materials had nothing of the beautiful about them and that ethnographical collections were intended only to enlighten. Among the most influential was E. F. Jomard, curator at the Bibliothèque Royale, who began in the 1820s to urge the creation of a full-dress ethnographical museum in Paris: "there is no question of beauty in these arts . . . but only of objects considered in relation to practical and social utility" (1831:423).

That position, however, was inherently problematic. The act of display itself suggested that beauty was somehow involved. Furthermore, many pieces, especially those from sophisticated material cultures like those of pre-Conquest America, fell into already well-established classes of artistic production—statuary, vases, bas-reliefs. Such objects seemed clearly to be born of aesthetic intentions, since they were decorative, formal, stylized, and unmistakably the products of careful labor and technical skill. Moreover, many European observers were susceptible to their aesthetic effects. Peruvian ceramics are the best case in point. Their beauty was admired even early in the nineteenth century by authorities such as Alcide d'Orbigny, a naturalist and

voyager who found little else to praise in American material culture (Soldi
1881:403–4). Although most later curators took Jomard's cue, repeating
throughout the nineteenth century that ethnographic pieces were solely instructive, there was a subliminal sense that certain of these objects reflected,
however imperfectly, the high aspirations of Art. They exerted a special
force, awakened a sense of intrigue, or evoked strangely harsh judgments on
their aesthetic nullity.

Pre-Columbian artifacts were a special source of wonder to European observers because of the high level of material development of ancient American civilization and its apparent independence from the fonts of Old World
creativity. The productions of the classical world could be easily arrayed along
a sequence of progress to the modern arts; the "oriental" world had lost its
feel of utter strangeness and been assimilated into European sensibility
through periodic vogues of chinoiserie; the "true" arts primitifs of Arctic,
African, and Oceanic peoples could be unambiguously categorized as the
work of savages. But the arts and civilization of pre-Columbian America were
a profound enigma. Chroniclers of the Conquest had testified to the brilliance of American civilization, but their works had largely disappeared from
view in the seventeenth and eighteenth centuries and were only beginning
to be read again from around 1750. Nor did they fully prepare nineteenth-
century observers for the wealth and complexity of the ars americana.
Because they were the writings of the conquerors themselves, they had an
equivocal and not wholly trustworthy status (Keen 1971:352–53, 393–94).
Moreover, their illustrations, if any, employed "naive" stylistic devices that
amused or irritated nineteenth-century "realist" readers.

It took a full century of reacquaintance with pre-Columbian civilization
before its material splendor was widely acknowledged (Lejeal 1903), and
even then ethnographers who willingly recognized the variety and complexity of pre-Columbian productions remained reluctant to grant them purely
aesthetic merit. This final task of revaluation of the ars americana was accomplished only in the wake of the "primitivist revolution" in European aesthetics, a process set in motion by avant-garde artists who appear to have
been little indebted to previous ethnographic labors among the "primitive
arts." The relation between the ethnographic rediscovery of the ars americana
and their ultimate aesthetic revaluation is the subject of the present essay.

Americanist Collections in France
to the Founding of the Trocadero

The study of ancient American material culture, and the building of pre-
Columbian collections, was but a part of the larger development in France
of américanisme—the general area study of the Americas of both continents

and all periods. Americanist scholars investigated diverse subjects, from the travels of Marquette, to the population and industry of modern St. Louis, to the history and remains of the Incas. Although interest in the Americas was slower to develop than that shown in "Orientalism" (cf. Said 1979), by 1875 French Americanists met with their European colleagues in the International Congress of Americanists (Comas 1954), and from 1896 they published in an independent journal, the *Journal de la Société des Américanistes*. The founding of these institutions in turn gave new impetus to *américanisme*, which by the end of the century increasingly emphasized collecting as an aid to study of American material culture.

The first American artifacts to enter a French collection (the Cabinet du Roi, later absorbed into the Bibliothèque Nationale and the Muséum d'Histoire Naturelle) had been sent back by Joseph Dombey from South America in the 1780s (Hamy 1889: 318–19). Subsequently, in the period 1800 to 1850, scattered pieces—mostly from Mexico but some from Peru— found their way into two private collections held in Paris. One was the possession of a parliamentarian named Allier; the other was formed by Jomard, who saw the assembling and methodical classification of artifacts as a primary function of an emerging science of "ethnography" (Longpérier 1850:9–10; Jomard 1831). The most extensive collection, however, was built in fits and starts at the Louvre itself. At the instigation of the antiquarian Henri de Longpérier, the Louvre had accepted donations of American pieces and finally in 1850 purchased a collection that Longpérier particularly admired— including some major pieces that had already been lithographed for Lord Kingsborough's *Antiquities of Mexico* (1831–48; cf. Longpérier 1850:7–10).

These newly purchased artifacts were displayed to the public as part of the first pre-Columbian exhibit ever opened in Paris. As Longpérier suggested in his catalog, few French scholars "had gotten a taste for American studies" (1); and indeed *américanisme* was neither his sole, nor even chief, interest. He was an antiquarian by profession, and in the field of "antiquities" concentration on a given area was less important than the basic disposition to work with the products of the "ancient arts." Thus Longpérier also prepared shows for the Louvre on Assyrian and Asian antiquities, French coins, and Gallic vases ("GE").

The Louvre pre-Columbian exhibit, as described by Longpérier's catalog, contained more than nine hundred pieces from varied sites in the ancient American world. There were sculptures in basalt, jasper, granite, and jade; numerous terra cotta figures including animal and human representations; shards of stone and terra cotta bas-reliefs; a wide range of ornamental objects including necklaces, bracelets, and plaques in jasper, jade, agate, obsidian, quartz, and crystal; and a number of utensils of daily life such as mirrors, needles, and weights (1850:17–128). Making no distinction between Central and South America, Longpérier presented these materials as the remains of a civilization that was "virtually wholly unknown" and of a highly "peculiar character" (5). He commented on the paucity of information available to scholars, but suggested that the lack of interest in the Americas was not surprising since their past was not, like the Egyptian, closely tied to Europe's own "sacred history" (1–10). Nor, he mused, would one be drawn to the study of American antiquities because of their inherent beauty. Instead of the beautiful, the Americans had devised "bizarre combinations" of forms and ideas reminiscent of the Oriental style; "their very [physiological] organization" seemed to have "denied to them that impulse toward the beautiful that alone engenders progress" (5–6). Despite these judgments, Longpérier's commentary on the actual pieces emphasized the strange fascination exerted by American artifacts, and he devoted considerable effort to explicating their origins and meaning. To do so, he consulted what materials were available at the Bibliothèque Nationale, including Mexican manuscripts and several codices, and he brought to the enterprise the greatest expertise any French scholar had yet developed in deciphering Mexican and Peruvian iconography (Hamy 1885:4).

Although the collection of pre-Columbian artifacts remained part of the Louvre's permanent holdings until 1880, it never served as the impetus to Americanist studies that Longpérier had envisaged (Hamy 1889:352). It was repeatedly moved in the years after the 1850 exhibit, the last time out of public view, and the handling of the materials was later strongly criticized by officials within the Ministry of Public Instruction (352). Nevertheless, Longpérier himself continued to devote time to Americanist pursuits. He later helped to produce an album of the drawings of Jean-Frédéric Waldeck, who had visited Palenque, Uxmal, and Chichen Itza in the 1830s (Waldeck 1866:v–xv). Then in 1859 he and a small circle of Americanists joined with colleagues in orientalist studies to found the Société d'Ethnographie américaine et orientale, although their emphasis was largely philological (Williams 1983:150–66).

During the following decade, the study of pre-Columbian America was given further impetus when Napoleon III's invasion of Mexico was accompanied by an "army of savants" modeled on that which the first Napoleon had assembled for the Egyptian expedition. In the course of the "imperial experiment" in Mexico, French scholars undertook large-scale excavations of ancient Mexican sites, the most extensive at Mitla (Keen 1971:436–37). Although many artifacts gathered in these undertakings found their way back to France, they were scattered in various public and private collections. Perhaps because of the ignominious end of the larger enterprise, their acquisition never led to any major exhibit of Mexican material culture.

Some of the artifacts acquired during the Mexican venture ended up at the Louvre, which in this period maintained not only its badly housed pre-

Columbian collection but also a separate "ethnographical collection" of some 2,000 objects of diverse origin, including some "rare and valuable" pieces. From 1850 forward, these were exhibited under the auspices of the Musée Naval, which had been housed in the Louvre since 1828 (Hamy 1889:347). This collection apparently had a certain success with the public, inspiring talk of building a permanent, extensive "museum of ethnography" at the Louvre. But the idea never met with favor among Louvre officials or bureaucrats in the Beaux-Arts administration, and by the 1860s it was clear to certain scholars that Paris was in sore need of a full-scale independent museum of ethnography (Hamy 1889:346–52). Not only were important pieces and collections being lost to provincial museums and "ignoble boutiques" (Jomard's phrase), but in 1868 the national pride of ethnographers was piqued when the Museum für Völkerkunde opened in Berlin under the direction of Adolf Bastian (Goldwater 1967:274). Thereupon, two scholars— Armand de Quatrefages, who was professor of anthropology at the Muséum d'Histoire Naturelle, and his protégé Ernest-Théodore Hamy—took the creation of a comparable museum in Paris as their special task. Neither Quatrefages nor Hamy had devoted much work to the collection or analysis of ethnographic artifacts, but both men strongly favored the idea of an ethnographical museum, in part because they were troubled by the predominantly "materialist" (physicalist) bent in French anthropology (Hamy 1882). After 1870 Hamy increasingly moved away from investigations in biological anthropology to historical and ethnographical concerns, work he hoped to see further stimulated through the agency of a museum.

From an early date Hamy took a special interest in things American, and it was a project to display pre-Columbian materials that gave the final impetus to the creation of the Musée d'Ethnographie du Trocadéro in 1878. In the mid-1870s the voyager and archeologist Charles Wiener returned from an excavating trip to Peru that had been financed by the Ministry of Public Instruction on the understanding that his finds would be handed over to the French government on his return (Wiener 1880:i–viii). Having sponsored Wiener's excavations, the Ministry was now obliged to mount some kind of an exhibit of the 4,000 objects he brought back. Combined with the constant urgings from Hamy and Quatrefages, this necessity encouraged the Minister to use the occasion to gauge public interest in the establishment of a permanent ethnographical museum. The Wiener Peruvian collection, along with a display of artifacts and natural history specimens from Colombia, Bolivia, and Ecuador, was assembled in the Palais de l'Industrie, and opened in the spring of 1878 (Hamy 1889:353–63). Attendance was high and press notices were favorable, and Hamy and Quatrefages now pressed for permanent arrangements. The Ministry agreed to sponsor a full-scale exhibit of Americana in connection with the Universal Exposition of 1878, and later

to convert the quarters into a permanent repository for ethnographic artifacts.

It is not easy to form a clear picture of the Peruvian exhibit from the
various accounts, but it appears that one of its primary purposes was to
achieve "life-like" effects that would intrigue and please the public. To do so,
Wiener engaged his friend the sculptor and medallionist Emile Soldi to assist
in preparing the display. The entryway to the exhibit simulated a facade from
the temple at Tiahuanaco, and immediately inside facsimiles of statuary were
displayed along with genuine pottery and other artifacts, all interspersed with
sculptures of human heads and figures Soldi created on the basis of Wiener's
notes and sketches. The exhibit made no consistent distinction between different locales or cultural areas, and objects from other collections were mixed
in with Peruvian materials. Mannequins were built to display necklaces,
headgear, clothing, and other ornamentation thought to be characteristic of
ancient Peruvian style, and objects and wares that formed pleasing "vi-
gnettes" were combined regardless of provenance or dating. Nonetheless it is
clear that both verisimilitude and artistic effect were major concerns; Soldi
sought, as he put it, to prepare "faithful reproductions" (Soldi 1881:335–
507; Hamy 1889:352–57).

Early Attempts to Overthrow the Naturalistic Aesthetic

Wiener's exhibit at the 1878 Exposition occasioned the publication of a major tract in defense of non-Western aesthetics, Soldi's Les Arts méconnus
(1881). Soldi was a follower of the architect Viollet-le-Duc, who had inspired and guided the neo-Gothic revival in modern architecture and was
among the best-known and most prestigious spokesmen for a nonclassical
aesthetic. Subtitled "les nouveaux musées du Trocadéro," Soldi's book was
written to promote the idea that an entire series of new museums must be
created to display those arts long neglected by academic tastemakers and
largely excluded from citadels of art like the Louvre. The first section covered
the "industrial arts," in which he included such pursuits as engraving, ca-
meos, and sculpture in precious gems; the other divisions corresponded to
given periods and regions—the art of the Middle Ages, then Persian, Khmer,
American, and Egyptian art. For each he had a special case to deliver, but
his overall argument rested on a rejection of the classical ideal in art, exemplified by the Greek, Roman, and High Renaissance traditions, whose productions were, "for the adepts of a certain school that is still too powerful,
the only superior productions of human genius, the only ones worthy of inspiring the artist" (3). In this view all other arts—he listed Egyptian, Assyrian, Hindu, Cambodian, Persian, Moorish, Mexican, Peruvian, Chinese,

Japanese, Byzantine, Lombard, and Gothic—were only sporadically interesting. Thanks to the efforts of antiquarians, the guardians of taste were being forced to abandon their narrow criteria for a more expansive vision, but in general the arts outside the classical tradition continued to be "disdained" (3–4).

Soldi's pleading for neglected artistic traditions was part of a long movement against classical aesthetics that began in the eighteenth century among collectors of archeological antiquities and encompassed such "primitivist" schools as the French *primitifs,* the German Nazarenes, the Pre-Raphaelite Brotherhood, and in Soldi's own day, the Nabis and Gauguin's school of Pont d'Aven (Curtis 1975). Yet within this context Soldi's style of argument is of special interest, in part because he made a case for arts, like the pre-Columbian, that attracted little attention even among aesthetic rebels. Furthermore, while other artists sought to transform aesthetic canons by themselves creating "primitivist" works, Soldi sought to achieve that end by public display and education through the medium of the museum, working in collaboration with ethnographers who were just beginning to establish their own authority in the management and display of the "primitive arts."

In preparation for the 1878 Exposition, Soldi and his circle had developed an ambitious plan for "an historical school of the sciences and the arts," which would include a "Museum of Ethnography" with collections representing all stages in the evolution of the arts (Soldi 1881:iii–vi). Along with sections on Old World antiquities and medieval art, these were to be housed in the new Trocadero, an eclectic Gothic-Byzantine-Moorish structure that was erected on the hill overlooking the Champs du Mars specially for the 1878 Exposition.

Soldi's grandiose scheme was rejected for requiring not only a great investment, but the raiding of other museums, including the Louvre, for large parts of their collections. His conception is, nonetheless, worth our notice. Aside from being the most forceful argument for studying the "primitive arts" in the period, it reveals some of the tensions and contradictions that bedeviled early attempts to overthrow the prevailing naturalistic aesthetic.

The "historical school of the arts and sciences" was intended to teach an evolutionist conception of the origins, nature, and development of the arts by showing how the arts began, what forms they took, and what materials were at the disposal of artists in diverse settings across the ages. It drew clear distinctions among arts that were "primitive," "advanced," "refined," and "decadent"—the last being a favorite term of Viollet-le-Duc's coterie, who believed that Occidental art of the High Renaissance was in a full phase of decadence from the art of the Middle Ages (Soldi 1881:69–71). This conception was never intended to suggest that all the arts were on a par, but rather that all the arts were worth looking at and that all arts could instruct.

In turn this new openness to variety in form, technique, and subject matter was expected to produce as a byproduct new valuations of the arts; and indeed Soldi's admiration of such traditions as the pre-Columbian demonstrated the benefits, in fresh vision, of rejecting the classical aesthetic.

Such an historical-evolutionist perspective on the arts had, however, its own criteria of excellence—standards by which "progress" and "decadence" could be gauged. And it was here that Soldi's favorite argument began to emerge, for along with his other purposes—promoting a historical museum of the arts and stating the case for his favorite *arts méconnus*—he also sought to promote a "materialist" theory of artistic production that eschewed inquiry into what he scornfully referred to as the "beautiful and the sublime" in favor of attention to the materials and tools available to artists and their level of technical competence (1881:xii–xv). This approach was a fruitful one for focusing wider attention on arts which, if judged by traditional aesthetic standards, were invariably dismissed as barbarous or, in the favorite term of the age, "grotesque." If the first desideratum was to make people *perceive*, then arguing for the historical and technical interest of alien arts was not a bad way to begin—and making people first perceive was the important function performed by exhibits such as the Trocadero show, and the function that, in effect, all ethnographic displays filled until the boundary between art and artifacts, the beautiful and the instructive, began to break down.

But if Soldi's materialism suggested a more positive valuation of exotic arts, he nonetheless found some pre-Columbian pieces repellent. In ranking the various traditions within pre-Columbian art, he drew directly upon Viollet-le-Duc, who had himself written on Mesoamerican ruins in an introduction to Desiré Charnay's *Cités et ruines américaines* (1863). Viollet-le-Duc's "racist/diffusionist" interpretation of Mexican architecture was directly inspired by propositions on the creative impulse found in Gobineau's *Essai sur l'inégalité des races humaines* (Keen 1971:437–38). Working from Gobineau, Viollet-le-Duc developed an analysis linking material techniques in architecture with specific racial groups—the use of mortar indicating, for example, the presence of a "Turanian-Finnish" element in the American races (Viollet-le-Duc 1863:26–27). Viollet-le-Duc argued that the "pure" artistic impulse at work in the ancient Americas was best expressed in the mature style of the Toltecs (3–4), whose "medieval" brilliance he equated with his own beloved European Middle Ages. Soldi reproduced Viollet-le-Duc's argument intact, adding his own observation that Incan art was much superior to the Aztec, which, with its "hideous forms" and sanguinary imagery, was clearly a "decadent" phase (Soldi 1881:343). Aztec monumental sculpture had produced "bizarre results"; Aztec work in obsidian and chalcinite was "barbarous"—utterly failing to capture the human figure and wholly lacking in fluid line because "technical grossness" made it impossible to sculpt in such materials

(347–48). In one case, he noted, the artist had so little control over his materials that he "had not even tried" to render true eyes, but had settled for two "slits" in the hard stone (351–54).

Although Soldi generally favored Peruvian art, he was no less harsh in judging the megalithic sculptures of Tiahuanaco. "Dominated by the material," this tradition of sculpture was "in infancy": human forms were square rather than fluid, the limbs were never freed from the body, simple holes sufficed for eyes and blocks for ears (363–71). Thus although Soldi was moved by many features of pre-Columbian art—which in one place he called "as great as any the world had produced in grandeur and beauty"—the naturalistic aesthetic died hard with him, too. In a perfect peroration to his evolutionist argument, he concluded: "The ingenuity and patience with which American sculptors designed human forms, in using procedures such as these, are worthy of all our admiration despite the gross aspect of the final result" (379).

Limited as Soldi's challenge to the naturalistic aesthetic was, his "materialist" theory of the evolution of art still did not gain easy acceptance in French aesthetic or ethnographic circles. French analysts of the "primitive arts," like their counterparts elsewhere, adhered strictly to an evolutionist scheme of artistic development (cf. Jacknis 1976). But they were little interested in the suggestion that technique or the artist's materials were of chief importance. Rather they concentrated on divining the causes and origins of the artistic impulse. Salomon Reinach, for example, attributed the artistic impulse to magical origins, specifically to the desire of primitive peoples to "evoke" by means of artistic representation the beneficent forces or spirits of the animals they hunted for food (1903). A more important opponent was Hamy, who became curator of the Trocadero on its founding and who in his writings on the pieces held there took strong issue with Soldi's contention that materials determined artistic form. Hamy insisted that the intellectual, cultural, and religious inspiration of the artist was primary (Hamy 1897:16), and his own understanding of the "evolution" of art was grounded in a broader scheme of cultural progress that placed peoples and civilizations along a continuum leading to the European standard. Thinking in this way, he was disinclined to appreciate and certainly never developed what potential there was in Soldi's "materialist" scheme for a revaluation of the "primitive arts."

The Pre-Columbian Collection at the Trocadero

Although figures on attendance at the pre-Columbian exhibit at the 1878 Exposition are not available, the show was successful enough to convince the Beaux-Arts authorities to proceed with opening the permanent Trocadero museum. Its founding began a new chapter in the display of pre-Columbian art in Paris, for from this point on, pieces from the ancient Americas were continuously on exhibit. Although the Trocadero museum was underfunded and ill maintained, it led a steady existence and provided ready access to art and artifacts that could be seen nowhere else.

To some extent the Trocadero preempted the role of the "world expositions" in satisfying the Parisian taste for pre-Columbian exotica. Sources on the 1889 Exposition Universelle include only a few references to pre-Columbian displays. A mock village of ancient Mexico was part of a larger exhibit of archaic dwellings that struck Van Gogh as "primitive and very beautiful" (Read 1964:48). And the businessman and assiduous *américaniste* Eugène Goupil displayed his collection of statuettes and diverse "industrial productions" from pre-Conquest Mexico (Boban 1891:8). But near the end of the nineteenth century public interest in exotica came increasingly to be focused on those regions of the world—West and Central Africa, Southeast Asia, Melanesia—where France had colonial "interests," and the later expositions responded accordingly. The 1900 Exposition included a giant replica of a Khmer temple which was very popular despite criticism in the *Gazette des Beaux Arts* for its false conception and detail (La Nave 1904:326). The craving to see what France had gained with the empire was to lead eventually to a festival of national self-congratulation in the Colonial Exposition of 1931. But as public interest in exotica shifted to France's own colonial world, there was little need for ad hoc displays of the more esoteric exotica like the pre-Columbian, and the Trocadero became the acknowledged focus of interest in the art and artifacts of the Americas.

As established in 1880, the Trocadero's American collection drew on several different sources. Although the most important transfer from another institution was that of the Louvre's "American antiquities," which were moved to the Trocadero on its founding, the Muséum d'Histoire Naturelle and the Bibliothèque Nationale also sent certain pieces (Hamy 1889:352–53). A number of donations were also made to the Trocadero by individuals who could not privately house the pieces they had collected, or who gave them to the French government out of national feeling. Career diplomats were especially important in this regard; after devoting lifetimes to investigating their surroundings, they frequently transferred the material results back to the metropole. Perhaps because Peruvian laws governing the export of artifacts were weaker than the Mexican ones, those who served in Peru seem to have been particularly active in collecting. Léonce Angrand, French consul in Lima and Wiener's mentor in Peruvian studies, was typical of such diplomatic donors; and the Drouillon collection was also acquired in this fashion.

But by far the greatest number of pieces, at least in the American division of the museum, came from "missions" financed by the Ministry of Public

The exterior of the Trocadero Museum in Paris at the time of the 1878 Exposition, as shown in *The Illustrated Catalogue of the Paris International Exhibition* (courtesy of the Newberry Library, Chicago).

Instruction. Wiener's Peruvian sojourn was the most "profitable" of these ventures; but others, too, were highly successful. The voyager Alphonse Pinart, who received a Fr 125,000 subsidy from the government to travel for five years in the southwestern United States, Mexico, Central America, and the Andes, returned hundreds of pieces (not all of them authentic, it now appears) to the Trocadero (Parmenter 1966:21–28). Hamy's friend Jules Crévaux sent a number of artifacts back from travels on both continents before he was killed near the Pilcomayo River by Toba Indians in 1882 (Hamy 1884). On another Peruvian trip, Léon de Cessac sent fifteen boxes containing both material artifacts and physical remains from an extended period of excavation at Ancon (Hamy 1889). Shortly after 1900 the explorer Paul Berthon spent five years on an archeological mission to Peru, where he gathered a treasure of Nazca ceramics (previously rare in European collections) as well as mummies, textiles, baskets, and an assortment of "the humblest of objects" (Berthon 1911:27–34).

In later years the Trocadero began to buy American pieces on the open market, but since the museum was always financially hamstrung this was never an important source. The museum was first funded on a Fr 22,000 annual budget, which grew in tiny increments, until in 1908 funding was again reduced to the original amount (Verneau 1918–19:554). Since the lion's share of these sums went to salaries and physical operations, virtually nothing was left for acquisitions. According to Hamy's successor René Verneau, the sum typically available to him for making new purchases in any given year was only two hundred francs (547).

Open free of charge to the public, the Trocadero enjoyed a certain following even in the early years, before the vogue of *arts primitifs*. But it was a difficult, if not impossible, place to work: quarters were cramped, lighting and heating minimal, and the collections arrayed in a haphazard arrangement determined only by storage and display facilities (Verneau 1918–19). As director of the museum from 1880 to his death in 1908, Hamy seems to have accepted these physical defects with equanimity. Although he did press the authorities for improvements, he had no success. On the whole, he preferred to devote his time not to improving the display of artifacts, but to "decoding" the pieces and drawing from them whatever ethnographic or historical information they would yield.

E. T. Hamy and the Evaluation of "Primitive Art"

Although Hamy was a man of many interests, he devoted the largest portion of his time to the Trocadero's American section, which he thought ranked with the best in the world (1889:363). His prominent role in creating the

Trocadero and his writing on pre-Columbian pieces were later to draw the attention of the art historian Robert Goldwater in his important study *Primitivism and Modern Painting* (1938). Although in Goldwater's view the "primitivist" revolution was effected chiefly by working artists, he thought that it was anticipated by ethnographers whose collections made possible a long unconscious association between European artists and works of art from Africa, Oceania, and the Americas (42–43). In isolated instances, moreover, he found that European ethnographers "appreciated their objects as 'art' long before the artists," supplying E. T. Hamy as a case in point (xxii, 21–22).

Yet while it is true that Hamy had a profound love of things American, he seems in fact to have had little appreciation for the aesthetic values of pre-Columbian culture. His approach to study of the Trocadero's holdings was exclusively scholarly and pedagogic, and on the rare occasions when he took up aesthetic matters, he usually found the pieces in question "grotesque" or taxed their creators for failing to achieve realistic effects. His first major work

An assortment of Aztec statuary as displayed in the Galerie d'Amérique of the Trocadero Museum (courtesy of the Musée de l'Homme, Paris).

on the Trocadero's American collection was *Décades americanae: Mémoires d'archéologie et d'ethnographie américaines* (1884), a series of short essays in which he developed his characteristic style of exposition about individual artifacts. Each essay was devoted to one piece whose origins, function, and iconography he attempted to trace: a stone fragment from an Aztec sacerdotal staff; a terra cotta figure of a frog, found on the upper Orinoco; a tombsite at Los Tres Molinos in Ecuador; a motif on a vase from Truxillo (Peru); a hieroglyph from one of the Aubin manuscripts showing an Aztec *tzompantli* (skull rack); "Carib" ornaments he found among "anthropolithic" remains from Guadeloupe; and swastikas found on an assortment of artifacts from North and South America.

Hamy's erudition was vast; he knew in depth the codices, the Spanish ethnographic and historical accounts, and the scholarly work of his contemporaries in Europe and America. Since he expended considerable energy trying to prove the Old World origins of pre-Columbian civilization, much of his scholarship now seems errant; but even in these instances, his exposition was marked by close attention to iconographic detail, careful searching in extant written sources, and laborious sifting of ethnographic evidence. In all these exercises the point of Hamy's labors was decipherment; as he put it himself, he was striving "to solve . . . problems, more or less difficult" that were posed in the process of classification (5). Thus his interests were historical and ethnographic, and he confined himself to tracing descriptions in earlier sources and taking up problems of origin, dating, and periodization.

After two decades with the Trocadero collections, Hamy published another series of essays, entitled *La galerie américaine du Musée d'Ethnographie du Trocadéro* (1897). This work was assembled on the occasion of yet another "universal exposition," this time the 1893 World's Fair in Chicago. When asked to contribute to the fair, Hamy assembled photographs rather than sending actual artifacts (he was no doubt short of money), and in *Galerie américaine* he wrote extensive commentary on a select group of the pieces. The sixty plates were superb illustrations of some of the Trocadero's treasures. Ten were of more recent North American origin, but the rest were pre-Columbian, including a stone mask, a limestone statue of a Nahua god, Toltec ceramics, a rock-crystal death's head, a funerary urn from Oaxaca, samples of Peruvian textiles, and ceramics from diverse culture areas in Mexico, Colombia, and Peru. Although he selected pieces for their "rarity or historical character" rather than for aesthetic reasons (i), Hamy was in this work forthright in assessing artistic merit, delivering, for example, a harsh judgment of the sculptural aesthetics of a limestone deity from Vera Cruz:

> The choice for materials of an easily worked limestone . . . the inability to detach the upper limbs . . . from the surface of the trunk; the summary execution of the lower limbs, which remain attached one to the other, all this

manifestly denotes a relatively ancient work. I will pass over the matter of proportions, which give to our personage a bit less than four *têtes* and reduce his height in so shocking a fashion; Mexican sculptors persisted to the end in this perverse aesthetic.

(17)

Whatever the truth about other ethnographers of the period, it would seem that Hamy should not be cited for working to raise the perceived aesthetic status of "primitive art." Although he was alert to purely technical refinements in ceramics and metalworking and appreciated the variety of decorative motifs in Peruvian textiles (1896:20), these judgments on the "minor arts" did not fundamentally qualify his broad assessment of pre-Columbian civilization as aesthetically barbarous.

It is true, as Goldwater observes, that Hamy frequently argued for the universality of the aesthetic impulse. And in this regard he did stand apart from those who denied aesthetic capacity to primitive artists working outside a naturalistic aesthetic (Goldwater 1967:17). But the "universality of art" was only another in a series of questions disputed among French anthropologists and ethnographers who sought to prove the fundamental sameness or diversity of humankind—a late embodiment, in short, of the monogenist-polygenist question (Stocking 1968). French monogenists had long argued that religiosity, family feeling, and the like were "universal," contesting the polygenist view that the various races had independent origins and widely differing capacities (Cohen 1980:84–86). As "primitive art" began to draw increased attention, monogenists argued that this faculty too was universal and constituted further proof of the oneness of humankind (Hamy 1908).

That affirmation of the universal artistic drive did not necessarily imply appreciation of "primitive art" is indicated in an 1883 article on ancient American art by the Marquis de Nadaillac, an archeologist of some repute. In a discussion that veered confusedly from rock painting to Mayan bas-reliefs, Nadaillac argued that American sculpture was full of "grimacing figures that are repulsively ugly" (121–27). He explained the "bizarre qualities" of American sculpture by observing that the "ancient American races failed to comprehend the beautiful as we do, formed as we are by the immortal creators of great art in Greece" (126–27). Yet Nadaillac was less interested in whether American artists produced beautiful works than in their very existence amidst a barbarous civilization, and he drew from his survey the lesson that "art is an innate sentiment in man . . . more or less developed among all the races" (140). For both Hamy and Nadaillac, then, their commitment to artistic "universalism" reflected positions staked out in other controversies. They were speaking to the enduring monogenist-polygenist argument rather than urging any genuinely new perception of the "primitive art" of the Americas or elsewhere.

Hamy remained director of the Trocadero until his death in 1908, and his approach to pre-Columbian artifacts remained consistently scholarly and pedagogic in character. Although he was interested in showing off selected pieces to good effect, he chose these according to nonaesthetic criteria since matters of display were of no great import to him. Indeed, by the end of Hamy's tenure as director, the Trocadero showed clear signs of neglect. The collections were jumbled and crammed into wholly inappropriate space. Some were displayed in dusty cases and others were simply stood on the boxes in which they had arrived (Verneau 1918–19).

The Trocadero and the "Primitivist Revolution"

Hamy was succeeded as director by René Verneau, during whose years (1908–27) the Trocadero fell on even bleaker times. Unlike Hamy, Verneau was interested in mounting impressive displays and, as we shall see, he was slightly more sensitive than Hamy to the aesthetic qualities of the Trocadero's holdings. Nonetheless, Verneau suffered many woes in trying to maintain the museum with its limited personnel and pitifully small budget. During the first World War, when all the Museum's employees save one aging guard were mobilized, Verneau could do little else than watch the collections slowly deteriorate. Even before the disastrous circumstances of the war, however, the Museum's meager budget and facilities were described by one visiting ethnographer as a "bad joke" (Verneau 1918–19:556). Although Verneau was irked at his inability to buy anything on the growing commercial market in "primitive art," the collections continued to expand with gifts from donors. One such instance illustrates both the Trocadero's characteristic style of operations and something of Verneau's feeling for the pre-Columbian pieces in his charge. In 1913 he was approached by a trader from Cholula who offered to sell for a modest sum a collection that included, in Verneau's words, "rare and beautiful" pieces. Even at cut-rate Verneau could not afford the purchase, but loathe to lose the opportunity, he asked a benefactor (Prince Roland Bonaparte) to buy the collection for the Trocadero.

Verneau later described these pieces for the *Journal de la Société des Américanistes* and in his account there is a new note of pure delight in the figurative sensibility, and especially in the decorative skill, of the ancient artists. Verneau referred to one piece, a figure of a laughing head as a "caricature worthy of a true artist," and to another, a pottery plate, as a "magnificent piece" whose "richness in decoration" surpassed anything similar to it previously held by the Trocadero (1913:339). Nonetheless, this article and Verneau's other writings of the period indicate that he saw his task as guardian of the Trocadero holdings in much the same light as had Hamy: the history and ethnography of the pieces were of primary importance. Verneau was open to the idea (as Hamy had not been) that there was beauty in "primitive art" like the pre-Columbian. But he did little himself to promote the idea or to suggest that the traditional scholarly approach to products of the "primitive arts" was constricted or inadequate.

This being the case, we may judge Verneau's delight a minor sign of the times, which now saw the "primitivist revolution" begin to gain broad cultural momentum. The role of the Trocadero in this movement is replete with irony. The museum, its director and patrons all unwitting, was one site where avant-garde artists became intimately acquainted with *arts primitifs* (Paudrat 1984:141–42). It is especially ironic that the Trocadero's disarray, which caused pain and embarrassment to ethnographers (Verneau 1918–19), was a source of delight to surrealist artists and aesthetes, for whom the museum was "an unscientific jumble of exotica, a place one went to encounter curiosities, isolated esthetic objects" (Clifford 1981:554).

In the postwar years the enthusiasm for "primitive art" was fueled by multiple cultural charges, from weariness with Pound's "botched civilization" to a new fascination with "colonials" generated in part by African participation in some of the worst fighting of the war (Lunn forthcoming). In Europe, African and Oceanic art were the principal objects of what James Clifford has called a "fetishism nourished on cubist and surrealist aesthetics" (1983:122), but the "primitivist revolution" changed the canonical status of all artistic traditions the nineteenth century had considered "primitive." This process of revaluation revealed new tensions in its turn, for while modernists appropriated "primitive art" to undermine established aesthetic categories, traditionalists like Raoul d'Harcourt strove to draw arts like the pre-Columbian into the high culture canon or at the least to regroup them with what modern art historians label the "court and theocratic arts" of "Archaic" societies (Rubin 1984:3; 74–75). In any event it was now impossible summarily to dismiss arts outside the classical tradition; choices, gradations, and preferences had to be expressed in specifically aesthetic terms rather than in the placid generalities of conventions that sorted out good from bad virtually without seeing.

This change, wrought primarily by avant-garde artists, necessarily reverberated among ethnographers and encouraged a break with the scholarly/pedagogic approach to the "primitive arts" that was largely sustained up to the first World War. Although pre-Columbian art was never central to the "primitivist revolution," the effects on both scholarship and display of American works were pronounced. The years after the first World War witnessed the first shows devoted to pre-Columbian art as such. Exhibits appeared across Europe and in America: at the Burlington Fine Arts Club in London, 1920; the Pavillon du Marsan in Paris, 1928; the Metropolitan Museum of

Art in New York, 1933. With this development the process of reacquaintance with pre-Columbian civilization was transferred to a new cultural plane. Although ethnographic expertise was required for such exhibits, ethnographers began to lose their privileged role in the selection and display of *ars americana*. This change raised for ethnographers the new, "modern" problem of how to display objects now judged outside their halls to be full-fledged Works of Art. However, the conflict between aesthetic and scholarly possibilities in the contemplation of "primitive art" continues to the present day.

Despite the "primitivist revolution" the exhibits of the Trocadero—refurbished in the 1930s as the Musée de l'Homme—continued to emphasize the geographical origins, functions, and technical qualities of pieces that had struck avant-garde artists either by their universally magical qualities (Paudrat 1984:141–42) or for their startling resolutions of formal problems. Indeed, the appropriation of "primitive" aesthetic values by modernist aesthetes seems increasingly questionable to anthropologists (see the discussion in *Res*, a recently founded journal of the Peabody Museum). On the other hand, many contemporary artists (like their predecessors in the avant-garde) fault the scholar's approach for rendering prosaic objects of great beauty and aesthetic force (*Arts primitifs* 1967). Thus the legacy of nineteenth-century ethnographic museology—the opposition between beauty and instruction, which was restated as a conflict between aestheticized, and functional/interpretive display (Clifford 1981:558–59)—has yet to be resolved.

Acknowledgments

Research for this paper was supported in part by the Hermon Dunlap Smith Center for the History of Cartography at the Newberry Library in Chicago and by the National Science Foundation. I would like to thank James Clifford and George Stocking for their criticism of the original manuscript, and the staff of the Newberry Library for gracious assistance in the use of their collections.

References Cited

Les arts anciens de l'Amérique. Exposition organisée au Musée des arts décoratifs. Palais du Louvre—Pavillon du Marsan. Mai-Juin 1928. Paris.
Arts primitifs dans les ateliers d'artistes. 1967. Musée de l'Homme, Paris.
Berthon, P. 1911. *Etude sur le précolombien du Bas-Pérou.* Paris.
Boban, E. 1891. *Documents pour servir à l'histoire du Mexique.* Paris.
Clifford, J. 1981. On Ethnographic Surrealism. *Compar. Stud. Soc. & Hist.* 23:539–64.

————. 1983. Power and Dialogue in Ethnography: Marcel Griaule's Initiation. *HOA* 1:121–56.

Cohen, W. 1980. *The French Encounter with Africans: White Response to Blacks.* Bloomington, Ind.

Comas, J. 1954. Los Congresos Internationales de Americanistas: Síntesis histórica e indice bibliográfico general, 1875–1952. México, D.F.

Curtis, M. 1975. *Search for Innocence: Primitive and Primitivistic Art of the Nineteenth Century.* College Park, Md.

Fagan, B. 1977. *Elusive Treasure: The Story of Early Archaeologists in the Americas.* New York.

"GE." *La grande encyclopédie,* s.v. "Henri-Adrien Prévost de Longpérier."

Goldwater, R. 1938. *Primitivism in Modern Painting.* Rev. ed. New York [1967].

Hamy, E. T. 1882. Introduction. *Revue d'Ethnographie* 1:i–ii.

————. 1884. *Décades americanae: Mémoires d'archéologie et d'ethnographie améri-caines.* Paris. (Reprint, Graz, 1971).

————. 1885. Introduction to J. M. A. Aubin, *Mémoires sur le peinture didactique et l'écriture figurative des anciens mexicains.* Paris.

————. 1889. Les origines du musée d'ethnographie. *Revue d'Ethnographie.* 8:305–417.

————. 1896. Etude sur les collections américaines réunies à Gênes à l'occasion du IVᵉ centenaire de la découverte de l'Amérique. *Journal de la Société des American-istes* 1:1–31.

————. 1897. *La galerie américaine du Musée d'Ethnographie du Trocadéro.* 2 vols. Paris.

————. 1908. La figure humaine chez le sauvage et chez l'enfant. *L'Anthropologie* 19:385–407.

d'Harcourt, R. 1924. *La céramique ancienne du Perou.* Paris.

The Illustrated Catalogue of the Paris International Exhibition. n.d. London.

Jacknis, I. 1976. Savage icons: Victorian views of primitive art. Unpublished master's thesis, Univ. Chicago.

Jomard, E. F. 1831. *Considérations sur l'objet et les avantages d'un collection spéciale consacrée aux cartes géographiques diverses et aux branches de la géographie.* Paris (reprinted in Hamy 1889).

Keen, B. 1971. *The Aztec Image in Western Thought.* New Brunswick, N.J.

La Nave, H. 1904. L'art khmer et les restitutions du Trocadéro. *Gazette des Beaux-Arts* 3d ser., 32:328–40.

Laude, J. 1968. *La peinture française (1904–1914) et l'art nègre.* Paris.

Lejeal, L. 1903. L'archéologie américaine et les études américanistes en France. *Re-vue internationale de l'enseignement* 45:215–32.

Longpérier, H. de. 1850. *Notice des monuments exposés dans la salle des antiquités américaines au Musée du Louvre.* Paris.

Lunn, J. (forthcoming) Kande Kamara Speaks: An Oral History of Africans in France, 1914–18. In *Black Men in a White Man's War,* ed. M. Page.

Nadaillac, Marquis de. 1883. L'art préhistorique en Amérique. *Revue des Deux Mondes* 60:117–41.

Parmenter, R. 1966. *Explorer, Linguist, and Ethnologist: A Descriptive Bibliography of Alphonse Pinart.* Los Angeles.

Paudrat, J. 1984. The Arrival of Tribal Objects in the West: From Africa. In *"Primitivism" in 20th Century Art,* ed. W. Rubin. Museum of Modern Art, New York.

Read, H. 1964. *A Concise History of Modern Sculpture.* New York.

Reinach, S. 1903. L'art et la magie. *L'Anthropologie* 14:257–66.

Res. 1981—. Ed. R. Guidieri and F. Pellizzi. Peabody Museum, Cambridge, Mass.

Rubin, W. 1984. Modernist Primitivism: An Introduction. In *"Primitivism" in 20th Century Art.* New York.

Said, E. 1979. *Orientalism.* New York.

Soldi, E. 1881. *Les arts méconnus: Les nouveaux musées du Trocadéro.* Paris.

Stocking, G. W. 1968. The persistence of polygenist thought in post-Darwinian anthropology. In *Race, Culture and Evolution,* 42–68. New York.

Verneau, R. 1913. Une nouvelle collection archéologique du Mexique. *Journal de la Société des Américanistes* 10:3–40.

———. 1918–19. Le Musée d'Ethnographie du Trocadéro. *L'Anthropologie* 29:547–60.

Viollet-le-Duc, E. 1863. Introduction to D. Charnay, *Cités et ruines américaines.* Paris.

Waldeck, J. F. 1866. *Monuments anciens du Mexique.* Paris.

Wiener, C. 1880. *Pérou et Bolivie.* Paris.

Williams, E. 1983. The Science of Man: Anthropological Thought and Institutions in Nineteenth-Century France. Unpublished doct. diss., Ind. Univ.

de Wyzewa, T. 1889. L'exposition retrospective de l'Histoire du Travail au Palais des Arts Libéraux. *Gazette des Beaux Arts* 3d ser., 2:67–72, 531–49.

THE ETHNIC ART MARKET IN THE AMERICAN SOUTHWEST 1880–1980

EDWIN L. WADE

The rapid rise of ethnic art markets in the twentieth century represents a dynamically interactive form of culture change, wherein native peoples, grasping for cultural legitimacy and survival in the industrialized West, accept the economic option of converting culture into commodity (Beier 1968; Graburn 1976). The products of their aesthetic impulse, first as artifact and then as art, become the currency of an "irreducible triad" (Alsop 1978, 1981)—the art market, art collecting, and art scholarship. Although motivated by different values and interests, dealers, collectors, and scholars are symbiotically interdependent, sharing an overlapping socioeconomic niche in which they cooperate and compete for the control of both the processes and the products of native aesthetic culture (McNitt 1962; Wade 1976). If one considers the evolving role of certain native artists, then a fourth component is added to the triad, creating a volatile quartet.

The Southwest Indian art market offers an illuminating microcosm, in which from the earliest days there has been a tense see-sawing of power between collector/humanists and trader/dealers, with the arts and crafts as fulcrum point, and scholar/anthropologists adding weight now to one side, now the other. Traders, anxious to tap a burgeoning tourist market, encouraged mass production with its attendant technological and aesthetic changes; collectors, anxious to save the arts from commercialization, sought to preserve traditional modes. Despite an historical edge, and the early cooperation of anthropologists, traders consistently lost ground to the financial and social influence of the well-endowed patron collectors, who were increasingly

Edwin L. Wade is Curator of Native American Art and Curator of Non-Western Art at Philbrook Art Center, Tulsa, Oklahoma. He received his Ph.D. from the University of Washington, and was formerly assistant director and manager of collections at the Peabody Museum of Archaeology and Ethnology, Harvard University. Among his publications is *As in a Vision: Masterworks of American Indian Art.*

joined by anthropologists in supporting a preservationist approach. The process, however, has been replete with paradox—the preservation of "traditional" aesthetic culture straining against the forces of community development and individual cultural creativity. Over time, the two factions have grown closer in their ideas about the direction of Native American art, as dealers began to realize the marketability of cultural "authenticity," and collectors began to value native creativity in more universalistic aesthetic terms. But enough of the old rivalry remains to revive the game of teeter-totter just when Native American artists begin to feel that they could please both sides, and they now seem forced to make a choice between isolation in a ghettoized ethnic art market and entry into the mainstream of "fine art." (Wade:1976; Wade & Strickland 1981).

   This essay delineates the major phases of this convoluted history: the incipient market (1875–1915), in which an economic bond was forged between Indian traders and scholars, with the academics dependent on the dealers for the acquisition of their study collections; the art revivalist movement (1920–70), characterized by powerful art patrons and their preservationist associations, who manipulated the imagery of Native American art for philanthropic purposes, but in the process drove a decisive wedge between art dealers and scholars; and, finally, the expansive period (1968–present), which has witnessed the reorientation of both market and scholarship toward a fine arts posture.[1]

Museums, Scholars, and Pothunters

In 1880 the Atchison, Topeka, and Santa Fe Railroad came to Albuquerque. During that same year the Atlantic and Pacific Railroad began constructing a line at Isleta, New Mexico, which would reach to the West Coast and

---

1. Not until Nelson Graburn's (1976) breakthrough study of ethnic arts and art markets did anthropologists seriously begin to consider the acculturative impact of such institutions on transitional native societies. Government workers had realized very early, however, that great economic and social change could be effected in conservative societies through the introduction of a cash economy based on arts and crafts production. In many ways the successful Anglo-inspired cultural revivals among Southwestern Puebloan peoples in the 1920s provided the prototype for the Collier administration's New Deal Era policies. These policies reoriented the federal Bureau of Indian Affairs (Burton 1936) and were reflected in thousands of articles outlining "progressive" work programs to promote the cooperative arts and crafts industry published in the Indian Service's journal *Indians at Work*.

   Nevertheless, no studies have exclusively focused upon the internal relationships of participants within such an ethnic market. Coming closest to such an analysis was my 1976 dissertation, *Economics of the Southwest Indian Art Market*, which traced a five hundred-year period of Anglo intervention and finally usurpation of local Native American art production. The present article relies heavily upon that study as well as upon my fifteen years of intimate involvement in both the academic and the commercial side of this market.

connect as far east as the Indian Territories of Oklahoma. Inevitably, the pueblo of Laguna would be served, for better or worse, by this rail line, since a train station would be built within the confines of this previously isolated native village. Within less than a decade, rural New Mexico was forcefully ripped from feudal self-sufficiency and dropped into the bustling economy of an industrializing nation. For White America, it was a time of personal movement and exploration, and the railway allowed Victorian sophisticates and metropolitan adventurers the experience of meeting in person "pacified" Pueblo and Navajo Indians in their native habitats (Tietjen 1969). Many of these travelers were learned people, familiar with the prestigious eastern museums, the popularized scientific reports published in *Harpers* and the weekly tabloids, and occasionally even the detailed military and research institute reports that dealt with the indigenous peoples and arts of the southwestern frontier. Others came anticipating a grand affair, replete with scenic wonders and quaint mementos from a distant land populated by "savage" artisans.

To inflame the tourists' expectations, the passenger departments of the major railways began to commission scholars to produce popular handbooks on the Indian cultures, picturesque ceremonies, and arts and crafts to be encountered along the way, as well as outlining the paid side trips available. One such publication was *The Moki Snake Dance*, "a popular account of that unparalleled dramatic pagan ceremony of the Pueblo Indians of Tusayan" by Dr. Walter Hough of the United States National Museum, published through the passenger department of the Santa Fe Route (Hough 1899; cf. Dorsey 1903). Exotic but docile Indians proved profitable, and it remained in the railroad's commercial interest to choreograph as many varied events as possible. The tourist concession personnel began organizing the Indian artisans, who responded by tailoring their work more to White taste (McNitt 1962; Harvey 1963). Functional full-sized ceramic water jars, too bulky to transport easily by train, were replaced by smaller, decorative forms. New shapes appeared as well, as J. G. Bourke observed in the 1880s at the Rito Railroad Station in New Mexico:

> The sugar bowls and salt cellars were bric-a-brac that would have set Eastern collectors crazy with envy; they were ornamental ware, made by the pueblos of Laguna, six miles distant. A dozen or more of the Indians were hanging around the door, waiting to sell their wares to the passengers.
>
> (Bourke 1884:106)

The railroads even furnished free travel passes to craftsmen and their families if they agreed to sell their works at other depot towns like Albuquerque and Gallup (Minge 1970; Harvey 1978). Obviously this mobility aided in the promotion of Indian arts, yet more importantly it now allowed the artists personal contact with their alien buying public and its needs. No other influ-

Laguna Pueblo potters with ollas on the village railroad tracks, ca. 1900 (negative number 20269, courtesy of the Southwest Museum, Los Angeles, California).

ence, neither traders nor dealers nor scholars, would so broadly promote and transform Indian art as did the railroads and their tourist bureaus.

By the 1890s, the demand for Southwestern Indian arts and crafts was significantly outstripping the supply. In addition to curio dealers, Indian traders, and tourists, museums were becoming major consumers of both antiquities and ethnographic objects. By the turn of the century archeological expeditions organized around excavations would become common, but prior to that most museum-sponsored collecting expeditions were directed to purchase representative tribal study collections. It was here that the interdependence of dealer and scholar was first realized. James and Matilda Stevenson's famous Bureau of American Ethnology expedition of 1879 acquired, through purchase, representative Puebloan artifacts both from native artists and from individual collectors like the Hopi trader Thomas V. Keam and the Santa Fe curio entrepreneur Jake Gold (Wade & McChesney 1981). Adolf Bandelier acquired much of his Harvard University collection of antiquities from Gold and another prominent Santa Fe dealer, Charles H. Marsh, and later assembled a similar collection for the Berlin Museum (Lange & Riley 1966:72–73). Although motivated by scholarly purposes, the activities of Stevenson, Bandelier, and later museum buyers introduced to Southwest Indian communities a cash economy based on the production of arts and crafts, and simultaneously established the Indian art shop and its proprietor as quasi-sanctioned scholarly entities.

Preeminent among these early trader/dealers was Thomas V. Keam, who operated on the Hopi reservation in northeastern Arizona (Tietjen 1969:121–23). Keam was the quality supplier of Southwest Indian artifacts, and a major source of ethnographic information about the meaning of the pieces and the lifeways of the people who made them. As early as 1881, Keam already had hundreds of prehistoric and modern Hopi pots, as well as an impressive collection of arts from other Pueblo and nomadic tribes (Bourke 1884). Unquestionably, Keam's association with leading anthropologists—including Frank Cushing and Washington Matthews—strongly aided him in becoming the most widely recognized Southwest Indian art supplier for the Eastern museums. Assisted by his resident "Hopiologist," Scottish-born and educated Alexander M. Stephen, Keam excavated thousands of Hopi vessels from the ancient village sites of Awatovi, Sikyatki, and Jeddito. In 1892 the second Hemenway Expedition, under the direction of Jesse Walter Fewkes, purchased a collection of over 3,500 objects—for the then fabulous sum of $10,000—which is now at the Peabody Museum of Archaeology and Ethnology (Wade & McChesney 1980). In the early 1890s the Scandinavian archaeologist Gustaf Nordenskïold, who was just completing his excavations of the Anasazi ruins at Mesa Verde, Colorado, wrote to Keam requesting a price list for any Indian relics he might have available for sale (Wheat 1974). In 1897 George A. Dorsey purchased a collection of pottery and artifacts for the Field Columbian Museum, and a collection of 500 objects was also shipped to the Museum für Völkerkunde in Berlin.

The competition of museum anthropologists and tourists for Keam's limited supply of native artifacts had an effect on the process of their creation, contributing simultaneously to the encouragement of mass production and the beginning of a ceramic stylistic revival. Although usually associated with Fewkes and the Hopi woman Nampeyo, much of the credit for inspiring this revival properly goes to Keam and his assistant, Stephen. According to the collection catalog Stephen prepared for the Hemenway Expedition, Keam was already encouraging Hopi potters to incorporate prehistoric designs and shapes into their modern ceramics by 1890 (Wade & McChesney 1981)—at least five years before the commonly accepted date associated with Nampeyo's revival. According to the catalog, the purpose of the expedition was to construct an evolutionary sequence for the history of Hopi culture on the basis of a serial ordering of Hopi ceramics from the earliest prehistoric to the contemporary. Many of the finest pottery examples, however, especially those from the Sikyatki and later San Bernardo periods (fifteenth through sixteenth centuries) were badly damaged and unsuitable for exhibition. Keam then commissioned a number of unidentified potters to fabricate replicas of the prehistoric wares. It appears that during the process Keam and Stephen expanded the original intention and used the replica project as a testing mechanism to see whether the contemporary potters could completely reproduce the ancient styles, firing techniques, and surface treatments used by the earlier traditions. It was their opinion that the modern potters were culturally degenerate and incapable of the sophistication of their forebears; yet occasionally, they admitted, one or another potter showed promise (Wade & McChesney 1980:13–14, 75).

Early photographs of Keam's home and shop at Hopi reveal large quantities of decorative ceramic tiles, dippers, ladles, shallow bowls, and other nonfunctional knickknacks that give every visual indication of having been mass-produced for the tourist trade. Many of the vessels in the collection sported repetitive designs, were miniaturized versions of functional forms, and clearly had never been used (Wade & McChesney 1980:9). Such are the characteristics of curios. Keam went so far as to import wooden molds to insure the uniformity of the Hopi tiles he had ordered:

> In the course of inquiries concerning the fabrication of their Modern Ware, the Moki women made frequent reference to the method anciently employed to produce a paste of compact and equable texture, by first moulding the clay into tiles which, after baking, were ground to a fine powder. As they were thus traditionally familiar with tiles, it was suggested to them to make some and decorate them, but they only produced a great number of rude, shapeless objects. Wooden moulds were then given them and a high price was paid for the tiles exhibiting carefulness in their preparation, and every means were used to elicit the best specimens of modern decorative art.
>
> (Quoted in Wade & McChesney 1980:96)

It was in this context that Fewkes and Nampeyo made their contribution—which in Fewkes's case may have been simply that of hiring Nampeyo's husband Lesou for a dig crew. Nampeyo had previously taken an interest in the designs found on prehistoric potsherds littering the Hopi Mesas, and during the excavation of the site at Sikyatki, she and her husband came to the camp, "borrowed paper and pencil, and copied many of the ancient symbols found

Nampeyo, Hopi potter (negative number 26996, courtesy of the Peabody Museum, Harvard University).

on the pottery vessels unearthed," which—according to Fewkes—she "repro-duced of her own manufacture many times since that date" (1919:279). But there is no evidence to indicate that Fewkes helped Nampeyo market her wares, encouraged her work, or assisted in its preservation; rather he was known to have complained bitterly that her revival ware was being mistaken for authentic prehistoric pottery and that unscrupulous forces could use them fraudulently to dupe unsuspecting buyers (Frisbie 1973). Nampeyo's unprec-edented success both in selling and promoting her work was the result of the concerted efforts of missionaries, traders, and other museum anthropologists. Even Fewkes's archeological assistant, Walter Hough, enthusiastically sup-ported her endeavor and in 1896 purchased some of the earliest examples of her revival ware for the collections of the National Museum. Two years later she had come under the sponsorship of Professor Dorsey and the Reverend Voth, who brought her to Chicago to demonstrate pottery making. By 1904 the Navajo trading post operator Lorenzo Hubbell had brought her to the attention of the Fred Harvey Company, who then hired her to demonstrate pottery making at their lodge at the Grand Canyon.

But if Keam was the original guiding force behind the ceramic revival, it was Nampeyo who perfected a new style of Hopi pottery based upon the design elements and shapes employed by the ancient Sikyatki and Payupki potters. As would an archeologist or art historian, she carefully reconstructed the design system, including the spatial arrangement of motifs, ascertaining which elements were acceptable for contiguous use and which were not, when to color in a design and when to leave it blank, and which composi-tional patterns were best suited to various vessel forms. This new style, du-biously labeled "Sikyatki Revival Ware," differed radically from then current traditions such as Polacca Polychrome, which had been heavily influenced by Zuni tastes, and in a relatively short time the new style completely eclipsed all others (Wade 1980).

The ceramic revival was replete with paradox. On the one hand, it might be interpreted as a sorcerer's apprenticeship gone awry. What began as a sanc-tioned scientific experiment was rapidly transformed into a commercial ven-ture which, because of its remarkable popularity, swept away the "valid" ce-ramic tradition of the people Fewkes had mounted an expedition to study. Inadvertently, Fewkes had set in process the ultimate destruction of part of a material culture he had been commissioned to document. But from another (and perhaps more native) point of view, the revival may be seen as establish-ing arts and crafts as a steady source of income for the Hopi, and ultimately as altering the economic base of the First Mesa villages. An economy that had been entirely dependent on subsistence farming was modified to incor-porate cash derived from pottery making; and in drought years when crops failed, pottery could still be made and sold. Furthermore, Nampeyo was the first, and for many years the only, Native American artist known by name, and the museum purchase of her modern wares contributed also to the legitimizing of contemporary Indian arts and crafts as more than just the degenerate products of ancient traditions.

The early interest in prehistoric Southwestern antiquities was by no means limited within the boundaries of the Hopi reservation. Worsening economic conditions in the United States in the 1890s contributed to the rapid acceleration of officially sanctioned pothunting, especially after the Federal Government shifted to the gold standard in 1893, and workers in closing silver mines turned to whatever quick source of income was available. Earl Morris, one of the founders of Southwestern archeology, recalled that his father, to feed his family, sold pottery he collected when the demand for his services as freight hauler for the mines near Farmington, New Mexico, tapered off (Lister & Lister 1968:4–6).

But the premier pothunters were the Wetherill brothers of Manco, Colorado (Watson 1961:17–28; McNitt 1962; Lister & Lister 1968). Running cattle through the desolate Mesa Verda Plateau in the southwestern corner of Colorado on a bleak December day in 1888, they stumbled upon one of the greatest troves of Southwestern archeology, the enigmatic "cliff cities" of the Anasazi. The brothers, who had always been interested in Indian relics, set to work exploring and digging into the ruins, and were rewarded with the bounty of a lost civilization. The following year, the first of many exhibits of the recovered materials was shown in Denver, and to everyone's surprise they were bought by a collector for $3,000 (Watson 1961:26). The wealth of artifacts recovered from the ruins soon gained international attention. In 1891 Gustaf Nordenskiöld employed the Wetherills to assist him in finding and excavating additional cliff dwellings. He amassed a considerable collection, part of which was exhibited at the Chicago Columbian Exposition, and upon his death was transferred to the National Museum in Finland.

The Wetherills, particularly John, became the celebrity explorers of the Southwest, listing among their formidable accomplishments the first discoveries among the ruins in Chaco Canyon, New Mexico; various sites in Canyon de Chelly, Arizona; Kiet Siel, Inscription House, and other cliff dwellings within the eastern Navajo reservation; as well as Basket Maker remains at Grand Gulch, Utah. During their long and influential careers, one or another brother guided and consulted with many of the leading archeologists and historians of their time, including George Pepper of the Hyde Exploring Expedition, Byron Cummings, S. J. Guernsey, Neil Judd, and even Zane Grey and Teddy Roosevelt. The success of the Wetherills offered admirers and emulators, such as the Day family of Chinle, Arizona, a career model, proving that self-taught expertise, though frowned upon academically, was valuable (Trafzer 1973), that selling artifacts was profitable even if only quasi-

respectable among some classes, and that the trappings of national heritage
and pride were still being discovered.

Art Fairs, Philanthropist-Sponsors, and the "Revival"
of Native Artistic Traditions

During the 1920s and 30s, a number of well-intentioned philanthropic organizations were born whose principal goal was to save Native American art
from ruination at the hands of commercial traders—among them, the Southwest Indian Art Association, the Gallup Ceremonial, and the Museum of
Northern Arizona, which sponsored various Indian craft shows. They sought
to reinvest in the Indian a feeling of pride in his culture and in his indigenous
craftsmanship, and to provide a continuing positive sponsorship that would
allow Indian art to flourish for generations to come. Indian artists could now
expect that they would no longer be subjected to a curio dealer's or trader's
refusal to show a work because it was too innovative, or too traditional; now,
presumably, there was an alternative (Brody 1971; Love 1974).

As a matter of fact, arts and crafts fairs were originally the creation of
reservation traders (James 1974; McNitt 1962). As early as the 1890s, trading post operators such as Hubbell of Granado, Arizona, and C. H. Algert
of Fruitland, New Mexico, were sponsoring lavish annual feasts for their Native American clientele, using as their models trade gatherings and market
fairs that took place during Spanish Colonial times. Seventeenth- and eighteenth-century Spanish officials recorded the broad tribal participation in
such events: Puebloans, Utes, Apaches, Comanches, Kiowas, Cheyenne,
and occasionally even Northern Plains tribes like the Blackfeet, would peace-
fully gather at traditional trade centers such as Taos, New Mexico, and barter
for both utilitarian and rarer commodities. Socially, such feasts were ritual-
ized intertribal proceedings, vehicles for the renewal of trade relationships.
In the same way, the reservation trader used the public feast as a political
mechanism to reinforce the economic pact between himself and the Indians
who patronized his establishment. By the closing decades of the nineteenth
century a new element was added. Certain traders realized that they could
ensure both the quality and quantity of particular native products, initially
weaving, by instilling in the craftsmen a competitive spirit. Feast days traditionally provided the public stage for warriors to play out their personal rivalries; now, through the selective awarding of small prizes of foodstuffs or
currency, the trader could acknowledge the workmanship he preferred. In the
case of Navajo blankets, the winning textile was placed on public display
outside the trading post (Amsden 1934).

The interior of Jake Gold's old curio shop in Santa Fe, New Mexico, ca. 1900. From the 1870s to his release of his shop to J. S. Candelario, Gold became celebrated as a supplier of quality Indian artifacts to the early Southwest scientific explorations (negative number 10729 [photograph by Royal Hubbell], courtesy of the Photographic Archives of the Museum of New Mexico).

While the traders were busy cultivating competition among the local weavers, collectors and pothunters were having their own version of an arts and crafts fair in the Four Corners area of the Southwest. Farmington and Fruitland, New Mexico, became popular gathering places where collectors could convene periodically to show off their latest acquisitions, and to trade and buy from one another (Lister & Lister 1969:66). Although prehistoric pottery was by far the main attraction at these gatherings, eventually classic textiles and other choice art objects and relics became common. By the opening years of this century, the basic ingredients were present that would coalesce into the grand-scale arts and crafts exhibitions of the 1920s. A group of traders as well as collectors were now concerned with Indian art for more than just its utilitarian value.

One of the first individuals to pull these divergent market forces together was William Shelton, the superintendent of the Navajo Agency at Shiprock, New Mexico, who instituted an annual fair in 1909 with the hope that it would be an acceptable alternative to federally discouraged religious ceremonials. Craft competitions were held, with prize money furnished by both the Agency and the local traders, who had been strongly urged to participate.

The fairs rapidly became economically important to the Navajos, as traders and a growing number of collectors began vying with one another for choice items (James 1974:58). In 1921, with a few modifications, the addition of some Indian dances and a move down the road from Shiprock to the train line at Gallup, New Mexico, a new event was conceived: the Gallup Ceremonial.

Although traders benefited by having an increasingly wider variety of arts and crafts to choose from, in general these fairs were meant to be Indian events—unlike present day arts and crafts fairs—thus, the 1934 Annual Navajo Fair at Shiprock attracted more than 7,000 Indians who came to buy, sell, trade, and visit each other. Anglos in the audience were so insignificant that they went uncounted (USBIA). Similar Indian Service fairs occurred in the 1930s at Moenkopi and Oraibi for the Hopis, at Window Rock for the Navajos, and at White River for the Apaches (Cornwall 1933).

The Indian Service, however, was not the only organization involved in the staging of arts and crafts fairs. Several other groups, mainly philanthropic, promoted Indian art and supported various fairs and competitions. Such exhibitions were ostensibly for the betterment of the Indian people, but each year the events tended to be more *about* Indians, and less *for* them. Although philanthropic groups were definitely trying to entice tourists into buying Indian art, their ultimate goal was to convey the unique and special qualities of the Indian and to show the nation that this was a heritage worth preserving. Certain of these organizations, such as the Southwest Association on Indian Affairs, have been instrumental in the growth of commercial Southwest Indian art traditions. Since 1921 they have sponsored the Annual Indian Market in Santa Fe, New Mexico. Through their activities, by 1930 Santa Fe had become a focal point for the contemporary Native American art scene.

A distinguished body of Santa Fean scholars, poets, artists, and art collectors, including Mary Austin, John Sloan, Amelia Elizabeth White, Alice Corbin Henderson, Edgar Hewett, and Kenneth Chapman, began financing Indian art exhibitions across the United States, as well as at home (Love 1974). To this end, they choreographed magnificent native song, dance, and costume shows performed against a backdrop of arts and crafts booths. At the 1921 Santa Fe Indian Market, tourists were enthralled by the sounds of tortoise shell clappers and moccasined feet, swaying to the primordial beat of ancient America. As early as the 1920s it was maintained that upwards of 100,000 visitors came to Santa Fe's market and fiesta each summer for the ethnic extravaganza (Burton 1936:66). Unquestionably, the unwary tourist received a touched-up picture of Native American life; but humanists justified the glamorized image as a legitimate way to build popular sympathy for

The Second Annual Indian Market sponsored by the Southwestern Association of Indian Affairs, 1922, in the Santa Fe Armory (negative number 14288, courtesy of the Photographic Archives of the Museum of New Mexico).

Indian political and religious freedoms. They doubted whether tourists stopping at the White River fair would have left with the same supportive attitude had they seen adult male Indians in blue jeans and cowboy hats, children in suspenders, and women carrying pocketbooks. Out of costume, they were too much like other poor Americans, devoid of magic and the "nobility of the savage." Thus, on the surface, philanthropically-sponsored fairs were very similar to those organized by other interests. The following advertisement published by the Gallup Ceremonial Committee could have applied equally to any of the arts and crafts fairs sponsored by philanthropic organizations:

> They will perform dances age old before the coming of the Spaniard. They will perform dances without a single innovation in rhythm or theme since the first time the measured tread and low-pitched chant sent forth a prayer to the Great Spirits of the Upper and Lower Worlds. . . . . . Half-naked, painted bodies, decorated with treasured beads, wild animal skins, feathers and sacred orna-

ments, will sway in faultless rhythm to the throbbing beat of the log drum and strange chants of dancers.

(ITGCA 1925)

The real difference between the humanists and the dealers was in their motivation for promoting Indian art. For humanists, the preservation of Indian culture was uppermost. To them, arts and crafts were inseparable from the culture and if permitted to die or degenerate, would take with them a significant part of the culture. Less concerned about the changing nature of Indian societies, the traders sought to create a product popular enough to provide a relatively stable economic base for the reservations—since more money for Indian artists meant more money in their own pockets. To achieve commercial success they were quite willing to have the native artists discard traditional and generally time-consuming techniques, such as the use of vegetal dyes in textiles, or ancestral designs of limited interest to Anglos.

Inevitably, the two groups found themselves in an adversary relation. By the 1930s, many humanists were concerned that there had been an overall decline in the quality of Southwest Indian art. In a Denver Art Museum leaflet, Frederic Douglas described the sad state of Pueblo jewelry with undisguised distaste:

Pieces of old rubber phonograph records are replacing the old black jet or lignite. Coral imported from Italy has supplanted almost altogether the reddish-pink stone seen in the prehistoric inlay. Within the last five years large quantities of Chinese turquoise have been imported and sold to the Indians, who make it into ornaments or sell it in crude lumps. A synthetic turquoise, or an enamel resembling the stone in appearance, is rapidly taking the place of the real article. It is an importation from Europe. Attempts have been made by unscrupulous traders to sell imitation shell beads made at American button factories.

(Douglas 1931:2)

The most vigorous campaign waged against the traders was that of Harold and Mary Colton, who turned their 400-acre hunting lodge into the Museum of Northern Arizona. In 1929 they initiated an annual Hopi arts and crafts fair and judging competition, and then set rigid criteria for the participants. For pottery these included judging the item on its symmetry; thinness of the vessel walls; surface finish; firing and color; ring (the sound produced when a finger is tapped along the rim of the vessel—poor ring suggests the pot is not fired well or is cracked); shape; permanency of design (it should not rub off); clarity of painted designs; application of design; and balance of design. Similar stiff requirements had to be met for coiled and wicker baskets, blankets, rugs, ceremonial garments, and Katcinas (Bartlett 1936). To make certain that the Hopi were producing items that would measure up, Museum staff members were sent out twice a year, in fall and winter, to check on the craftsmen's progress and to make recommendations for improving the quality of their work. Then in the spring, just before the exhibition, the staff members would return, review the pieces offered, and select the ones to be included in the show.

Among the items that were flatly rejected were any blankets containing aniline dyes, which had been introduced by traders to the Hopi around 1890, along with a deep wastepaper basket shape. The new dyes were faster and easier to use, and the new shape had proved to be more appealing to tourists than the flat baskets, which had virtually no (western) functional value, and could only be hung on the wall as decoration. But the Museum of Northern Arizona was adamant about disallowing nontraditional shapes and techniques in the baskets that appeared in their exhibition. The traders were just as firm, complaining that it was already difficult to sell Hopi baskets, even with commercial modifications. The preoccupation with reviving the old techniques was increasing the already discouragingly high cost of Hopi crafts. The Hopi had to ask between $40 and $50 for their blankets because the

The 1933 Museum of Northern Arizona Hopi Craftsman Expedition. *Left to right:* Katharine Bartlett, Mrs. Harold S. Colton, Edmund Nequatewa, and Sam Shingoitewa (courtesy of the Museum of Northern Arizona Collections).

Museum of Northern Arizona insisted they persist in the laborious, time-consuming process of dying their wool with lump indigo (Whiting 1942; ITGCA 1930). The manager of an Indian curio shop in Flagstaff summarized the situation in the 1940s:

> Hopi blankets are hard to sell. Prices are too high. There is no pattern in them. Nothing but stripes and they are a lot easier to weave than the Navajo rugs. . . . They are using horrible brilliant native dyes. No, the native dyes do not sell better than the aniline.
>
> (Whiting 1942:156)

The Museum of Northern Arizona crusade among the Hopi was not the only problem with which the traders had to contend. Other philanthropists had made attempts among the Navajo to reinstitute the use of native dyes and classic designs, and even to originate styles all their own. Between the efforts of the traders and the patrons, Navajo rug styles began to multiply. Ambitious patrons promoted their favorite styles by offering prizes at the Gallup Ceremonial and other competitions. The top prizes at the 1930 Ceremonial, each $25, were contributed by Mary Cabot Wheelwright for "blankets of old pattern vegetable dye" (ITGCA 1930). There was in fact more opposition to the Navajo project than to the Hopi revivals. Traders objected that following detailed recipes in which chemical mordants and vegetable materials had to be precisely mixed and slowly simmered for hours added to the cost of the textiles. Navajo rugs were in constant high demand and the traders were unwilling to jeopardize their steady market by raising prices and introducing new colors and fine woven designs.

Many of the traders' misgivings about the marketability of the revival textiles proved correct. Nine years after the inception of the Hopi Craftsman Show, the museum proclaimed that the production of vegetable-dye textiles had doubled over preprogram years. But from the 1940s to the present, textile production has dwindled each year, and its survival as a commercial art is highly problematic. A few inferior pieces still appear at the Hopi Craftsman Show and the reservation guild, but most weavers find it too time consuming to manufacture finely woven wool blankets for the small monetary return.

The struggle to determine the future of Indian art was not confined solely to the trader and the humanist. Humanists often disagreed among each other, and sometimes a group would change its philosophy regarding the arts and crafts in midprogram. Apparently this happened with the Museum of Northern Arizona. After its failure to sustain Hopi weaving it began to lean more toward accepting and encouraging innovative work. The director's wife and members of the museum staff decided that the traditional silver jewelry made by the Hopi was too similar to that of the Navajo and Zuni—which was not surprising, considering that the Hopi had only learned the craft from the Zuni at the close of the nineteenth century and the Zuni had, in turn, learned it from the Navajo. But the Museum felt it was time for the Hopi to have their own distinctive style, even if that meant displacing what they had come to think of as their traditional form of jewelry.

Virgil Hubert of the Museum staff set out to collect designs from Hopi pottery and basketry as the basis for creating the new Hopi silverwork. Although Hubert supervised the development of the overlay metalworking technique, Paul Saufkie, a Hopi silversmith, was commissioned to turn the ideas into real jewelry, and his pieces were placed on exemplary exhibit. Proud of its creation, the Museum of Northern Arizona announced that "Here was an art that was definitely aided and inspired by the work of the Museum" (Bartlett 1953:47)—surely a radical turnabout from its earlier grassroots tradition revivalism. Although Museum visitors showed considerable interest in the silverworking that resulted, their enthusiasm was not shared immediately by the Hopi. At first no native smith would use the designs or the overlay technique. It was only in 1947 that the new style became generally accepted and the Hopi Silvercraft Guild adopted overlay silver jewelry as their official tribal technique.

Another paradoxical product of the revivalist movement was the introduction of prehistoric Anasazi and Mimbres pottery motifs among the potters of Acoma Pueblo in the 1950s. Dr. Kenneth Chapman of the Laboratory of Anthropology, Santa Fe, New Mexico, showed members of the Lewis and Chino families examples of thirteenth-century Mimbres designs and advised them how to adapt these to their current styles. Though it is doubtful Chapman believed this was much more than an interesting experiment, others hailed it as a revival of Acoma's ancestral art. Apparently they assumed that the ancient Mogollon-Mimbres were the ancestors of the Acomas, even though the prehistoric sites ascribed to the respective cultures were hundreds of miles apart and there is little archeological support for postulating a mass exodus of Mimbres out of southernmost New Mexico into the Western Keres area of the Rio Grande Valley, where Acoma is located. The only time when such migrations could have occurred would have been in the late 1400s. The fact that Acomas at that time were producing glaze ware with strong similarities to the Zuni and Little Colorado styles, however, seems to rule out much influence from the Mimbres.

The interest of Anglo patrons and philanthropic organizations in reviving old art traditions has continued to the present—as witness the revival of old-style Mojave effigy pots and frog figurines with the encouragement of the Gila River Arts and Crafts Center in the 1970s (Wade 1976). But viewing the revivalist movement as a whole, it is hard to avoid the conclusion that it has been caught from the beginning between not easily reconcilable forces. Although Anglo philanthropists saw themselves in opposition to private profit-

Kenneth Chapman showing an Acoma pot to Acoma potter Lucy Lewis (© 1979, Laura Gilpin Collection, Amon Carter Museum).

oriented traders, over time they also became of necessity increasingly concerned with monetary matters. Derived honestly from a desire to reward Native American artists (and sustain the communities from which they came)—as well as from the desire to record some public indication of success—the emphasis on sales intensified as art dealers and curio merchants continued to run their own art fairs. When financially successful, these drew the most talented native artists away from the humanists. Irrespective of good intentions, the philanthropists soon realized that money spoke. The larger the sales, the greater the commitment of the artists; the certainty of an object's purchase, since it conformed to the ideals of the fair sponsors, guaranteed that its style would be emulated. Trying to insure the purity of traditional native art, the humanists were caught up in the greater forces of an art market of which they were never more than a single component (Wade 1976).

The Limitations of Revivalism and the Liberation of Artistic Vision

The inability of philanthropically motivated organizations to live up to their ideals has been a factor in the recent harsh criticism of such organizations by militant Indian groups and independent artists. In the early 1970s, the American Indian Movement, Indians Against Exploitation, several Navajo National Chapters, and the Coalition for Navajo Liberation publicly expressed serious objections to the way in which some of these activities have been conducted. The most scathing criticism—reinforced by a petition signed by 1,200 people—has been directed against the Gallup Ceremonial, which A.I.M. charged rewarded Indians for perpetuating a Hollywood caricature of their traditional life, and committing sacrileges through the public performance of sacred ceremonies (*Navajo Times* 1972:34; Wassaja 1973:21). Events sponsored by nonprofit philanthropist organizations, including the Santa Fe Indian Market, have also fallen victim to criticism.

In this context, certain limitations of revivalism as an historical movement and a cultural strategy (in both the aesthetic and the anthropological sense) demand consideration. Certain of the programs were, by important criteria, quite successful—the Museum of Northern Arizona's invention of the silver-working style gave the Hopi a sorely needed means for bringing more income to the reservation. But the question may still be asked: Was traditional Indian art really saved?

A true revival requires extensive knowledge about traditional techniques and the repertoire of design elements, as well as the function the art tradition fulfilled in its society. By such standards, commercially successful revivals must often be judged wanting. Thus while the newer Navajo textiles have found a place in the tourist market, there is no basis for the claim that classic Navajo weaving was saved. Designs were often modified and simplified—as in "Crystal," "Wide Ruins," and "Chinle" rugs. Even the revival "Chief's" textiles had little in common with those produced from the 1850s to the 1880s. Orangey aniline reds were often used in place of the deep, lustrous ones produced by natural cochineal dye; and revival weavers often substituted coarsely carded grey wool for the dark brown bands used so effectively in the early blankets to set off the brilliant indigo blue stripes.

Alternatively, the few revivals that have accomplished the goal of bringing back the pristine traditions have not always succeeded financially—as witnessed by the Northern Arizona Hopi blanket project. In this respect the Gila River Arts and Craft Center's efforts to reward Pimas who would weave accurate renditions of the old willow and devil's claws baskets has been perhaps the most successful. Today weavers like Naoma White and Gladice Anteone are creating baskets that rival the finest works made before the decline of the 1920s.

Yet citing examples of revival programs that succeeded simply raises the further question of the irreducible selectivity of the whole revival process, and the criteria of choice. At the same time that Hopi basket weavers were persuaded to return to the use of vegetal dyes, many of the greatest basket traditions—Chemehuevi, Washoe, Panamint, and Western Apache—were being lost. Although in some cases geographical isolation of the producing groups was no doubt a factor, one still wonders how museum and other philanthropic groups who wanted to save Indian art could allow so much of the brilliance of these traditions to waste away. From the viewpoint of art specialists, saving the superior art traditions would have seemed most logical. From this perspective, revival programs in the Southwest have typically been overly subjective and inconsistent regarding who to promote, what to save, what to discard, what to discriminate against, and what to tolerate. Organizations commonly waver back and forth on policy, as in the case of the Museum of Northern Arizona's fierce persistence in stamping out aniline dyes in Hopi weaving, then introducing a commercial silverworking project at the expense of a native tradition.

Inevitably, one is led to consider the way most decisions have been made. Characteristically, a philanthropic patron acts either on his own or in concert with an organization of his associates concerned with the plight of the American Indian. The patron and his fellows usually have friends in surrounding Indian communities whom they encourage and sometimes support financially in arts and crafts endeavors. If they have the facilities, they invite the Indians to perform their arts and crafts specialities on the organization's grounds. If the arts seem to be failing, or if the particular community is not doing well economically, the group may decide to hold fairs or special exhibitions where cash prizes are awarded and the Indian artists are promoted. The patron and his organization find themselves so completely immersed in the problems and accomplishments of one group they may never find time for anyone else. In their enthusiasm they lose sight of other Indian peoples' problems, and they continue to sponsor the same group, pour money into their community, and devise one program after another even after that community may have gotten back upon its feet.

In view of this, it is not surprising to find Hopi yucca baskets, with crude coiling, being turned out now in larger quantities than ever while the unsurpassable artistry of the Washoe and Chemehuevi has been lost. The Rio

Grande pueblos drew attention, as they were convenient to Santa Fe and Albuquerque. Patrons could visit them whenever they liked. Today people know the names of Maria, Nampeyo, and Lucy Lewis, but the names of the top Chemehuevi basket weavers, Mary Snyder, Maggie Painter, Mary Hill, and Anne Land are virtually lost. The logic that most humanist groups seem to apply in deciding which arts (or more accurately, which Indian communities) to preserve is to save their friends, or those most cooperative and willing to be saved. To a disconcerting degree, revivals seem thus to have been based on three underlying factors: the convenience of travel to local Indian populations; the personal whim of the patron, and the maleability of the people in allowing Anglo control and manipulation of their arts and crafts.

But even if revival programs had been less subject to such decision-making factors, even if they had been successful in reconstituting traditional Native American arts, many today—including both artists and art specialists— would argue the legitimacy of an alternative strategy. Art is not necessarily served by resurrecting ancient designs and techniques that perished centuries before—especially when this demands the focused energies of talented native craftspersons and artists who must emulate an obscure tradition rather than developing their own visions (Milton 1969; Highwater 1985).

The liberation of Native American artistic vision is, however, inevitably constrained by the art market that receives or rejects its products. By now, the future of the antique sector of the Southwest art market is no longer problematic; prehistoric and historic Southwest Indian art has attained a secure place in the international market for "primitive art." But contemporary creations and the artists who produce them have had a harder course, and their future is less secure. Irrespective of the degree of Westernization of the contemporary Native American artists, their art is not exhibited in the same galleries where Anglo-American and European art is shown. Indian art is a separate, distinct aesthetic movement in the United States. Native American artists have their own competitions, such as the Scottsdale National and the Heard Museum shows, and their own fairs and exhibitions (Wade & Strickland 1981; Brody 1971).

Several factors have caused this segregation of contemporary Native American art from mainstream American art movements. First, modern Native American art owes most of its forms, designs, and themes to the traditional tribal arts. The galleries and other commercial outlets for Native American arts and crafts have capitalized on this heritage. In the mind of the patron a great deal of the "specialness" of this art lies in its primitive roots; and though the Native American today is not primitive, both Native Americans and Native American art bear an ethnic trademark. Indeed, ethnicity is their best promotional asset (Ashton 1973).

This protective veil of ethnicity, however, can erode the innovative vigor of the art. Those who wish to retain the benefits of their Native American association and exploit the exclusivity of an ethnic market will forever float between the lower tiers of the "fine art" mainstream and the quaintness of folk crafts. They will have to operate within the aesthetic constraints imposed by humanist organizations, whose inadvertent legacy has tainted Native American artistic expression with the paternalistic sanctions of historic trust, removed from objective criticism, and as a consequence has limited creative self sufficiency.

In the 1970s an alternative contemporary Native American art movement arose: the Individualists (Wade & Strickland 1981:4). Founded in the polemical, anticolonial stance of the Institute of American Indian Arts, this movement has rapidly grown beyond its original primarily political posture. Though proud of their Indian heritage, and acknowledging its influence, artists like Ric Danay, Bob Haozous, George Morrison, George Longfish, Truman Lowe, Emmi Whitehorse, David Bradley, James Havard, and others strive for artistic excellence first and ethnic association second—if at all. No longer artistically content with the restrictive themes and styles sanctioned by the ethnic market, they openly explore their creative inspirations, unconstrained by media or medium. Charles Loloma has not hesitated to produce gold jewelry despite the fact that Indians are supposed to work in silver. He set diamonds, opals, and ivory in his jewelry when Southwest Indian art patrons were clammering for huge chunks of turquoise and coral. His designs are Charles Loloma designs, not reinterpretations of Navajo and Zuni motifs. And the Indian art patrons purchased his pieces enthusiastically. Fritz Scholder brought to his paintings something new, not just to the Indian art market, but to the modern art world: he demonstrated a new way to use color in stressing his explosive imagery. The modern Indian artist who feels that contemporary Native American art is far too narrowly defined and aesthetically dominated by Anglo patrons can follow the precedents set by Loloma and Scholder. Scholder purposely challenged the Studio Tradition of Southwest Indian painting and held his work up as a way out of the old cliched approaches. R. C. Gorman echoed the challenge: "Traditional Indian painting is a bore. . . . . I say, leave traditional Indian painting to those who brought it to full bloom . . . . The younger painter must certainly look and work within himself, within his own generation" (Milton 1969:91).

Not surprisingly, conservative Native American artists and supporters of Indian art feel that such views are harbingers of doom, and both the Individualists and their critics are amply represented by artists, supportive scholars, patrons, and the newest of market creations, Indian art galleries. Debate rages broadly as to what, if anything, constitutes legitimate Native American

Robert Haozous, son of traditional Mescalero Apache sculptor Allen Houser, and a leading exponent of "individualistic" art, standing in his Santa Fe studio with his sculptures (courtesy of Robert Haozous).

artistic expression, and the ethnic art market is in a state of some turmoil. It seems certain that Indian art in the traditional sense, replete with ethnic identifiers, will continue to be produced, and that fairs, judging competitions, and preservationist societies will continue to promote and oversee it. Increasingly, however, it will be relegated to the realm of American folk art traditions, and from the ranks of its producers will arise more individuals who, because of skill, vision, or proximity to alternative traditions, will shed their specifically Indian identity for that of the mainstream artist. In this context, the folk craft market may become the protective placement service for the fine arts, and the Native American experience may provide a much-needed inspirational jolt to tired aesthetic traditions of the West.

References Cited

Alsop, J. 1978. Art history and art. Art Collecting: The Renaissance and Antiquity, *Times Lit. Supp.* No. 3982 (28 July 1978); No. 3983 (4 August 1978).

―――. 1981. *The rare art traditions: The history of art collecting and its linked phenomena wherever these have appeared.* New York.

Amsden, C. 1934. *Navaho weaving.* Santa Ana, Cal.

Ashton, B., ed. 1973. *American Indian art show and sale* [catalog]. Boulder, Col.

Bartlett, K. 1936. How to appreciate Hopi handicrafts. *Mus. Notes* 9:1 Flagstaff, Ariz.

―――. 1953. Twenty-five years of anthropology," *Plateau,* 26 (No. 1, July).

Beier, U. 1968. *Contemporary art in Africa.* New York.

Bourke, J. 1884. *The Snake-dance of the Moguis of Arizona.* New York.

Brody, J. 1971. *Indian painters and white patrons.* Albuquerque.

Burton, H. 1936. *The re-establishment of the Indians in their Pueblo life through the revival of their traditional crafts.*

Cornwall, C. 1933. Apache Fair—White River. *Indians at work,* 2 (No. 9, December 15).

Dorsey, G. 1903. *Indians of the Southwest.* Passenger Department, Atchison Topeka and Santa Fe Railway System.

Douglas, F. 1931. *Denver Art Museum leaflet* No. 30 (August). Denver.

Fewkes, J. 1919. Designs on prehistoric Hopi pottery. *33rd Ann. Rept. Bur. Am. Ethn.* Washington, D.C.

Frisbie, T. 1973. The influence of J. Walter Fewkes on Nampeyo: Fact or Fancy? In *The changing ways of Southwestern Indians,* ed. A. Schroeder. Glorieta, New Mex.

Graburn, N., ed. 1976. *Ethnic and tourist arts: Cultural expressions from the fourth world.* Berkeley, Cal.

Harvey, B., III. 1963. The Fred Harvey collection, 1899–1963. *Plateau* (Fall).

―――. 1978. Personal communication.

Highwater, J. 1985. What is controversial in Native American art? In *What is Native American Art?,* ed. E. L. Wade. New York.

Hough, W. 1899. *The Moki Snake Dance.* Passenger Department, Atchison Topeka and Santa Fe Railway System.

ITGCA [Inter-Tribal Gallup Ceremonial Association]. 1925. Inter-tribal Indian ceremonial. [promotional pamphlet] August 26, 27, 28. Gallup, New Mex.

―――. 1930. Premium list, Inter-tribal Indian ceremonial. August. Gallup, New Mex.

James, G. 1974. *Indian blankets and their makers.* Reprint ed. New York.

Lange, C., & C. Riley, eds. 1966. The Southwest journals of Adolph E. Bandelier, 1880–1882. Albuquerque, New Mex.

Lister, R. & F. 1968. *Earl Morris and Southwestern archaeology.* Albuquerque, New Mex.

―――. 1969. *The Earl H. Morris memorial pottery collection.* Univ. Colorado Studies, Series in Anth. No. 16.

Love, M. 1974. A history of the Southwest Association on Indian Affairs. *Quart. Southwest. Assn. Indian Affs.* 9:1.

McNitt, F. 1962. *The Indian traders.* Norman, Okla.

Milton, J., ed. 1969. *The American Indian speaks.* Vermillion, S.D.

Minge, W. 1970. Personal communication.

Navajo Times. 1972. IAE Release Report on Ceremonial Protests! 13:34.

Tietjen, G. [1969]. *Encounter with the frontier.* Los Alamos, New Mex.

Trafzer, C. 1973. Anglos Among the Navajos: The Day Family. in *The Changing Ways of Southwestern Indians,* ed. A. Schroeder. Glorieta, New Mex.

USBIA [United States Bureau of Indian Affairs]. 1934. A new step in merchandising Indian arts and crafts. *Indians at Work.* 2 (No. 9).

Wade, E. 1976. *Economics of the Southwest Indian art market.* Unpublished doct. diss. Univ. of Washington.

———. 1980. The Thomas Keam collection of Hopi pottery: A new typology. *Am. Ind. Art Mag.* 5 (No. 3).

Wade, E., & L. McChesney. 1980. *America's great lost expedition.* Phoenix, Ariz.

———. 1981. *The Thomas Keam collection of Hopi ceramics.* Paps. Peabody Mus. Cambridge, Mass.

Wade, E., & R. Strickland. 1981. *Magic images: Contemporary Native American art.* Norman, Okla.

Wassaja. 1973. Ceremonial at Gallup resisted by Gallup Indians. Vols. 1 & 2.

Watson, D. 1961. *Indians of the Mesa Verde.* Mesa Verde Nat. Park, Col.

Wheat, J. 1974. Personal communication.

Whiting, A. 1942. Hopi Crafts. [Report prepared for the Arts and Crafts Board] Mus. North. Ariz. Arch.

ON HAVING A CULTURE

Nationalism and the Preservation
of Quebec's Patrimoine

RICHARD HANDLER

It even happens frequently in anthropological collections that a vast field of thought may be expressed by a single object or by no object whatever, because that particular aspect of life may consist of ideas only.

(Boas 1907:928)

Twenty years after his debate with Otis Mason and J. W. Powell over the proper arrangement of ethnological objects in museums, Franz Boas returned to the pages of *Science* to discuss the relative place that popular education and scientific research should occupy in the hierarchy of objectives of a great museum. The argument against arbitrary classification he had sketched only tentatively in 1887 (cf. Stocking 1974:2, 57) was now elaborated with the confidence of one who had long since won his point: "any attempt to present ethnological data by a systematic classification of specimens will not only be artificial, but will be entirely misleading." Decontextualized in museum cases, specimens or objects were fundamentally inadequate to portray cultural realities:

> The psychological as well as the historical relations of cultures, which are the only objects of anthropological inquiry, can not be expressed by any arrangement based on so small a portion of the manifestation of ethnic life as is presented by specimens.

(Boas 1907:928)

Richard Handler is Assistant Professor in the Department of Sociology and Anthropology at Lake Forest College. He is completing a book on nationalism and the politics of culture in Quebec. His other research and writing concerns the anthropology of Jane Austen's novels, and the literary and aesthetic aspects of the work of Edward Sapir.

Yet for Boas the existence of unsolvable problems connected with the display of material culture (cf. Jacknis, this volume) did not mean that anthropology museums were to be abandoned. The "function of the large museum," he wrote, was to preserve "vanishing" specimens for future scientific research:

> We collect these [specimens] because they are the foundation of scientific study. . . . It is the essential function of the museum as a scientific institution to preserve for all future time . . . the valuable material that has been collected, and not allow it to be scattered and to deteriorate.
> (Boas 1907:929–30)

Apparently Boas, preoccupied with the problems of "salvage" ethnography, did not consider the collecting of ethnographic specimens—that is, their removal from living cultural milieus—as an example of arbitrary decontextualization. Perhaps because he believed that many "primitive" cultures would soon cease to exist, Boas wanted a tangible record of their contribution to human history preserved in metropolitan museums. There at least they could be studied by the appropriate specialists, and protected from physical destruction.

The problem of the proper contextualization of museum specimens, however, has not disappeared in the intervening years. If anything, the postcolonial, often militant self-consciousness of "tribes" who have become "ethnic groups" (Cohen 1978), of former colonies that have become new nations, and of "underdeveloped" nations attempting to develop, has reoriented and embittered disputes about the contextualization issue. It is no longer simply particular methods of display, but the very right of old and established museums to the objects in their possession that is now contested. In the eyes of their critics, these museums have not merely misrepresented other cultures, they have oppressed and plundered them. From this point of view, no appeal to scientific necessity can justify the removal of what has come to be called, tellingly, cultural property: only the people who created artifacts, or the people whose "identity" they represent, can place them in a proper context.

Conflict over the collection and preservation of cultural property in museums is as old as the museum itself. The Louvre was founded during the French Revolution to house art treasures confiscated from the Crown and Church and transferred to the ownership of the sovereign people. Napoleon systematically extended the collections of the Louvre by "liberating" the art of Europe from its aristocratic and royal owners, but after Waterloo the French were required to return much of what they had taken—while the Paris mob watched in despair as their treasures were dispersed. Subsequent European revolutions saw similar programs of cultural expropriation intended to democratize access to previously inaccessible cultural treasures, as well as to protect them from the revolutionary mob: "Rescued from the fury of the people by revolutionary art lovers and scholars, the visual objectifications of tyranny, superstition and oppression were, through the alchemy of the museum, transformed into the National Heritage, the most precious possession of the people" (Nochlin 1972:15).

Yet, as the case of the Louvre suggests, a collection that represents their national heritage to the citizens of one political entity may well represent a patrimony-in-exile to those of another. We see today attempts at a "worldwide repatriation movement of cultural properties" (Halpin 1983:269)—or, more sensationally, "culture wars" in which "nations fight for treasures in exile" (Miller 1984). If Boas despaired of the possibility of exhibiting objects so as to convey cultural context, he hardly imagined that the museum itself, an institution that "must stand first and last," as he put it (1907:933), "for the highest ideals of science," would become the target of "accusations of vandalism, cultural imperialism, destruction of meaning, and outright theft" (Nochlin 1972:10).

It is not my intention in the present essay to pronounce upon the proper function of museums or the just distribution of cultural property. Rather, I am concerned with what Harris (1981:36) has called "the logic of cultural institutions"—and specifically, the logic of "high-cultural" institutions such as museums and the objects they contain. By focusing on the idea of cultural property, as manifested in some sixty years of historic-preservation legislation in the Canadian province of Quebec, I seek to explicate what might be called the fetishism of material culture that animates governments, citizens, and museum curators alike in their zeal to preserve their "heritage." *Whose* heritage a particular collection represents is often open to question; but the idea that objects, or material culture, can epitomize collective identity—and, epitomizing it, be considered as the property of the collectivity—is rarely disputed. Indeed, the repatriation of heritage objects often comes down to placing them in one's own museum—an act which perhaps establishes ownership, but only by reinterpreting cultural things in terms of the ideas of those who plundered them.

Cultural-Property Legislation in Quebec

In Quebec *le patrimoine* is a term common in popular usage and central in nationalist discourse. To speak of the *patrimoine* is to envision national culture as property, and the nation as a property-owning "collective individual," to use Dumont's term (1971). The simplest definition of the *patrimoine* is "old things." A school child, for example, told me that "the *patrimoine* is old things. Like that chair—if that chair is maybe twenty-five years old, it's part of the *patrimoine*." Similarly, the early reports of the Historic Monuments Commission of Quebec plead "en faveur des *vieilles choses*" (1923:xvi). And people unsympathetic to historic preservation would ridicule the *patrimoine* by explaining to me that it was nothing but "old junk." In contrast, the broadest definition of *patrimoine* equates it with national culture. During a parliamentary debate in which the narrow versus the broad meaning of the concept was specifically at issue, one member of the Assemblée Nationale offered the following definition: "The word *patrimoine* designates the totality of what we possess, and what is added to it. Thus it refers not only to the conservation of what we call traditional goods, but of everything that can be called cultural property" (ANQ 1972:XII, 4585) Taking the narrow and broad senses together, we can isolate three aspects of the significance of *patrimoine:* (1) age combined with (2) proprietorship that is (3) collective. People weight these elements differently, but for the moment I would stress that the concept typifies what may be called an objectifying logic (cf. Handler 1984a). It allows any aspect of human life to be imagined as an object, that is, bounded in time and space, or (amounting to the same thing) associated as property with a particular group, which is imagined as territorially and historically bounded.

Although it can also be seen as typifying a worldwide interest in cultural property that is if anything more acute in peripheral or "emerging" polities than in older metropolitan centers where people are culturally self-confident, historic-preservation legislation in Quebec has followed European trends. Private efforts to preserve Quebec's heritage can be found in the mid-nineteenth century (Fregault 1963), but the provincial government first acted in this domain in 1922, when it passed the Historic or Artistic Monuments Act.[1] That law called for the "classification" of "monuments and objects of art, whose preservation is of national interest from an historic or artistic standpoint." Once classified (in the *Quebec Official Gazette*), immovable property could not be destroyed, repaired, restored, or otherwise altered without the consent of the Provincial Secretary, who was to be advised by a five-member Historic Monuments Commission (hereafter H.M.C.). Privately owned movable property could not be classified without the consent of its owner, but no classified objects were to be alienated without the consent of the Provincial Secretary—although the sanctions were only vaguely specified.

The 1922 Act was followed by one in 1935 which attempted to preserve

---

1. 12 Geo. V, Chapter 30. I cite the English version of all laws, which, until 1977, had official status in Quebec, as did, of course, the French version.

the historic character of the Ile d'Orleans, just down the St. Lawrence River from Quebec City. The act called for the improvement of roads, the creation of parks, and the erection of historic markers, and placed restrictions on the construction of restaurants and gas stations as well as "the putting up of posters [e.g., billboards]" (25–26 Geo. V: Ch. 8). In 1952 the Historic or Artistic Monuments and Sites Act added (but did not define) 'sites' to the "monuments and objects of art" of the earlier law. It also specified that the category of "immoveables susceptible of classification" was to include "prehistoric monuments, lands containing remains of ancient civilization and landscapes and sites having any scientific, artistic or historical interest," as well as "immoveables the possession of which is necessary to isolate, clear or otherwise enhance a classified monument or site" (15–16 Geo. VI: Ch. 24).

The laws of 1935 and 1952 foreshadowed later developments in historic-preservation legislation. The former focused not on single objects but on a sociogeographic area; the latter expanded the category of properties deemed worthy of protection, and also attempted to give government a more active role. The provincial government, however, was not disposed to exploit such possibilities until the "Quiet Revolution" transformed it from a patronage organization whose scope of activity was limited, to a welfare-state bureaucracy seeking to influence practically all aspects of life in Quebec. Henceforth the provincial government—in competition, it should be noted, with the Canadian federal government, which had been expanding rapidly since the second World War—would be the major actor in the preservation of Quebec's heritage.

One of the first pieces of legislation of the Quiet Revolution government was the creation, in 1961, of a provincial Ministère des Affaires culturelles (hereafter M.A.C.), which sponsored the new Historic Monuments Act passed in 1963 (*Rev. Stats. Prov. Queb.*, 1: Ch. 62). In addition to the monuments, objects and sites of previous legislation, the new law provided protection for "any municipality or part of a municipality where a concentration of immoveables of historic or artistic interest is situated." Construction, alteration, or demolition within any such "historic locality" was forbidden without a permit from the H.M.C., which was also authorized to regulate "posters and signboards." The law prohibited export of classified property without the permission of the H.M.C., and also authorized the M.A.C. to acquire classified property, as well as to aid private individuals and organizations to maintain or restore classified property in their possession. Finally, it established the Historic Monuments Service within the M.A.C., to provide bureaucratic and academic expertise to both the Minister and the H.M.C— which was reduced to a more purely advisory, rather than administrative, body (MAC 1965:172).

Although the M.A.C.'s third annual report called the provision for historic localities "the most radical modification" of older laws (1964:52), the institutionalization of expertise and the creation of a governmental bureaucracy to deal with heritage was to be as significant as the widening of the category of what could be protected. Though the Service, like the M.A.C. generally, had difficulty in the beginning finding personnel (MAC 1966:153), by the late 1960s Quebec universities were turning out enough social scientists to meet the government's demand for their expertise (cf. Tremblay & Gold 1976:26). The 1960s also witnessed a rapid increase in the number of items classified. The Deputy Minister, historian Guy Fregault (1963), listed 122 properties classified between 1922 and 1963, whereas the tenth annual M.A.C. report puts the total at "nearly 700" (1971:79). The same report mentions that the Service studied more than 1000 demands for construction permits that year, as compared to sixty-seven in 1963 (MAC 1964:53–55). Finally, the Service consciously sought to rationalize its procedures, in order to improve efficiency and put itself "in accord with the most progressive formulas being studied or applied in other countries" (MAC 1968:56).

The expansive effect of the institutionalization of heritage preservation is evidenced in sweeping new legislation, the Cultural Property Act (*Stats. Queb.* 1972: Ch. 19) which the M.A.C. sponsored to replace the 1963 Act. The 1972 law opened with a list of definitions, including those for "cultural property"; "work of art"; historic property, monument, site, and district; archeological property and site; "natural district" ("a territory . . . designated as such . . . because of the aesthetic, legendary or scenic interest of its natural setting"); and "protected area" ("an area whose perimeter is five hundred feet from a classified historic monument or archaeological site"). This array of cultural properties was complemented by intricate regulatory provisions, including two methods for controlling heritage objects: "recognition" and "classification." The M.A.C. could regulate alienation, export, and alteration of both "recognized" and "classified" property; it was to keep an official registry of all such property, and would hold a right of preemption in case of alienation. The Minister was given the right to classify property without the owner's consent, to grant tax incentives to help individuals maintain patrimonial property, and to establish around any classified object a "protected area" in which the same restrictions applied as were applied to the object itself. The M.A.C. was empowered to "make an inventory of cultural property that might be recognized or classified," to authorize inspections by experts, and to block other government agencies when their actions endangered protected cultural property—as well as to issue "archaeological research permits" and to be notified of archeological discoveries. The maximum fine for violation was raised from $500 to $5,000—which in 1978 was raised to $25,000. With this amendment, the legal framework for preserving *le patrimoine* reached its present form.

Nationalism, Government Regulation, and the Creation of Cultural Property

The fundamental assumption of all versions of French-Canadian and Québécois nationalist ideology is that an individuated—that is, bounded and distinctive—nation exists.[2] This collective individual is imagined (like a biological organism) to be precisely delimited both physically and in terms of a set of traits (its culture, heritage, or "personality") that distinguishes it from all other collective individuals. The nation is said to "have" or "possess" a culture, just as its human constituents are described as "bearers" of the national culture. From the nationalist perspective, the relationship between nation and culture should be characterized by originality and authenticity. Culture traits that come to the nation from outside are at best "borrowed" and at worst polluting; by contrast, those pieces or aspects of national culture that come from within the nation, that are original to it, are "authentic." Yet specifying the components or content of an authentic national culture is a secondary operation which follows the assumption that a culture-bearing nation exists. Thus descriptions of cultural content, and the criteria for determining authenticity, can vary widely, and there are recurrent debates over what should be included in the national heritage, or whether a particular piece of material culture is or is not historical. Yet there is relatively little debate over the question of whether an individuated French-Canadian or Québécois nation exists (cf. Belanger 1974:42). In sum, nationalist ideology privileges the fact of existence over its characteristics, formal boundedness over substantive interrelationships.

This nationalist worldview permeates both the letter and the spirit of cultural-property laws in Quebec. The various activities that the H.M.C. initiated or championed in the 1920s indicate that its primary mission was to make both French Canadians and the members of other nations aware of the existence of French Canada's historical and cultural possessions. Crucial to this goal was the work of "inventorying" cultural property in dossiers with extensive photographic documentation in order, first, to preserve "at least the memory" of patrimonial objects and, second, to aid in the "practical task" of "conservation and preservation" (HMC 1923:xi). For similar reasons the H.M.C. advocated the creation of an historical museum and an ethnographic museum—the first, as "a temple of national devotion" (xiv); the

2. The terms "French-Canadian" and "Québécois" are not equivalent, though they may be used to refer to the same group. I use both terms to refer, roughly, to French-speaking citizens of Quebec, but, following indigenous trends, use "French-Canadian" when speaking of the pre-1960 nationalist outlook, and "Québécois" when discussing developments since 1960. For a nationalistic analysis of the evolution of terms of self-identification in French Canada, see Rioux (1975:5–21).

second, to secure "specimens of each of the objects that our ancestors used" against the increasingly voracious appetite of American tourists for French-Canadian antiques (1925:xvii). Other duties included the unveiling of patriotic statues (1923:xi–xii) and the erection of new monuments and commemorative roadside markers. According to the H.M.C., to increase historical awareness—"of what we once were and what we must be today"—was among the surest means to "develop the patriotic spirit of a people" and to give tourists a better image of the nation (1925:xiv). Finally, the H.M.C. made its inventories available to the public in such works as *The Old Churches of the Province of Quebec, 1647–1800* (1925) and *Old Manors, Old Houses* (1927), both attributed to P. G. Roy, provincial archivist and member of the H.M.C. Reprinting an appreciative review from the London *Times* literary supplement (1/27/1927), the H.M.C. called the publication of the volume on churches "the event of the year," suggesting that such praise from abroad should make French-Canadians more respectful of their national heritage (1926:vii).

In its inventories the H.M.C. divided cultural property into ten categories: (1) commemorative monuments; (2) churches and chapels; (3) forts of the French Regime; (4) windmills; (5) roadside crosses; (6) commemorative inscriptions and plaques; (7) devotional monuments; (8) old houses and manors; (9) old furniture; and, somewhat vaguely, (10) *"les choses disparues"*—things that have disappeared (HMC 1926:xii–xiii). Its classification shows that the H.M.C. defined national culture in terms of the conservative, clerical nationalism that dominated Quebec in the first half of the twentieth century. In that ideological perspective the substance of national identity and culture depended on French origins and Roman Catholicism. As the leading nationalist ideologue, the historian Abbé Groulx, put it in an address to French-Canadian youth: "Students of Catholic faith and French race. Here, it seems to me, is your definition; it is your originality; you have no other" (1935:188). Groulx's definition corresponds to the H.M.C.'s categories, which privilege buildings dating from New France, monuments referring to that period, and religious architecture and relics.

Roy (1927:vi) mentions a second and related categorization for buildings that may properly be considered "patrimonial": (1) those possessing "both historic character and antiquity," (2) those "whose merit lies entirely in their being of another age," and (3) those "typifying Canadian architecture." In other words, cultural property can arouse veneration because of age alone or age combined with historically important events, or because it epitomizes national existence. For Roy, buildings rooted in an historically specific past or typifying a national-cultural style "possessed originality and symbolised truly the soul of an entire people" (v). By contrast, newer houses were not "really of our tradition," nor could French Canadians be "truly at home in them" (vii). In sum, what is historical and typical is authentic, truly French-Canadian; and it is assumed that authenticity is objectively ascertainable, even though, as we shall now see, the criteria to determine what is historical, typical, or patrimonial can change.

The Quiet Revolution of the early 1960s saw the displacement of clerical-conservative nationalism by a forward-looking nationalism typified by the *indépendentiste* Parti Québécois (founded in 1968). The emergence of the provincial government as a welfare state was by no means unprecedented in North America, but in the Canadian context that institutional transforma-tion interacted with a long-standing national polarization (French versus En-glish Canada) to produce a renewed "Québécois" nationalism. As the previ-ously passive but now rapidly expanding Quebec government came into conflict with a federal government which was also expanding, traditional concerns for pan-Canadian French-Canadian "survival" were transformed among the political elites of the province into the desire for "national devel-opment" *within* Quebec, which could now be viewed as a global society pos-sessing an autonomous state—the provincial government (McRoberts & Postgate 1980:94–123). Québécois routinely describe their changed outlook by saying that an exclusive concern with *la survivance* was replaced in the 1960s by the desire to live a full and creative national existence within the boundaries of Quebec.

Accompanying the new outlook were new interpretations of Quebec's his-tory and culture that challenged and then replaced the clerical-conservative vision of a French and Catholic Quebec gazing eternally backward to New France. For example, G. E. Lapalme, the political leader responsible for the creation of the M.A.C., typified a generation of Montreal intellectuals and artists who sought, in the 1940s and 1950s, a secular, contemporary French-Canadian culture intimately connected to the internationally prestigious high culture of France. Lapalme seems to have been immensely influenced by André Malraux (appointed Minister of State for Cultural Affairs by De Gaulle in 1959), as well as by European high-cultural institutions and the efforts of national governments and international agencies such as UNESCO to promote cultural development. He equated culture with "a civilization, an art of living, or, as André Malraux has put it, 'the best of what survives of men's works'" (1973:96; cf. Malraux 1953:630–42). Lapalme's cultural ori-entation was written into the charter of the M.A.C., whose goal, as de-scribed by law, was to "promote the development of arts and letters in the Province and their diffusion abroad" (*Rev. Stats. Prov. Queb.* 1: Ch. 57).

Although Lapalme was committed to "democratizing" culture, this did not entail an appreciation of popular or anthropological culture, but rather rais-ing the cultural level of the masses by exposing them to high culture. But the Quebec government's bureaucratization of cultural politics between the 1963 and 1972 cultural property laws was increasingly accompanied by appeals to anthropological definitions of culture (Handler 1984b). The concept of a national culture anthropologically defined was better suited than a definition restricted to high culture for justifying the provincial government's growing concern to intervene in all aspects of Quebec society and culture. Thus the list of "cultural property" covered in the 1972 law was much more extensive than the "historic and artistic monuments" of previous legislation, a fact that generated much discussion among the members of Quebec's Assemblée Nationale who discussed the bill before its passage.

The Minister of Cultural Affairs introduced the bill by stressing the insufficiency of the 1963 law with regard to the natural and archeological *patrimoine* and movable cultural properties. The new bill, she explained, was based on the most progressive concepts from Mexico, France, Israel, Italy, and UNESCO, and was designed to protect Quebec's *patrimoine* from the ravages of economic development (increasingly threatening to traditional architecture), from the booming art market, and from "museums outside the province" (ANQ 1972:XII, 1844). All deputies who responded to the Minister recognized the validity of the expanded notion of cultural property. As one remarked, the interdependence of all social and cultural phenomena had become increasingly obvious in past discussions of the M.A.C.'s role, and thus in the proposed law "the notion of culture has just taken a step forward" (1845).

The evocation of a broad, anthropological notion of culture did not resolve the problem of defining what properly belongs to Quebec's heritage. The deputies were agreed that "nowhere in the world is there an architecture more Québécois, that corresponds better to us, than that which we are aiming . . . to protect" (1855)—but the problem was to determine the content of such categories as "Québécois architecture" or "national heritage." For example, one deputy objected to the vagueness of the term "cultural property"—did it indicate Québécois, Canadian, or North American properties, or items from around the world housed in Quebec museums (1845)? Other discussants pondered the cases of persons maintaining dual residences, of immigrants, and of others who change nationality—how long must a person reside in Quebec before his property could be counted as part of Quebec's *patrimoine* (4617–20)? One deputy, arguing for ethnic diversity in the composition of the new Cultural Property Commission (which replaced the H.M.C.), stressed that all who live in Quebec are Québécois, hence their property is part of the *patrimoine* and they too should be able to "rediscover [their] identity" in the official heritage (1863–64). In contrast, other deputies discussed grounds for excluding items from the national heritage. One speaker bemoaned the fact that Québécois art is lost to the nation when, as often happens, it comes to rest in the private collections of "English" Québécois (1861). And ever re-

current was the problem of separating the Québécois and Canadian heri-
tages—how could Ottawa be prevented from claiming pieces of Quebec's *patrimoine* as Canadian, either by acquiring Canadian national monuments in
Quebec or by bringing Québécois movables to Ottawa museums?

A related issue was that of the temporal limits of the *patrimoine*. Some
deputies were puzzled by the broad definition of archeological property (any
object "indicating . . . human occupation"). How old must something be
before it could be considered archeological or historical property? "History
begins at what date" (4640)? They also questioned the fifty-year limit specified in the article concerning the Minister's right of preemption in the case
of classified property offered for sale. Might it not be desirable for the Minister to acquire objects less than fifty years old, for example, those associated
with persons holding important offices (4625–29)?

Some discussants were willing to rely on the advice of experts. The Minister of Cultural Affairs refused to change the broad definition of archeological property because archeologists had insisted on it; and to the question
about the limits of history she responded, "you have to ask the historians"
(4590, 4640). Another speaker, who wanted even more reliance on expertise
written into the law, argued that only anthropologists, historians, and archeologists—as opposed to "amateurs"—could "identify a cultural property and
. . . place it in the category corresponding to [its] reality" (1847). But another deputy contested expertise, arguing instead for the necessity of citizen
involvement in heritage preservation: "who knows better than the citizen of
a particular region the history of his region" (1863)?

The potential consequences of the 1972 law were signalled almost immediately by the newly created Cultural Property Commission (hereafter
C.P.C.). In its first annual report the C.P.C. (1973:7) stressed that the law
went beyond conservation to promote systematic development of heritage
properties and sites; later reports elaborated a view of the Cultural Property
Act as a tool to prevent urban destruction. For example, it meant to defend
against the "visual" pollution of historic buildings by new construction, and
suggested the indirect regulation of zoning "by classifying an entire street in
order to save not only buildings . . . but a sociological milieu" (1975:133,
143). Nor was the C.P.C. the only organization to envision such possibilities,
for citizens' groups increasingly turned to the 1972 law to fight pollution and
to defend neighborhoods against real estate speculation as well as to preserve
their local heritage. In brief, the anthropological conception of culture embodied in the law could be used in defense of lifeways as well as material
property.

Nowhere were these new concerns more salient than in the debate over
"Place Royale"—a recently created name attached to several blocks of Quebec City's oldest section. Although the interest of the provincial government

dates from the late 1920s, when the H.M.C. declared the church of Notre-Dame-des-Victoires an historical monument, little more was done until the late 1950s, when the H.M.C. and then the M.A.C. began to restore isolated buildings near the church. In 1967 the government passed an act respecting Place Royale at Quebec City (15–16 Eliz. II: Ch. 25), which created a geographically delimited Place Royale (as, in effect, an historic locality) and authorized the M.A.C. to undertake its development. By 1970 the M.A.C. had acquired some forty of the sixty-four buildings in the locality, while this decaying section of Quebec City was partially evacuated. At that time the M.A.C. (1979:18–19) intended "to privilege the French character of the locale." It would preserve buildings and parts of buildings dating to the French Regime, demolish those from later epochs and replace them with reconstructions "as faithful as possible, in their external appearance, to those which existed in the 17th or 18th centuries." The project was to combine historical restoration, urban renewal, and touristic and economic development.

Because the Place Royale project was the largest of its kind ever undertaken in Quebec, it was seen as epitomizing the M.A.C.'s approach to heritage preservation. By the middle 1970s, however, "authentic" restorations focusing exclusively on the heritage of the French Regime were increasingly called into question. With the displacement of clerical-conservative nationalism by a secular nationalism oriented to the present and future, and the new-found equation of *patrimoine* with anthropological "culture," the Place Royale project became the target of an array of citizens' groups and cultural-affairs activists who disputed both the politics of historic preservation and the constricted view of the national past that it represented.

In late 1978 the M.A.C. sponsored a conference to bring together all parties interested in Place Royale. Specialists from the Historic Monuments section of the M.A.C. presented the case for the reigning restoration philosophy. They described four stages in the architectural history of Place Royale (Amerindian, French, British, and twentieth-century) and justified their decision to focus exclusively on the French period. The architecture of that period, they explained, housed a homogeneous and original style of life that succumbed, not at the Conquest, but in the mid-nineteenth century, to the "abusive intensification of commercial activities" associated with British and American architecture. Because Place Royale represented the most important "concentration of [architectural] elements from the French period," it was crucial to the identity of the entire (Québécois) nation. Thus the specialists reaffirmed their commitment to the reconstruction of a French-Regime Place Royale. As they put it, for Québécois seeking their national identity, Place Royale "becomes a privileged tie between the French Canada of yesterday and Quebec of today." To walk through Place Royale is "to be transported into

View of the "Old City," Quebec City, in 1970 (courtesy of the Ministère des Relations internationales and the Ministère des Affaires culturelles Quebec).

the past," and such contact with "our deepest roots" (*nos origines profonds*)
is crucial to the ongoing vitality of national culture (MAC 1979:165–69; cf.
Fitch 1982:55).

Criticism of this position came from architects, social scientists, citizens'
groups, and cultural-affairs facilitators (*animateurs*), almost all of whom
agreed on two complaints. First, in privileging French-Regime architecture
to the exclusion of all else, the project had favored fakery at the expense of
the authenticity of an evolving system of styles. Second, the Place Royale
project had arbitrarily isolated part of a neighborhood, turning it into an
artificial museum while destroying the authentic social life that once existed
there.

Taking the architectural critique first: critics argued that restoration at
Place Royale had proceeded on the basis of an arbitrary judgment as to the
superior value and authenticity of French-Regime styles. In their view such
judgments were relative, subject to shifts in historiographical fashions.
Furthermore, "restoration itself is merely one more action to which a build-

View of Place Royale, Quebec City, in 1981 (courtesy of the Ministère des Relations internationales and the Ministère des Affaires culturelles, Quebec).

ing is subjected . . . in the course of its long life" (MAC 1979:25). Thus critics urged that restoration respect all styles and epochs represented in a site. Some even redefined authenticity as the accumulation of styles contained in the latest state of a building, "a state resulting from a normal evolution" (157). And some suggested a new reading of history to justify that position: rather than abandoning the nineteenth century to the commercial invasion of English speakers, they argued that nineteenth-century architecture, with its diverse influences, be seen as an expression of "the adaptive faculty of Quebecois builders" (152). Finally, these critics demanded that restoration be "readable" and even "reversible." Since the restorations of today will become simply one more phase in the life of a building, future generations must be enabled to identify them as the work of the current generation of restorers-occupants, who should even leave a record of the reasoning behind their choices (25, 157).

Turning to the sociological critique, we find the same concern for the continuity of a broadly integrated culture. Critics argued that the law establishing the boundaries of Place Royale had created a geographic and administrative entity arbitrarily isolated from the larger neighborhood. The subsequent

Hotel Louis XIV, Quebec City, in 1966. Note pattern of windows on second and third floors (courtesy of the Ministère des Relations internationales and the Ministère des Affaires culturelles, Quebec).

"museumification" of Place Royale destroyed 200 years of continuous social life (49) and turned it into a "concentration camp for culture" (39). Moreover, the culture displayed there was typical of what culture has become in a society that privileges economics above all else: an isolated and reduced commodity (35). In contrast, these critics wanted an urban-renewal strategy that would privilege the residential function of the neighborhood, combined with a judicious mix of other functions such as education, tourism, recreation, and business. Only by establishing Place Royale as a "natural" social milieu could it be made to live again. Otherwise, as G. E. Lapalme noted, "at the approach of winter there would be nothing but the silence of a vast museum. . . . Only a normal life can conquer winter" (12). In sum, these critics deplored what they saw as the reduction of the *patrimoine* to a fragmented,

The Dumont and Le Picart houses, Place Royale, restored to their eighteenth-century forms (courtesy of the Ministère des Relations internationales and the Ministère des Affaires culturelles, Quebec).

commercialized image of the past; instead, they envisioned it anthropologically, as "the mark of a community of men in a particular space"—a witness to "the continuity of a human milieu" (37–38).

These critiques, both architectural and sociological, correspond to some extent to my analysis of the nationalistic objectification of culture. I have argued elsewhere (1984a) that those who seek the sources of national identity reinterpret aspects of a social world as typifying that world, which is then understood to be territorially and sociologically bounded ("the nation"), and in possession of "a" culture composed of detached, object-like "traits." The critics of Place Royale contested the interpretation of "authentic" identity and history represented by the project. Yet they did not reject the notion of an "authentic" culture (cf. Handler & Linnekin 1984) but merely located it elsewhere: in the ongoing life of ordinary citizens. Their argument reflects

Pierrot Cafe, Quebec City, in 1969. Note right-hand door on ground floor (courtesy of the Ministère des Relations internationales and the Ministère des Affaires culturelles, Quebec).

the ascendancy of a holistic, anthropological conception of culture, yet such a conception depends on an objectification at least as extreme as that of narrower conceptions of the *patrimoine,* for it focuses on life itself as the object to be preserved, documented, and displayed, whether in a museum or on the stage of an outdoor theater (cf. Handler 1983). The Place Royale critique rejects the artificial stage of a museumified site, but transforms "ordinary" life into a stage. Even the restorers are viewed as actors, and urged to leave an objective record of their motivations!

On Having a Culture

The preceding review of heritage legislation in Quebec indicates a steady expansion of the category of patrimonial things—an expansion we can compare to what Durkheim called the contagiousness of the sacred. Early legis-

La Maison Leber, Place Royale, after its restoration (courtesy of the Ministère des Relations internationales and the Ministère des Affairs culturelles, Quebec).

lation sought discrete pieces of culture, monuments and objects of art originating in a well-defined sociohistorical era, and sacralized them by surrounding them with rules designed to isolate them from social space and historical time (cf. Maccannell 1976:42–45). In later legislation the category of things that could be sacralized grew. The sacred past expanded forward and backward to include relatively recently created properties and the pre-French, prehistoric Amerindian civilization of Quebec. Sacred space grew, as historic and natural localities were added to buildings and art objects in the category of culture to be protected. The sacralized objects themselves became contagious, spreading their sacredness into the "protected" zones surrounding them. Even the "view" attached to patrimonial sites became inviolable.

There has also been a proliferation in the number of social domains considered capable of generating heritage. The initial concern with religion, New France, and great men has widened to include a variety of historical epochs and sociological milieus. Today people talk about the "industrial *patrimoine*" (for example, early factories) and the contribution of ordinary people, as well as of diverse ethnic groups, to Quebec's heritage. Official attention to the archeological *patrimoine* extended the realm of the sacred beneath the earth's surface. Finally, the 1972 law established degrees of sacredness by adding the procedure of "recognition," for less worthy property, to that of "classification."

To document the spread of the sacred does not, however, identify its source, which I would locate in the relationship of patrimonial property to the collective individual. Dumont, following Tocqueville, has stressed the individualistic basis of what is presumably a model of the group: nationalist ideology. According to Dumont (1971, 1977), in Western common sense the nation is perceived as a collection of individuals, each of whom replicates, and who together constitute, a collective individual—a formula that accords perfectly with Québécois nationalist ideologies. For example, to claim that Québécois houses express the soul of a people is to personify the collectivity; and to claim that only in such houses can individual Québécois feel at home implies both the essential likeness that unites those individuals, and the replication of each in the collective individual.

Yet to understand the sacredness of the *patrimoine* we need to look at the particular relationship that links the individual to property. C. B. Macpherson (1962) has suggested the term "possessive individualism" to describe that relationship as it was initially formulated in Locke's labor theory of value. Locke's problem was to explain how individuals could appropriate for themselves portions of the earth and its resources, which God had given to all men as common property. His solution was to treat a person's body as his own property, along with the labor of his body and the "works of his hands" (1690:305). By objectifying labor as an individual's property, Locke allowed the individual to mix detachable pieces of himself into natural objects. Yet the individual does not thereby alienate his labor; rather, he draws the contacted objects to himself. He annexes them, and they become, in effect, extensions of himself: "Whatsoever then he removes out of the State that Nature hath provided, and left it in, he hath mixed his *Labour* with, and joyned to it something that is his own, and thereby makes it his *Property*" (ibid.). Thus can self-sufficient (and, it should be noted, presocial) individuals isolate, objectify, and attach what is "common" and unbounded. In brief, in the individualist worldview there is an almost mystical bond uniting the agent with the things he acts upon. Moreover, if on the one hand those things become his property, on the other hand the individual comes to be defined by the things he possesses. For example, Locke grounded society itself in the need of individuals to protect their possessions—a theory that Marx found well-suited to a society "in which relations between men are subordinated to relations between men and things" (Dumont 1977:5; cf. Marx 1867:81–96).

The preceding analysis sheds light on the relationship uniting nation and culture, the collective individual and its *patrimoine*. "We are a nation because we have a culture"—nationalists in Quebec and elsewhere have elaborated that assertion in many forms. It suggests that existence is a function of possession: "You [on] can live without [formal] instruction [but] you do not exist, you will leave no trace, if you are without culture" (Lapalme 1973:226). Moreover, what the nation possesses is often conceived to be part of it, so that cultural content becomes the very body of the nation; Finlay (1977: 13) relies on this argument in a plea for tougher export controls for cultural property:

> The artistic possessions of a country are a great part of its heritage, . . . they are part of us and their outgoing diminishes us. There is a difference between coveting something for a particular collection and saving for the nation something which is part of it.

As we have seen, the most basic assumptions of nationalist ideology concern the existence of a geographically, historically, and culturally unique nation. That nation is believed to be "born of" and indissolubly linked to a bounded territory and a particular history; those links are conceived as natural, and arbitrary.

This set of assumptions is rarely questioned from within the nationalist perspective of a given nation; but when questioned from outside, by spokesmen for competing national groups, it is often fervently and creatively defended. For example, the British reformer Lord Durham, who wrote in 1839 that French Canadians were "a people with no history, and no literature" (Lucas 1912:II, 294–95), is recognized as both the "villain and catalyst" who stimulated the beginnings of French-Canadian historical and literary self-consciousness (Trofimenkoff 1982:81–83). A similar episode, at exactly the same time, occurred in the history of Greek nationalism; the German scholar J. P. Fallmerayer's denial of the Greek claim "to descent from the ancient Hellenes" stimulated half-a-century's folklore scholarship in Greece (Herzfeld 1982:75–80).

To meet the challenge of an outsider's denial of national existence, nationalists must claim and specify the nation's possessions: they must delineate and if possible secure a bounded territory, and they must construct an account of the unique culture and history that attaches to and emanates from the people who occupy it. It is at this point that disputes about the ownership of cultural property come into play. However constituted or mobilized, and however situated with respect to given political boundaries, a self-conscious national or ethnic group will claim possession of cultural properties as both representative and constitutive of cultural identity. Yet the ability of such groups to validate ownership claims, and then to act on them, will differ widely.

We might imagine a typology of cultural property claims, constructed from three opposing pairs of features of objects and the groups that claim a relationship to them: actual possession of an object versus lack of possession;

control of the cultural identity or affiliation of an object versus the lack of such control; and sovereignty versus the lack of it—that is, political autonomy versus minority status or collective encompassment. Combining these, we find six possibilities:

(1) A sovereign group possesses an object, and controls its identity (example: the Liberty Bell).

(2) A sovereign group possesses an object, but does not control its identity—that is, cannot claim that the object is unambiguously and exclusively affiliated to its culture (example: the Elgin Marbles in the British Museum).

(3) A sovereign group does not possess an object but claims to control its identity (example: the Elgin Marbles, from the Greek point of view).

(4) An encompassed or minority group possesses an object, and controls its identity. This situation is often seen to justify the encompassed group's aspirations for political autonomy: "we are a nation because we have a culture" (example: those pieces of the Quebec *patrimoine* securely housed in provincial museums).

(5) An encompassed group possesses an object whose identity is disputed (example: those pieces of the Quebec *patrimoine* controlled by the provincial government but also claimed by the Canadian government as constitutive of Canadian identity).

(6) An encompassed group controls or claims to control the identity of an object, but does not possess it (example: those pieces of the Quebec *patrimoine* housed in federal museums outside Quebec).

We can further elaborate this typology by considering the responses of disputing parties to the claims of their opponents. For example, in the second situation—that of a sovereign group possessing an object whose affiliation is disputed—we can imagine these additional possibilities:

(a) The owning group can make no legitimate claim to control the identity of the object in question, and responds by attacking the validity of others' claims to it. As one art dealer, justifying his traffic in Greek antiquities recovered in Turkey, put it: "Do the descendants of the Turks who drove out the Greeks from Asia Minor have a better right [than citizens of other nations] to the art made by the ancestors of the Greeks?" (quoted in Meyer 1973:112).

(b) The owning group can make no legitimate claim to control the identity of an object, and responds by rejecting nationalistic or particularistic limitations on the object's affiliation. In these cases the object is said to belong to a universal human heritage, and the owners become its "self-styled guardians" (Miller 1984:2).

(c) The owning group asserts its right to control the [disputed] affiliation of an object by claiming to encompass the contesting group that claims the object as its own. For example, the federal government in Canada claims that the Québécois *patrimoine*, or that of any Canadian minority or Native

American group, is also part of Canada's heritage, because the minority groups themselves "are Canadian."

(d) The owning group claims that sustained ownership establishes a new cultural affiliation: "This is our heritage now."

In Canada the third of these additional possibilities has become increasingly relevant, as the Canadian federal government asserts its own nationalism in response to the claims of Quebec and other Canadian minority groups and to the changing relationship of Canada to Great Britain and the United States. For example, a recent review of federal cultural policy (the Applebaum-Hébert Report) asks that in Canadian national museums greater attention be devoted to "Native art and archival material." This involves changing the status of Native material culture from artifact to art—that is, from being viewed as the remains of a vanquished "Other," to being included as part of the "high culture" of the mainstream. Thus the report recommends that a proposed "Contemporary Arts Centre" house Indian art currently collected in an anthropology museum (the National Museum of Man) in order to "remove the unfortunate and unnecessary connotation that works of contemporary Native art are understood best as artifacts and . . . are neither contemporary nor art" (Canada 1982:111, 148–49).

Yet the report also recognizes that regional and ethnic minorities within Canada are sensitive to issues of control with respect to "their" heritage:

> It is entirely reasonable that institutions in each region should develop collections and exhibitions which reflect the distinctive characteristics of that region. . . . the National Museums of Canada, in pursuing the objectives of the National Programmes, has not always been as sensitive as it could have been to provincial and regional priorities, interests and standards, and has sometimes acted in a directive rather than a reactive way toward the non-national museums.
>
> (118)

From the point of view of militant minorities, this is drastically understated. Québécois nationalists, for example, have consistently attacked what they see as the Canadian federal government's attempts to annex their culture. What to federalists may seem a legitimate aspiration to include all Canadian "subcultures" as full-fledged constituents of a greater Canadian whole, is to nationalists in Quebec nothing more than cultural imperialism:

> Ottawa's action appears to us to proceed . . . from a firm . . . will to *create a Canadian culture*. To do this it is logically impossible for the federal government to . . . recognize . . . the existence of a distinct, homogeneous and dynamic Québécois culture. . . . It is thus not surprising that it wishes . . . to absorb the components of Québécois culture into a Canadian totality.
>
> (MAC 1976:98)

Similar arguments have been made by Native Canadian groups, and, more generally, by militant and self-conscious ethnic groups throughout the world who now protest what they see as the alienation of their cultural property by governments and museums of the West. Such examples indicate that claims on cultural property are made to an international audience. It is not enough to have culture and history; the collectivity's proprietary claims must be recognized by others. As in Locke's social contract, cultural-property legislation aims to protect and demonstrate the collective individual's existence by protecting what it possesses from the claims of other collective individuals. As the Quebec case shows, to do this entails inventory, acquisition, and enclosure. First the collectivity or its representatives (whether self-appointed leaders or a duly constituted government) must take stock of what it has—hence the widespread passion for the inventory in cultural-property management as well as in nationalist literature more generally (cf. Belanger 1974:358–59). Next, what has been shown to be "ours" must be acquired—either by the state, or by private citizens—and enclosed, whether by isolating property with special rules, constructing museums, or gathering relevant information and images within the covers of books.

Inventory, acquisition, and enclosure can involve making explicit one's implicit but undisputed claim to cultural property, disputing the proprietary claims of others, or recognizing something as national heritage that was not so recognized previously. A francophone official of the Montreal Museum of Fine Arts told me that he would like to "nationalize" that institution by relabelling, in terms of Quebec's regions, art objects that are now labelled "Canadian." Currently, he explained, "Canadian" means "national" and anything from Quebec is merely "regional." A different type of creative labelling occurs in the creation of "heritage" out of previously unmarked bits of daily life. A patrimonial object can be created by locating its origins within the bounds of national territory and history. For example, a custom or an antique is said to "come from" a region and period, as if its "birth" characterized it once and for all: "Child's Rattle, Beauce County, ca. 1910."[3] On the other hand, for a multi-ethnic national *patrimoine*, properties become patrimonial when their human possessors-creators accept citizenship and thereby subordinate their ethnicity to their newly chosen national identity. In sum, all properties that can be claimed to emanate from the collective individual, or

3. To suggest that an object "comes from" a region evokes a naturalistic image (birth from the land) associated with "objective fact." Yet "comes from" is an ambiguous notion at best, often indicating no more than the locale where a researcher encountered a cultural thing. Ellis has argued (1983:26–27) that the Grimm brothers deliberately manipulated the practice of naming a region in order to disguise the fact that many of their German folktales were obtained from their middle-class relatives—who, though they indeed lived in various German "regions," were of French origin and spoke French at home.

from the human beings who constitute it, can be included in the collective heritage.

As is inevitable in a world made meaningful in terms of our individualistic moral and legal codes, the proprietary claims of some will challenge those of others, and a successful assertion of rights to cultural property can exclude the rights of others in the same property. Yet despite often bitter disagreements, the disputants in contemporary "culture wars" share an understanding of what cultural property is; that is, all disputants—current, would-be, and former imperialists, as well as oppressed minorities, ex-colonies, and aspiring new nations—have agreed to a worldview in which culture has come to be represented as and by "things." More and more anthropologists tell tales of natives whose self-conscious authenticity depends on anthropological records of the lives of their ancestors (e.g., Linnekin 1983:245; Smith 1982:130), and more and more anthropologists are hiring themselves out as "cultural worker[s]" (Guedon 1983:259) to protect or reconstruct the culture that "belongs" to the groups that employ them. Thus it is not surprising that groups who succeed in repatriating items of cultural property often put them in their own museums. Indeed, one of the responses of Western museum administrators to Third World repatriation claims is to send foreign aid—to build and staff museums (Miller 1984:2). Boas despaired of using a language of objects to portray cultural ideas adequately in museums; could he have foreseen that objects would become a privileged symbol of the idea of culture?

Acknowledgments

The research discussed in this paper was supported by a fellowship from the University Consortium for Research on North America, Center for International Affairs, Harvard University. A preliminary draft was presented at a symposium on "Material Culture in Eastern Canada" during the 1984 meeting of the Maine Council for Canadian Studies, University of Maine, Orono. The comments of the symposium participants, as well as those of James Clifford, Ira Jacknis, Daniel Segal, George Stocking, and Pauline Turner Strong have helped me in revising earlier versions of the paper. I particularly thank Claude Girard and other members of the Quebec Government Delegations in Boston and Chicago for facilitating my research on cultural property legislation in Quebec, and helping to obtain the illustrations from the Ministère des Relations internationales.

References Cited

ANQ [Assemblée nationale du Québec]. 1972. *J. des debats*, Vol. 12. Quebec City.

Belanger, A. J. 1974. *L'apolitisme des idéologies québécoises, 1934–1936*. Quebec City.

Boas, F. 1907. Some principles of museum administration. *Science* 25:921–33.

Canada (Government). 1982. *Report of the Federal Cultural Policy Review Committee*. Ottawa.

Cohen, R. 1978. Ethnicity: Problem and focus in anthropology. *Annual Rev. Anth.* 7:379–403.

Cultural Properties Commission of Quebec. 1973, 1975, 1976. *Rapport annuel*. Quebec City.

Dumont, L. 1971. Religion, politics, and society in the individualistic universe. *Procs. Roy. Anth. Inst.*:31–45.

———. 1977. *From Mandeville to Marx: The genesis and triumph of economic ideology*. Chicago.

Ellis, J. M. 1983. *One fairy story too many: The brothers Grimm and their tales*. Chicago.

Finlay, I. 1977. *Priceless heritage: The future of museums*. London.

Fitch, J. M. 1982. *Historic preservation: Curatorial management of the built world*. New York.

Fregault, G. 1963. Le Ministère des Affaires culturelles et la tradition artistique du Canada français. *Le Devoir* Aug. 20:6.

Groulx, L. 1935. *Orientations*. Montreal.

Guedon, M. F. 1983. A case of mistaken identity. In Manning, ed. 1983:253–61.

Halpin, M. M. 1983. Anthropology as artifact. In Manning, ed. 1983:262–75.

Handler, R. 1983. In search of the folk society: Nationalism and folklore studies in Quebec. *Culture* 3:103–14.

———. 1984a. On sociocultural discontinuity: Nationalism and cultural objectification in Quebec. *Cur. Anth.* 25:55–71.

———. 1984b. Cultural policy-making in Quebec and Canada. Paper read at the Center for International Affairs, Harvard.

Handler, R., & J. Linnekin. 1984. Tradition, genuine or spurious. *J. Am. Folklore* 97:273–90.

Harris, N. 1981. Cultural institutions and American modernization. *J. Library Hist.* 16:28–47.

Herzfeld, M. 1982. *Ours once more: Folklore, ideology, and the making of modern Greece*. Austin.

HMC [Historic Monuments Commission of Quebec]. 1923. *Prémier rapport*. Quebec City.

———. 1925. *Deuxième rapport*. Quebec City.

———. 1926. *Troisième rapport*. Quebec City.

Lapalme, G. E. 1973. *Le paradis du pouvoir. Mémoires, tome III*. Ottawa.

Linnekin, J. S. 1983. Defining tradition: Variations on the Hawaiian identity. *Am. Ethnol.* 10:241–52.

Lucas, C., ed. 1912. *Lord Durham's report on the affairs of British North America.* 3 vols. New York (1970).

Locke, J. 1690. *Two treatises of government.* Cambridge (1960).

MAC [Ministère des Affaires culturelles du Québec]. 1964, 1965, 1966, 1968, 1971. *Rapport annuel.* Quebec City.

———. 1976. *Pour l'évolution de la politique culturelle.* Quebec City.

———. 1979. *Colloque place Royale: Les actes du colloque.* Quebec City.

Maccannell, D. 1976. *The tourist.* New York.

Macpherson, C. B. 1962. *The political theory of possessive individualism: Hobbes to Locke.* Oxford.

McRoberts, K., & D. Postgate. 1980. *Quebec: Social change and political crisis.* Toronto.

Malraux, A. 1953. *The voices of silence.* Garden City, N.Y.

Manning, F., ed. 1983. *Consciousness and inquiry: Ethnology and Canadian realities.* Ottawa.

Marx, K. 1867. *Capital.* New York (1906).

Meyer, K. E. 1973. The plundered past: The flying facade and the vanishing glyphs. *New Yorker* Mar. 24:96–121.

Miller, N. 1984. Culture wars. *Chicago Tribune* 14 August, Section 5:1–2.

Nochlin, L. 1972. Museums and radicals: A history of emergencies. In *Museums in crisis,* ed. B. O'Doherty, 7–41. New York.

Rioux, M. 1975. *Les québécois.* Paris.

Roy, P. G. 1927. *Old manors, old houses.* Quebec City.

Smith, M. E. 1982. The process of sociocultural continuity. *Curr. Anth.* 23:127–142.

Stocking, G. W., Jr. 1974. *The shaping of American anthropology, 1883–1911: A Franz Boas reader.* New York.

Tremblay, M. A., & G. Gold. 1976. L'anthropologie dans les universités du Québec: L'émergence d'une discipline. *Procs. Can. Ethn. Soc.* 3:9–49.

Trofimenkoff, S. M. 1982. *The dream of nation: A social and intellectual history of Quebec.* Toronto.

WRITING THE HISTORY OF ARCHEOLOGY

A Survey of Trends

BRUCE G. TRIGGER

The earliest historical studies of archeology (Haven 1856; Morlot 1861) date from the mid-nineteenth century, when Joseph Henry, first Secretary of the Smithsonian Institution, sought with considerable success to purge American archeology of useless speculation and to encourage an interest in factual scientific research (Hinsley 1981:40). For the next century, however, most histories of archeology were accounts written for the general public (for a comprehensive bibliography see Daniel 1975:401–6). Although some authors claimed to supply more balanced surveys (Casson 1934), there was a strong emphasis on the romance of exploration and on spectacular discoveries. Some books offered noninterpretative accounts of specialized aspects of archeology, such as barrow digging (Marsden 1974), or largely narrative biographies of leading archeologists (Woodbury 1973; Thompson 1977; Green 1981; Hawkes 1982). Most of them, however, chronicled the archeology of the ancient civilizations, especially in the Near East, where discoveries had attracted the greatest public interest (Ceram [Marek] 1951). Although there are several excellent histories of archeological exploration by professional archeologists (Lloyd 1947; Fagan 1975), the image of archeology as a discipline devoted to recovering exotic remains neglects the work of archeologists whose main contributions have been to the interpretation rather than the recovery of archeological data, as well as the accomplishment that most

Bruce G. Trigger is Professor of Anthropology at McGill University and a Fellow of the Royal Society of Canada. He has published on African archaeology, North American ethnohistory, and the theory and history of archaeology; among his publications is *Time and Traditions: Essays in Archaeological Interpretation.* He is currently completing a study of the relevance of anthropological research for understanding the early history of New France.

professionals claim to prize most highly: progress in the interpretation of archeological data in terms of human behavior.

A popular style that to some degree remedied this shortcoming was pioneered in Geoffrey Bibby's *The Testimony of the Spade* (1956). Although archeological exploration remained a key element of his narrative, Bibby skilfully interwove accounts of how various archeologists learned to interpret archeological data with summaries of what they had found out about European prehistory from Paleolithic times to the late Iron Age. Michael Hoffman (1979) recently employed an identical format in his treatment of the archeology of predynastic Egypt. While the approach can be applied only to the archeology of single regions, it has a close affinity to the chapters outlining the history of local archeology that are becoming increasingly common in culture-historical syntheses of archeological research (e.g., Milanich & Fairbanks 1980; Walthall 1980).

During the last decade interest in the history of prehistoric archeology has increased greatly, and is now engaging the attention of archeologists in all parts of the world. Research topics have become more specific and, as scholars multiply and cease to work in isolation, growing debate is improving the quality of their work. Although archeologists still predominate, some historians of science (Freeland 1983) and other professional historians (Killan 1983) are also exhibiting an interest in the field. Formal techniques, such as citation analysis (Sterud 1978) and thematic analysis (Zubrow 1972, 1980), are starting to be employed, and at least one important early manuscript source has been published in a scholarly fashion (Brongers 1973). These developments have in turn ignited a debate about the relevance of the history of archeology for archeological research.

Intellectual History and the Positivist Impulse

The development of a more strictly professional interest in the history of archeology has centered on what Glyn Daniel (1975:10) has called "changes in the conceptual basis of prehistory." Not surprisingly, the growing awareness that the archeologist's understanding of the past is influenced not only by fresh data but also by changing styles of interpretation developed first in Western Europe, where by the 1930s generational differences among professional archeologists and the accumulation of a corpus of essential literature brought into focus the contrast between the evolutionary interpretations of the nineteenth century and the diffusionist culture-historical explanations that had replaced them. A few prehistoric archeologists became convinced that discovering the reasons for such changes was essential for understanding what was happening in their discipline. Some were also influenced by the popularity of Marxist modes of analysis at that time (Crawford 1932), and by the writings of the philosopher-archeologist R. G. Collingwood (1939, 1946), who stressed the idea of history and archeology as subjective disciplines in which the scholar relives the past in his own mind.

Much of the significant pioneering work on the intellectual history of archeology surveyed its subject matter on a grand scale. The first major study was Stanley Casson's *The Discovery of Man* (1939), which sought to trace from earliest times how humanity had come to study itself objectively. Beginning in ancient Greece, severely set back in Roman and medieval times, resumed during the Age of Discovery, the struggle against ignorance and superstition reached a new and definitive stage in the nineteenth century, when evolutionism transformed and for the first time unified the study of mankind. While only archeology could document humanity's physical and cultural development, Casson regarded it as heavily dependent on ethnology for its understanding of human behavior. Although both disciplines were portrayed as strongly influenced by broader intellectual traditions, Casson defined these traditions extremely vaguely. Often they amounted to little more than a *zeitgeist*, such as the spirit of intellectual freedom resulting from the discovery of the New World (143). Moreover, while Casson noted that industrial activity and a growing leisured class had favored the development of archeology, he examined the relationship between archeology and changing social conditions in a still more superficial manner. The great accomplishment of his book was to suggest that an intellectual history of archeology was possible and worthwhile.

It was Glyn Daniel's *A Hundred Years of Archaeology* (1950; cf. 1975), along with some of his later and more popular books (Daniel 1962; 1981a) that really initiated the systematic study of the history of archeology. Daniel traced the development of archeological interpretation from the Renaissance to the present, with particular emphasis on the period from 1840 to 1900. Although he depended to a considerable degree on secondary sources, and failed to resolve in his own mind the relative importance of the roles played by the early nineteenth-century Scandinavian archeologists and later English and French Paleolithic specialists in creating a discipline of prehistoric archeology, his interpretation of this period was a lasting contribution to the history of archeology. He felt less confident about his ability to see the work of the twentieth century in a proper historical perspective, and his account of it remained largely a catalogue of discoveries.

Daniel stressed the important role played by new scientific techniques of analysis, especially radiocarbon dating, in shaping the development of archeology. But like Casson, he saw it influenced mainly by changing scholarly fashions. Although social conditions had at times made people eager for archeological information, they had no significant impact on the interpretation of archeological data (1975:53). The real driving force was individuals willing and able to seize opportunities to advance their discipline.

Adopting a minimum of formal periodization, Daniel stressed that change took place gradually and largely adventitiously. Yet the main theme of his book was the rise and decline of evolutionary interpretations and their replacement by a culture-historical perspective. Like most contemporary English historians, he refused to assign absolute validity to any particular model or theory that purported to explain the past. Because each was the product of specific historical circumstances and subject to inevitable limitations, a healthy situation was one in which a number of alternative models competed. The main lesson to be learned from studying the history of archeology was that the "final truth" of any given period inevitably breaks down as new facts accumulate and new explanations are developed (1975:374). Although he saw archeology as being influenced by randomly shifting intellectual fashions rather than developing inevitably in a specific direction, Daniel did not doubt that certain states were healthy for the discipline, while other ones definitely were not. He clearly privileged an historical orientation, conceptualized in a broad and seemingly atheoretical fashion, arguing that without it archeology would degenerate from a discipline studying human behavior into a new object-oriented antiquarianism.

Daniel was a member of a larger circle of British scholars who, inspired in part by Kenneth Clark's *The Gothic Revival* (1928) and Christopher Hussey's *The Picturesque* (1927; cf. Piggott 1976:v), have written more focused monographic studies relating changes in British archeology to the broader history of ideas and literary fashions. Thus T. D. Kendrick (1950) interpreted the development of antiquarianism during the Tudor period as a triumph of Renaissance over medieval thought. M. C. Hunter (1975) argued that John Aubrey's archeological research was shaped by the scientific methods based on Baconian principles that were promoted by the early Royal Society. Stuart Piggott (1950, 1968, 1976) has attempted to demonstrate how the shift from rationalism to romanticism reoriented British antiquarian research during the eighteenth century. In his biography of William Stukeley, he went so far as to suggest that had this change in fashion not occurred Stukeley might have continued his early analytical studies and not begun to indulge in lavish fantasies about the Druids (Piggott 1950:183).

For the most part, monographic work on the intellectual history of British archeology has dealt with earlier periods; very little, apart from biographies (McNairn 1980; Green 1981), deals with the twentieth century. This may reflect a need for discretion in a small and until recently strongly hierarchical academic community. My biography of Gordon Childe, which in a loose fashion appears to adhere to this tradition, sought to understand how broader intellectual movements (especially Marxism) influenced his work but, in keeping with the nature of that work, mainly examined how these influences reached him through the writings of other archeologists (Trigger 1980; 1984a).

In addition to this work on British archeology, a major contribution to the emerging intellectual history of archeology was Annette Laming-Emperaire's *Origines de l'archéologie préhistorique en France* (1964), which traced the development of archeology from medieval times into the late nineteenth century, when, she believed, archeology achieved essentially its modern form. Seeking to account for the current divisions of theory, method, organization, and attitude within prehistoric archeology in France—especially those that differentiated the study of the Paleolithic period from that of more recent prehistory—her primary emphasis was on the interaction between the various scientific disciplines that played a role in the development of prehistoric archeology. In contrast to earlier studies of the Celtic peoples who had lived in France at the time of the Roman conquest, which relied very heavily on written texts, true prehistoric archeology was created in the nineteenth century as a result of the combined influence of geology, paleontology, physical anthropology, and ethnology. Towards 1900 this rupture between a natural science and an historical approach to prehistory was narrowed somewhat, as French historical studies became increasingly social rather than political in orientation. Yet Paleolithic archeology maintained its close links to the natural sciences, while the study of later periods of prehistory has become more closely tied to history.

While primarily interested in the influences of other developing disciplines on prehistoric archeology, Laming-Emperaire was also concerned with broader intellectual trends. Thus she argued that the synthesis of antiquarian and natural science interests was long delayed because it required "a new conception of man and his place in nature" (156), ultimately supplied in the nineteenth century by a growing interest in both cultural and biological evolution. She somewhat neglected the impact of developments elsewhere in Europe on French prehistoric archeology; but she studied in far more detail than Daniel the way structures of teaching and research, as well as professional associations and their journals, reflected and shaped the development of archeology. Although she did not answer the question posed at the beginning of her book—whether the contradictions in modern prehistoric archeology are a permanent reflection of the requirements of studying different periods or merely a transient result of the heterogeneous origins of the discipline—her book marked a significant step forward in studying the history of archeology.

If in Great Britain and France the history of archeology has moved toward intellectual historical contextualization, in the United States it has taken a more "positivistic" turn. Although the history of archeology was often surveyed in graduate courses, and brief discussions appeared in publications dealing jointly with archeology and anthropology, relatively little was published prior to the 1960s (for a bibliography see Willey and Sabloff 1980:7). The main exception was Robert Heizer, whose two books *The Archaeologist at Work* (1959) and *Man's Discovery of his Past* (1962) reprinted articles that were of major importance for understanding the development of archeological knowledge in the Old and New Worlds (cf. Daniel 1967; Hawkes 1963). The general upheaval produced by the "New Archeology" in the 1960s, however, encouraged interest in the history of American archeology. The first substantial result was D. W. Schwartz's *Conceptions of Kentucky Prehistory* (1967), which argued that three broad trends had successively characterized American archeology: an original speculative approach, followed after 1850 by an empirical trend, and after 1945 by an explanatory one. Although each new trend was seen as supplementing rather than replacing previous ones, the overall effect was to transform archeology (see also Schwartz 1968).

The first comprehensive treatment of the history of New World archeology was Willey and Sabloff's *A History of American Archaeology* (1974; cf. 1980). Arguing that the "critical self-appraisal" going on in American archeology required a review of the development of the discipline and its concepts, the authors concentrated on the archeology of the United States, and especially on developments since 1960. Willey and Sabloff stress the value of relating changes in archeological practice to the intellectual climate of the past; to theoretical developments in other fields, such as ecology, systems analysis, and art history; to the availability of new analytical techniques, such as radiocarbon dating and computers; and to changing patterns of funding. But to them the most crucial influences on archeology are ideas derived from ethnology and social anthropology. Thus, although they observe that evolutionism was rejected by most of the social sciences towards the end of the nineteenth century, they attribute the failure of American archeologists to adopt an evolutionary perspective at that time specifically to the influence of Franz Boas and the inadequacy of the archeological data base; a position that Meltzer (1983:38–39) has demonstrated to be incorrect. They are even more wary of correlating developments in archeology with social or political factors, although they do suggest that virulent anti-Communism in the United States inhibited the advocacy of theories of cultural evolution after the second World War (1980:184).

Willey and Sabloff divide their history into four periods: the Speculative (1492–1840); the Classificatory-Descriptive (1840–1914); the Classificatory-Historical, subdivided into an early phase concerned primarily with chronology (1914–40) and a later one marked by a growing interest in reconstructing context and function (1940–60); and the Explanatory (1960–present). Although partly derived from Schwartz (Willey 1968), each unit was treated as a specific period of time, not as a potentially overlapping trend, on the not very persuasive ground that the concept of "period" was more appropriate than that of "trend" for purposes of historical analysis. Schwartz's locally adapted scheme of Kentucky archeology (not the same as his three overall trends) as well as some of the more developed regional archeological histories collected in James Fitting's *The Development of North American Archaeology* (1973) do suggest, however, that at this time many American archeologists were prone to conceptualize the history of their discipline in terms of successive periods. Some of them had begun to regard the advent of the New Archeology as a "paradigm shift" of the sort Thomas Kuhn (1962) had described in *The Structure of Scientific Revolutions* (Sterud 1973), and although Willey and Sabloff did not draw attention to Kuhn's work, it was relatively easy for others to interpret the transition between each of their periods as examples of such shifts.

Yet in contrast to Kuhn (and the European writers previously discussed), Willey and Sabloff adopted a strongly "positivist" approach, presenting their successive periods as a logical and largely inevitable development. Only after American archeology had advanced from speculation to description to culture-historical synthesis were archeologists in a position to begin really to explore their data. While they noted considerable continuity between one period and the next, and took some pain to demonstrate that many features that characterized the New Archeology had evolved during the preceding period, they did not hesitate to evaluate previous theories and interpretations in terms of their current validity rather than the state of archeology at the time they were formulated. In general, they denied any substantial significance to explanations of archeological data or prehistory that had been offered prior to the 1960s. Finally, Willey and Sabloff observed that what held true for American archeology was also likely to apply everywhere: the methodological approaches devised by the New Archeology "are clearly of worldwide scope and are being so conceived by an increasing number of archeologists" (Willey & Sabloff 1974:210).

The original edition of *A History of American Archaeology* thus offered an historical legitimization for the New Archeology, while at the same time providing a critique of what Willey and Sabloff regarded as the excesses of the new movement. Vindicating the close association between archeology and anthropology long advocated by many American archeologists and now reasserted by the New Archeology, it proclaimed that American archeology was poised for a great stride forward: now for the first time archeologists could hope to verify their speculations about the nature and causes of cultural change (1974:209). In the second edition of their book, they celebrated the accomplishments of the New Archeology and praised its growing theoretical sophistication, flexibility, and adaptability. Thus they provided "processual" archeology with a far more inevitable pedigree than Daniel had accorded to culture-historical archeology or Casson had belatedly supplied to evolutionary archeology. It was also a pedigree that, by restricting the factors that influenced the development of archeology largely to the discipline of anthropology, corresponded admirably with the positivist view of knowledge embraced by the New Archeology, which sees the development of archeology as controlled solely by the discovery of fresh data and of sounder, scientifically valid methods for interpreting these data. Because of this, it is not surprising that this book has been widely used as a textbook in courses on prehistoric archeology.

Just as the intellectual-contextual approach has produced monographic as well as general studies, so also there have been in recent years more specific studies displaying a narrowly positivist orientation, in the sense that their principal concern has been to understand how interpretations have been developed in relationship to a specific archeological problem as new data have accumulated, with little interest in the influence of broader intellectual trends or social conditions. The most specific of these studies is Robert Cunnington's *From Antiquary to Archaeologist* (1975), in which an amateur historian examines the collaboration between his ancestor William Cunnington and Richard Colt Hoare, as they together studied the prehistoric monuments of Wiltshire in the late eighteenth and early nineteenth centuries. The main theme of this book is how Cunnington, rejecting traditional antiquarian sources, relied solely on archeological data in his effort to classify and date the burials that he excavated. Chronicling the alterations in Cunnington's' understanding in his analyses of successive discoveries, the author provides detailed insight into the sophistication that was possible at this time, as well as the limitations of an analysis based on a narrow range of excavated material.

A study of more general interest is Bo Gräslund's *Relativ datering: Om kronologisk metod i nordisk arkeologi* (1974; since summarized in English in Gräslund 1976). Most of this book provides a detailed, step-by-step account of how the dating system of Scandinavian archeology was established during the eighteenth century. Gräslund stresses the strongly empirical nature of this research, which from the beginning was based largely on the comparative analysis of the contents of graves and other "closed finds" that ensured the simultaneity of their deposition, and on the chronological ordering of these finds in terms of stylistic similarity. Although some of the basic concepts employed by this system appear to have been suggested by earlier numismatical studies, Gräslund interprets its elaboration as a process that was almost entirely internal to archeology. In particular, he rejects the widely held view that concepts derived from biological evolution played a significant role in the origins and development of typology. Such concepts only began to be

used by Scandinavian archeologists late in the nineteenth century as illustrative analogies to justify their already established analytical techniques as a
scientific method.

The most recent major work of this sort is D. K. Grayson's *The Establishment of Human Antiquity* (1983), which traces a series of steps, beginning
with the differentiation between stone tools and fossils, each of which made
easier the recognition in 1859 that human beings had inhabited the earth
many times the traditional biblical span. Although Grayson acknowledges
that theological views impeded the early recognition of human antiquity in
Great Britain, he argues against the commonly accepted belief that a conservative theological orientation necessarily hindered such recognition while
an agnostic and scientific orientation inevitably promoted it. He also acknowledges that social factors influenced this process, inasmuch as the high
antiquity of human beings had to be accepted by the "inner circle" of zoologists and geologists, who were not the people actually collecting the relevant
evidence. Nevertheless, he concludes that the establishment of human antiquity ultimately depended on internal verifiability, which involved providing irrefutable evidence of human activities in undisturbed geological contexts that were demonstrably more than 6,000 years old. Yet the force of his
argument is blunted by his own observation that Marcel-Jérôme Rigollot's
convincing evidence was rejected "from the sheer belief that such things
could not be" (206). Grayson has also been criticized for following Laming-
Emperaire's claim that prehistoric archeology developed as a result of the
recognition of human antiquity—ignoring the achievements of Scandinavian and Swiss archeologists prior to 1859 (Trigger 1983; Daniel 1984).
What he is really describing is the origin of Paleolithic archeology, which
appears to have evolved in France and England relatively independently of
the Scandinavian and Swiss studies of the later phases of prehistory.

The Social Basis of National Archeological Traditions

In terms of the traditional opposition in the history of science, positivistic
and intellectual/contextual histories of archeology may be contrasted as "internalist" and "externalist"—insofar as the latter take into consideration influences impinging on archeology from the outside. If the New Archeology
encouraged an "internalist" view of the history of the discipline, there have
been among American historians of archeology since the 1960s some who
argued the importance of external social and ideological factors. Although
the equation of paradigm shifts and periods could sustain a positivistic view
of the development of archeology, Kuhn's view of scientific development
could also (and perhaps more appropriately) be used to sustain a critique of

positivistic viewpoints, and even to some extent the consideration of social factors in the history of archeology. Thus Fitting interpreted *The Development of North American Archaeology* in Kuhnian terms, characterizing the period before 1850 as preparadigmatic, the period that followed as that of a culture-historical paradigm, and the 1960s as a time of scientific crisis. Unlike Sterud (1973) and Willey and Sabloff (1974), however, he rejected the cumulative character of archeological understanding and stressed the socially determined nature of paradigms. Construing these in an exaggerated fashion as indicating "that subjective truth is relative and science basically irrational" (12), he argued that "prerevolutionary science is neither more nor less scientific than postrevolutionary science" (290). Because of the essential subjectivity of archeology, it was necessary to be familiar with the history of the discipline in order to understand current interpretations of archeological data.

Other American writers ventured in more detail into the realm of "external" ideological and social influences. Thus Schwartz (1967) traced the long-lasting impact on archeological research of the eighteenth-century belief that Indians had never lived in Kentucky but had only fought over it, and therefore had no valid land claim that White settlers must respect. Similarly, R. E. Silverberg (1968) explored in detail the links between the nineteenth-century belief in Mound Builders as a civilized, non-Indian people who had inhabited North America in prehistoric times and the denigration of native peoples that accompanied the spread of white colonization across North America. Although a popular study, it exerted considerable influence among archeologists as the first substantial treatment of a major problem relating to the history of North American archeology.

A more specific and detailed study relating to the Mound Builder controversy was Marshall McKusick's (1970) monograph describing the discovery of fraudulent inscribed slate tablets and elephant pipes by members of the Davenport Academy of Science in Iowa and the heated national debate that these finds occasioned concerning the antiquity of man in North America. McKusick treats these debates as an example of the disorder which could occur in the small private scientific clubs that flourished in the United States during the nineteenth century and of the widespread antagonism between these organizations and "big science," as embodied in the Bureau of American Ethnology. This controversy was sustained by suspicions and jealousies, as well as by professional and political competition, that made its resolution impossible.

More recently, D. J. Meltzer (1983) has examined the role played by the Bureau of American Ethnology in discouraging other claims that America had been inhabited in the remote past by native peoples who were culturally different from those known in historic times—a view reinforced by the tacit acceptance by most archeologists and ethnologists of the popular belief that Native Americans had never been capable of change. Meltzer concludes that in the absence of conclusive evidence for or against the presence of human beings in America prior to Holocene times, social and institutional factors played a crucial role in determining the interpretation of what evidence was available.

The anti-positivist emphasis on "external" influences has been given impetus by the growing interest in the history of archeology outside of Western Europe and North America, which has been nurtured by Glyn Daniel through his editorship of the Thames and Hudson *World of Archaeology* series, and the role that he and Ole Klindt-Jensen played in organizing the first international Conference on the History of Archaeology in Aarhus in 1978 (Daniel 1981b). *Antiquity and Man,* a *festschrift* recently presented to Glyn Daniel (Evans et al. 1981), contains papers on the history of archeology in various parts of the world, and two successive issues of *World Archaeology* (Trigger and Glover 1981, 1982) are composed of studies that attempt to account for variations in national archeological traditions by examining them in historical perspective. The latter clearly demonstrate that, despite an internationally shared corpus of methods, the questions archeologists ask and the answers they are predisposed to accept as scientifically supported vary widely from one society to another. The cultural patterns of individual societies and the expectations of particular groups within these societies influence these differences, as do the formal organization of archeology and sources and levels of funding for archeological research.

The first major European study to consider the relationship between archeology and its social context was Klindt-Jensen's *A History of Scandinavian Archaeology* (1975). After surveying the progress of antiquarian studies in Scandinavia during the Renaissance and Enlightenment, he attributed the beginnings of scientific archeology in the early nineteenth century to emergent nationalism which, as a product of galling military defeats, combined with the romantic movement to encourage a more widespread and intense interest in the history and origins of the Scandinavian peoples. In tracing subsequent developments, Klindt-Jensen paid careful attention to the changing political and economic conditions within each Scandinavian country, the early training of individuals who later became professional archeologists, the manner in which prominent Scandinavian archeologists influenced each other's work, and the impact of differing institutional structures. Although he treated the influence of Scandinavian archeologists on archeology elsewhere in Europe, he paid little attention to the substantial recent influences of foreign (mainly British and American) archeology on the study of prehistory in Scandinavia. In general, his treatment of the twentieth century was largely anecdotal. Moreover, the analysis of social factors was carried on in a holistic fashion at a regional or national level, rather than in terms of sectional or class interests—matters which have since been explored in K. Kristiansen's (1981) investigation of the changing social background of support for archeology in Denmark since 1805.

A more explicitly sociological approach is offered in Karel Sklenář's *Archaeology in Central Europe: The First 500 Years* (1983), which traces developments in the region between the Rhine Valley and Russia from the Middle Ages to the end of the second World War. In addition to the influence of pan-European intellectual movements such as the Enlightenment, romanticism, and positivism, Sklenář emphasizes the changing sense of national identity among the diverse ethnic groups that have occupied this region, demonstrating in great detail how prehistoric archeology was used by particular social classes within ethnic groups to pursue their own social, political, and ideological objectives. Such activities have involved both the encouragement and suppression of archeological activities, as well as favoring specific interpretations of archeological data. He provides a particularly chilling account of the role played by archeology in the development of German nationalism and *Ostpolitik* after 1870.

On the other hand, Sklenář pays almost no attention to influences from Western Europe, or to the work of foreign archeologists, such as Gordon Childe, who studied the prehistory of Central Europe. Such an approach precludes an understanding of tendencies such as the "positivism" he argues had a beneficial influence on Central European archeology in the late nineteenth century—since this orientation was clearly shaped by the "international archeology" that evolved in Western Europe after 1860 (Trigger 1984b). Sklenář's isolationist perspective is all the more curious in view of his claim that Central European archeologists generally were familiar with the work of their more famous Western European colleagues, despite the neglect of their own work because of the obscure languages in which it was published.

The most successful national history is Ignacio Bernal's *A History of Mexican Archaeology* (1980), which traces the study of Mexican prehistory from the Spanish conquest to 1950. Bernal takes account of studies of prehispanic Mexico by European, North American, and Mexican scholars and demonstrates not only how their work reflected their national traditions, but also how scholars from different countries influenced one another. Noting how they were all influenced by successive modes of pan-European thought—Renaissance, rationalist, romantic, and positivist—he documents in considerable detail the differing attitudes towards the study of archeology taken by Spanish officials and creoles prior to Mexican independence, by liberals and conservatives during the nineteenth century, and by the Mexican government since 1910. He also traces in detail the evolution of the institutional setting of Mexican archeology, showing how it was molded by political events and in turn influenced the character of indigenous Mexican archeology. Bernal has gone further than any other historian of archeology in accounting for the influence of international scholarly trends, foreign scholarship, internal social, political, and economic conditions, as well as institutional settings for teaching and research, on the development of archeology in a single country. One can only regret his decision to halt his study at 1950.

Turning once again to Great Britain, two recent works that examine social influences on the development of archeology are worth noting. Kenneth Hudson's A *Social History of Archaeology: The British Experience* (1981) is a collection of essays on topics such as the changing meaning of archeology among the general public; the class affiliations of members of Victorian archeological societies; the impact of railways on such societies; the popularization of archeology; the changing relationship between professional and amateur archeologists; and social factors involved in the development of popular support for Industrial Archeology. Stuart Piggott has also discussed some of these problems, in particular the origins of county archeological societies (1976:171–93). While Hudson, as a social historian, is interested primarily in the occupational and class characteristics of the membership of these societies and the impact of railways on their activities, Piggott, in keeping with his concern for intellectual history, emphasizes the role played by the Oxford Movement and the Northern Revival in encouraging their formation—although he notes the role of more efficient modes of communication in transmitting new intellectual fashions to the rural-dwelling middle class. Clearly, the barrier between intellectual and social history is a nebulous one.

Although Hudson's essays are somewhat lacking in scholarly depth and marred by too free an expression of his personal biases on a variety of topics, one can only applaud his attempt "to relate the practice of archaeology to the social conditions of the time, to see how money, the educational and political system and the class structure have determined both the selection and ambitions of archaeologists and the way in which they have set about their work" (1). It is to be hoped that this book will encourage others to carry out more detailed research on the social history of British archeology.

The History and the Practice of Archeology

Generalizing from the works here considered, it seems that a "positivist" viewpoint tends to produce a narrowly "internalist" history, weighted heavily toward the present, both in the sense of devoting more space to recent theory and method, and in the sense of using them as criteria for interpreting the past. In the extreme case, positivistically inclined archeologists would dispense with history entirely.

Thus some processual archeologists question the value of studying the history of archeology at all. Michael Schiffer (1976:193) has argued that graduate programs in archeology should dispense with histories of thought and concentrate instead on defining the known principles of the discipline and indicating future lines of inquiry. In positivist terms, this argument is attractive. The more logically inevitable are the theoretical formulations that characterize the mature stages of a discipline, the less important it is to know the history of that discipline in order to understand these formulations and the problems that scholars are confronting. If clearly formulated techniques of analysis and a growing corpus of data can produce increasingly accurate approximations of reality, the history of a discipline becomes irrelevant to its functioning.

There can be no doubt that the findings of social historical studies of archeology pose a direct challenge to the positivist view that a growing corpus of archeological data and proper methods for analysing these data can lead to an ever more thorough and accurate understanding of human behavior and history. Increasing familiarity with the development of archeology in different parts of the world indicates that social, political, and cultural differences influence not only the questions archeologists ask but also the answers that they are prepared to accept as credible. It is also the case that such findings can be invoked as support for a currently growing trend in archeology to reject the notion that archeological interpretations can achieve validity that is independent of the societies that have produced them (Leone 1982; Hodder 1982).

In a sharp reaction against this trend, L. R. Binford (1983:233, n. 14) has denounced what he calls the "irrationalist" position that archeological interpretations are influenced as a result of social factors having an impact on the worldviews of scientists—an outlook he associates with the work of Kuhn. Others, however, use Kuhnian assumptions to bolster positivism. Thus David Clarke (1979:154) attributed regional variations in archeology to the infancy or preparadigmatic status of traditional archeology, suggesting that in due course the "unformulated precepts of limited academic traditions" would be winnowed and consolidated to produce a "single coherent empirical discipline of archaeology." While we have seen a certain tendency for contextual studies to focus on earlier periods, it does not appear that national variations in the interpretation of prehistory are disappearing or even significantly diminishing, despite growing international contacts and increasing agreement on many methodological issues. Today, no less than in the past, general views of prehistory appear to reflect the concerns of the present (Trigger 1981).

Another positivist response to historical contextualism is Binford's (1981) distinction between general theories, which are common to all of the social sciences and seek to explain human behavior, and middle-range theories, which tend to be specific to archeology and seek to establish systematic relationships between material culture and human behavior. It could be argued that the latter theories, which are fundamental to all archeological interpretations, are considerably less affected by social biases than are broader concepts of human behavior. Yet even the relationship between material culture and human behavior appears to be sufficiently nuanced and complex that the biases of the observer can influence how the latter is inferred from the former. This is particularly so if, as Ian Hodder argues, material culture is not always a direct reflection of social behavior, and interpretations must take account of contextually restricted meanings and ideologies (Hodder 1982). Under these circumstances, as Collingwood (1939; 1946) pointed out long ago, a complete understanding of archeological interpretations is impossible without knowing the biases of the interpreter as well as the data that he has at his disposal. This would reinforce the claim that studying the history of archeology is not something incidental to archeology but a vital contribution to disciplinary self-awareness and effectiveness. Most historians of science do not advocate the utility of their history to the ongoing work of science, and they are in this respect often the opposite side of the coin to the ahistorical disciplinary practitioner. Yet it is almost certainly no accident that such claims are made for the human sciences far more often than for the sciences generally; this being a reflection of the greater complexity of interacting factors that determine human behavior by comparison with what is encountered at the biological or physical level (Trigger 1982).

On the other hand, even to the anti-positivist historical contextualist, the history of archeology reveals the study of prehistory as something more than an uncontrolled projection of current beliefs and prejudices into the past. Insights have been gained into the nature of the past that have stood the test of time, and some of these have powerfully influenced a general understanding of humanity. No archeologist today doubts that all cultures developed from a rudimentary and ultimately a precultural state, however much archeologists may disagree about how or why these changes have taken place. Acknowledging that social conditions may influence the sort of research that is done and the conclusions that are reached in archeology does not mean that it is impossible to gain a more complete and objective understanding of the past by recovering more archeological data and searching for new analytical techniques and better correlations between material culture and human behavior. On the contrary, knowing more about the social factors that influence archeological research should increase the self-awareness of archeologists and permit a more objective understanding of their interpretations. Viewed from this perspective, the results of such research appear to be of interest even to archeologists who subscribe to a strongly positivistic view of archeological studies (Binford 1983:241, n. 11).

The history of archeology must therefore be pursued on two fronts. On the one hand, there is a need for archeologists to understand how the continuous recovery of archeological data and the pioneering of new techniques for analysing it have influenced an understanding of prehistoric times. On the other hand, it is necessary to investigate all the factors influencing the interpretation of archeological data: the funding and organization of archeological research; scholarly traditions within archeology; the broader cultural traditions within which archeologists operate; social, political, and economic conditions; and the impact of foreign archeological studies, especially those carried out in countries with major research traditions.

Archeologists, as amateurs, have pioneered in the study of the history of their own discipline, identifying in a piecemeal fashion a large number of factors that have influenced the development of archeology. They will no doubt continue to have a special contribution to make, especially in relation to the development of theory and method. On the other hand, studying the history of archeology clearly requires all the resources of intellectual and social history. Increasing professionalism will be required if progress is to continue and the relative importance of the factors involved in individual situations and their mutual interconnections is to be ascertained more precisely. The work done so far suggests that, instead of diverting energy from the basic concerns of archeological studies, investigating the history and sociology of archeology can enhance the quality of archeological interpretations of prehistory. Glyn Daniel's science seems close to coming of age.

References Cited

Bernal, I. 1980. *A history of Mexican archaeology*. London.

Bibby, G. 1956. *The testimony of the spade*. New York.

Binford, L. R. 1981. *Bones: Ancient men and modern myths*. New York.

———. 1983. *In pursuit of the past*. London.

Brongers, J. A. 1973. *1833: Reuvens in Drenthe*. Bussum.

Casson, S. 1934. *Progress of archaeology*. London.

———. 1939. *The discovery of man*. London.

Ceram, C. W. [Kurt Marek]. 1951. *Gods, graves, and scholars: The story of archaeology*. New York.

Clarke, D. L. 1979. *Analytical archaeologist*. London.

Collingwood, R. G. 1939. *An autobiography*. London.

———. 1946. *The idea of history*. London.

Crawford, O. G. S. 1932. The dialectical process in the history of science. *Soc. Rev.* 24:165–73.

Cunnington, R. H. 1975. *From antiquary to archaeologist.* Princes Risborough.

Daniel, G. 1950. *A hundred years of archaeology.* London.

———. 1962. *The idea of prehistory.* Cleveland.

———. 1967. *The origins and growth of archaeology.* Harmondsworth.

———. 1975. *A hundred and fifty years of archaeology.* London.

———. 1981a. *A short history of archaeology.* London.

———, ed. 1981b. *Towards a history of archaeology.* London.

———. 1984. Review of *The establishment of human antiquity* by D. K. Grayson. *Am. Scientist* 72:312.

Evans, J. D., B. Cunliffe, and C. Renfrew, eds. 1981. *Antiquity and man.* London.

Fagan, B. M. 1975. *The rape of the Nile.* New York.

Fitting, J. E., ed. 1973. *The development of North American archaeology.* Garden City, New York.

Freeland, G. 1983. Evolutionism and arch(a)eology. In *The wider domain of evolutionary thought,* ed. D. Oldroyd & I. Langham, 175–219. Dordrecht.

Gräslund, B. 1974. *Relativ datering: Om kronologisk metod i nordisk arkeologi. Tor* 16. Uppsala.

———. 1976. Relative chronology: dating methods in Scandinavian archaeology. *Norwegian Arch. Rev.* 9:69–126.

Grayson, D. K. 1983. *The establishment of human antiquity.* New York.

Green, S. 1981. *Prehistorian: A biography of V. Gordon Childe.* Bradford-on-Avon.

Haven, S. F. 1856. *Archaeology of the United States.* Smithsonian Contributions to Knowledge, 8(2). Washington.

Hawkes, J. 1963. *The world of the past.* 2 vols. New York.

———. 1982. *Mortimer Wheeler: Adventurer in archaeology.* London.

Heizer, R. F. 1959. *The archaeologist at work.* New York.

———. 1962. *Man's discovery of his past.* Englewood Cliffs.

Hinsley, C. M., Jr. 1981. *Savages and scientists: The Smithsonian Institution and the development of American anthropology, 1846–1910.* Washington.

Hodder, I. 1982. *The present past.* London.

Hoffman, M. A. 1979. *Egypt before the Pharaohs.* New York.

Hudson, K. 1981. *A social history of archaeology: The British experience.* London.

Hunter, M. 1975. *John Aubrey and the realm of learning.* London.

Kendrick, T. D. 1950. *British antiquity.* London.

Killan, G. 1983. *David Boyle: From artisan to archaeologist.* Toronto.

Klindt-Jensen, O. 1975. *A history of Scandinavian archaeology.* London.

Kristiansen, K. 1981. A social history of Danish archaeology (1805–1957). In *Towards a history of archaeology,* ed. G. Daniel, 20–44. London.

Kuhn, T. S. 1962. *The structure of scientific revolutions.* Chicago (2nd ed., 1970).

Laming-Emperaire, A. 1964. *Origines de l'archéologie préhistorique en France des superstitions médiévales à la découverte de l'homme fossile.* Paris.

Leone, M. P. 1982. Some opinions about recovering mind. *Am. Antiq.* 47:742–60.

Lloyd, S. 1947. *Foundations in the dust: A story of Mesopotamian exploration.* London (2nd ed., 1981).

McKusick, M. 1970. *The Davenport Conspiracy.* Iowa City.

McNairn, B. 1980. *Method and theory of V. Gordon Childe.* Edinburgh.

Marsden, B. M. 1974. *The early barrow-diggers*. Park Ridge, New Jersey.

Meltzer, D. J. 1983. The antiquity of man and the development of American archaeology. In *Advances in archaeological method and theory*, ed. M. B. Schiffer, 6:1–51. New York.

Milanich, J. T., & C. H. Fairbanks, 1980. *Florida archaeology*. New York.

Morlot, A. von. 1861. General views on archaeology. *Ann. Rept. Smithsonian Inst.*, 1860:284–343. Washington.

Piggott, S. 1950. *William Stukeley: An eighteenth-century antiquary*. Oxford.

———. 1968. *The druids*. London.

———. 1976. *Ruins in a landscape: Essays in antiquarianism*. Edinburgh.

Schiffer, M. B. 1976. *Behavioral archeology*. New York.

Schwartz, D. W. 1967. *Conceptions of Kentucky prehistory: A case study in the history of archaeology*. Lexington.

———. 1968. Archaeology in historical perspective. *Actes du XIᵉ Congrès International d'Histoire des Sciences*, Vol. 2:311–15. Warsaw and Cracow.

Silverberg, R. 1968. *Mound builders of ancient America: The archaeology of a myth*. Greenwich, Connecticut.

Sklenář, K. 1983. *Archaeology in Central Europe: The first 500 years*. Leicester.

Sterud, G. 1973. A paradigmatic view of prehistory. In *The explanation of culture change*, ed. C. Renfrew, 3–17. London.

———. 1978. Changing aims in Americanist archaeology: A citation analysis of *American Antiquity*. *Am. Antiq.* 43:294–302.

Thompson, M. W. 1977. *General Pitt-Rivers: Evolution and archaeology in the nineteenth century*. Bradford-on-Avon.

Trigger, B. G. 1980. *Gordon Childe: Revolutions in archaeology*. London.

———. 1981. Anglo-American archaeology. *World Arch.* 13:138–55.

———. 1982. Archaeological analysis and concepts of causality. *Culture* 2(2):31–42.

———. 1983. Human history legitimated: Review of *The establishment of human antiquity*, by D. K. Grayson. *Science* 220 (4595):834–35.

———. 1984a. Childe and Soviet archaeology. *Australian Archaeology* 18:1–16.

———. 1984b. Alternative archaeologies: Nationalist, colonialist, imperialist. *Man* 19:355–70.

Trigger, B. G., & I. Glover, eds. 1981–82. Regional traditions of archaeological research I, II. *World Arch.* 13(2); 13(3).

Walthall, J. A. 1980. *Prehistoric Indians of the southeast*. University City, Alabama.

Willey, G. R. 1968. One hundred years of American archaeology. In *One hundred years of anthropology*, ed. J. O. Brew, 25–53. Cambridge, Massachusetts.

Willey, G. R., & J. A. Sabloff. 1974. *A history of American archaeology*. San Francisco. (2nd. ed., 1980).

Woodbury, R. B. 1973. *Alfred V. Kidder*. New York.

Zubrow, E. 1972. Environment, subsistence and society: The changing archaeological perspective. *An. Rev. Anth.* 1:179–226.

———. 1980. International trends in theoretical archaeology. *Norwegian Arch. Rev.* 13:14–23.

OBJECTS AND SELVES—
AN AFTERWORD

JAMES CLIFFORD

Entering
You will find yourself in a climate of nut castanets,
A musical whip
From the Torres Straits, from Mirzapur a sistrum
Called Jumka, 'used by aboriginal
Tribes to attract small game
On dark nights', coolie cigarettes
And mask of Saagga, the Devil Doctor,
The eyelids worked by strings.

James Fenton's poem, "The Pitt-Rivers Museum, Oxford" (1984:81–84),[1] from which this stanza is taken, rediscovers a place of fascination in the ethnographic collection. For this visitor, even the museum's coolly descriptive labels seem to increase the wonder ("'. . . attract small game / on dark nights'") and the fear. Fenton is an adult-child, exploring territories of danger and desire. For to be a child in this collection ("'Please sir, where's the withered / Hand?'") is to ignore the serious admonitions about human evolution and cultural diversity posted in the entrance hall. And it is to be interested instead by the claw of a condor, the jawbone of a dolphin, the hair of a witch, or "a jay's feather worn as a charm / In Buckinghamshire. . . ." Fenton's ethnographic museum is a world of fetishes, of intimate encounters with inexplicably fascinating objects. Here collecting is inescapably tied to obsession, to personal recollection. Visitors "find the landscape of their childhood marked out / Here, in the chaotic piles of souvenirs" . . ."box-room of the forgotten or hardly possible."

1. Quoted with permission from *Children in Exile: Poems 1968–1984*, copyright 1984 by Random House, Inc.

James Clifford is Associate Professor of the History of Consciousness at the University of California, Santa Cruz, and the author of *Person and Myth: Maurice Leenhardt in the Melanesian World*. He has recently edited, with George Marcus, *Making Ethnography*, forthcoming from the University of California Press.

Go
As a historian of ideas or a sex-offender,
For the primitive art,
As a dusty semiologist, equipped to unravel
The seven components of that witch's curse
Or the syntax of the mutilated teeth. Go
In groups to giggle at curious finds.
But do not step into the kingdom of your promises
To yourself, like a child entering the forbidden
Woods of his lonely playtime:

Do not step into this tabooed zone ". . . laid with the snares of privacy and fiction / And the dangerous third wish." Do not encounter these objects except as *curiosities* to giggle at or as *evidence* to be understood scientifically. The tabooed third way, followed by Fenton, is a path of too-intimate fantasy, recalling the dreams of a solitary child "who wrestled with eagles for their feathers," or the fearful vision of a young girl—her turbulent lover seen as a hound with "strange pretercanine eyes." And this path through the Pitt Rivers Museum ends with what seems to be a scrap of autobiography, the vision of a personal "forbidden woods"—exotic, desired, savage, and governed by the (paternal) law:

He had known what tortures the savages had prepared
For him there, as he calmly pushed open the gate
And entered the wood near the placard: 'TAKE NOTICE
MEN-TRAPS AND SPRING-GUNS ARE SET ON THESE PREMISES.'
For his father had protected his good estate.

Fenton's journey into otherness leads to a forbidden area of the self. His third way of engaging the exotic collection finds only an area of desire, marked off and policed. This law is preoccupied with *property*.

C. B. Macpherson's classic analysis of Western "possessive individualism" (1962) traces the seventeenth-century emergence of a sense of self as owner. The ideal individual surrounds itself with accumulated properties and goods. Richard Handler's essay in this volume on the construction of a Québécois cultural "Patrimoine" draws on Macpherson to unravel the assumptions and paradoxes involved in "having a culture," selecting and cherishing an authentic collective property. Extending his point, it can be said that this form of identity, whether cultural or personal, presupposes the act of collection, a gathering up of properties in arbitrary *systems* of value and meaning. These systems, as various essays in this volume show, have changed historically. But they are always powerful and rule-governed. One cannot escape them. At best, Fenton suggests, one can transgress ("poach" in their tabooed zones), or make their self-evident orders seem strange. In Handler's subtly perverse analysis a common system of retrospection—revealed by a Historic Monuments Commission's selection of ten sorts of "cultural property"—becomes a taxonomy worthy of Borges' Chinese Encyclopedia:

> (1) commemorative monuments; (2) churches and chapels; (3) forts of the French Regime; (4) windmills; (5) roadside crosses; (6) commemorative inscriptions and plaques; (7) devotional monuments; (8) old houses and manors; (9) old furniture; (10) "les choses disparues."

In his discussion, the "collection" or preservation of an authentic domain of identity cannot be natural or innocent. It is tied up with nationalist politics, with restrictive law, and with contested encodations of past and future.

Some sort of "gathering" around the self and the group—the assemblage of a material "world," the marking off of a subjective domain which is not "other"—probably is universal. And all such collecting produces hierarchies of value, exclusions, rule-governed territories of the self. But the notion that this gathering involves the accumulation of possessions, the idea that identity is a kind of wealth (of objects, knowledge, etc.) is surely not universal. The individualistic accumulation of Melanesian "big men" is not possessive in Macpherson's sense. For in Melanesia one accumulates not to hold objects as private goods, but to give them away, to redistribute. In the West, however, collecting has long been a strategy for the deployment of a possessive self, culture, and authenticity.

Children's collections are revealing in this light: a boy's accumulation of miniature cars, a girl's dolls, a summer vacation "nature museum" (with labeled stones and shells, a hummingbird in a bottle), a treasured bowl filled with the bright-colored shavings of crayons. In these small rituals we observe the channeling of obsession, an exercise in how to make the world one's own, to gather things around oneself tastefully, appropriately. The inclusions in all collections reflect wider cultural rules, of rational taxonomy, of gender, of aesthetics. An excessive, sometimes even rapacious need to *have* is transformed into rule-governed, meaningful desire. Thus the self which must *possess*, but cannot have it all, learns to select, order, classify in hierarchies—to make "good" collections.[2]

Whether a child collects model dinosaurs or dolls, sooner or later she or he will be encouraged to keep the possessions on a shelf, in a special box, or to set up a doll house. Personal treasures will be made public. If the passion is for Egyptian figurines, the collector will be expected to label them, to know their dynasty (it is not enough that they simply exude power or mystery), to

2. A highly suggestive source on collecting as a strategy of desire is the catalog (Hainard & Kaehr, eds. 1982) for an exhibition at the Musée d'Ethnographie, Neuchâtel, 5 June–31 December 1981—an analytic collection of collections and *tour de force* of reflexive museology.

tell "interesting" things about them, to distinguish copies from originals. The good collector (opposed to the obsessive, the miser) is tasteful and systematic. Accumulation unfolds in a pedagogical, edifying manner. The collection itself, its taxonomic, aesthetic structure, is valued. And any private fixation on single objects is negatively marked as fetishism. Indeed, a "proper" relation with objects (rule-governed possession) presupposes a "savage" or deviant relation (idolatry or erotic fixation).[3] In Susan Stewart's gloss: "The boundary between collection and fetishism is mediated by classification and display in tension with accumulation and secrecy" (1984:163).

Stewart's wide-ranging study, *On Longing*, traces a "structure of desire" whose task (following Lacan) is the repetitious and impossible one of closing the gap that separates language from the experience it encodes. She explores certain recurrent strategies pursued by Westerners since the sixteenth century. In her analysis, the miniature, whether a portrait or doll's house, enacts a bourgeois longing for inner experience. She also explores the strategy of gigantism (from Rabelais and Gulliver to earthworks and the billboard), the souvenir, and the collection. She shows how collecting—and most notably the museum—creates the illusion of adequate representation of a world by first cutting objects out of specific contexts (whether cultural, historical, or intersubjective) and making them "stand for" abstract wholes—a "Bambara mask," for example, becoming a metonym for Bambara culture. Next, a scheme of classification is elaborated for storing or displaying the object so that the reality of the collection itself, its coherent order, overrides specific histories of the object's production and appropriation (162–65). Paralleling Marx's account of the fantastic objectification of commodities (their "fetishization"), Stewart suggests that in the modern Western museum "an illusion of a relation between things takes the place of a social relation" (165). The collector discovers, acquires, salvages objects. The objective world is given, and thus historical relations of power in the work of acquisition are occulted. The *production* of meaning in museum classification and display is mystified as adequate *representation*. The time and order of the collection overrides and erases the concrete social labor of its making.

Stewart's work, along with that of James Bunn (1980), Daniel Defert (1982), and Johannes Fabian (1983), among others, brings collecting and display sharply into view as crucial processes of Western identity formation. Gathered artifacts—whether they find their way into curio cabinets, private living rooms, museums of ethnography, folklore, or fine art—function within a developing capitalist "system of objects" (Baudrillard 1968). By virtue of

3. My understanding of the ideological role of the fetish in Western intellectual history—from De Brosses to Marx, Freud, and Deleuze—owes a great deal to the so far unpublished work of William Pietz, especially "The Problem of the Fetish" (1984).

this sytem, a world of *value* is created and a *meaningful* deployment and circulation of artifacts maintained. For Baudrillard, collected objects create a structured environment that substitutes its own temporality for the "real time" of historical and productive processes: ". . . the environment of private objects and their possession—of which collections are an extreme manifestation—is a dimension of our life that is both essential and imaginary. As essential as dreams" (135). The history of anthropology needs to accommodate a perspective on collecting that embraces both a form of Western subjectivity and a changing set of powerful institutional practices. The history of collections (not limited to museums) is central to an understanding of how those social groups that invented anthropology have *appropriated* exotic things, facts, and meanings. ("Appropriate": to make one's own; from the Latin, *proprius*, proper, property.) It is important to analyze, as a number of the essays in this volume do (Williams, Wade, Handler), just how powerful discriminations, made at particular moments, constitute the general system of objects within which non-Western artifacts circulate and make sense. Far-reaching questions are thereby raised.

What criteria validate an authentic cultural or artistic product? What are the differential values placed on old and new creations? What moral and political criteria justify "good," responsible, systematic, collecting practices? (Why, for example, do Frobenius' wholesale acquisitions of the early century now seem excessive?) How is a "complete" collection defined? What is the proper balance between scientific analysis and public display? (In Santa Fe, a superb collection of Native American art is housed at the School of American Research in a building constructed, literally, as a vault, with access restricted to research scholars. The Musée de l'Homme exhibits less than a tenth of its collection; the rest is stored in steel cabinets, or heaped in corners in the vast basement.) Why has it seemed obvious, until recently, that non-Western objects should be preserved in European museums, even when this means that no fine specimens are visible in their country of origin? How, at different historical moments and in specific market conditions, are "antiquities," "curiosities," "art," "souvenirs," "monuments," and "ethnographic artifacts" distinguished? (Why, for example, have many anthropological museums in recent years begun to display certain of their objects as "masterpieces"? Why has tourist art only recently [Graburn, ed. 1976] come to the serious attention of anthropologists?) What has been the changing interplay between natural history collecting and the selection of anthropological artifacts for display and analysis? The list could be extended.

The history of collecting is concerned with what, from the material world, specific groups and individuals choose to preserve, value, and exchange. Although the complex history of this symbolic system from at least the Age of Discovery remains to be written, Baudrillard provides an initial framework within which the deployment of objects in the recent capitalist West can be conceived. In his account, it is axiomatic that all categories of meaningful objects—including those marked off as scientific evidence and as great art— function within a ramified system of symbols and values.

To take just one current example: the *New York Times* of December 8, 1984, reported the widespread, illegal looting of Anasazi archeological sites in the American Southwest. Painted pots or urns thus excavated, in good condition, could bring as much as $30,000 on the art market. The same issue contained a photograph of Bronze Age pots and jugs salvaged by archeologists from a Phoenician shipwreck off the coast of Turkey. One account featured clandestine collecting for profit, the other scientific collecting for knowledge. The moral evaluations of the two acts of salvage were starkly opposed. But the pots recovered were all meaningful, beautiful, and old. Commercial, aes- thetic, and scientific worth in both cases presupposed a given system of value. This system finds intrinsic interest and beauty in objects from a past time, and it assumes that collecting everyday objects from ancient (preferably van- ished) civilizations will be more *rewarding* than collecting, for example, charmingly decorated thermoses from modern China, or original T-shirts from Oceania. Old objects are endowed with a sense of "depth" by their historically minded collectors. Temporality is reified and salvaged as beauty and knowledge.[4]

This archaizing system has not always guided Western collecting, and it is presently contested. The curiosities of the New World gathered and appre- ciated in the sixteenth century were not primarily valued as antiquities, the products of primitive or "past" civilizations. They occupied, frequently, a cat- egory of the marvelous, or of a real, present "Golden Age" (Honour 1975; Mullaney 1983; Rabassa 1984). In recent years the systematic, ideological, bias of Western appropriation of the world's cultures in a mode of retrospec- tion has come under critical scrutiny (Fabian 1983; Clifford 1985), and at least two of the essays gathered here (Handler and Wade) strongly suggest

---

4. This system may perhaps be brought into sharper relief by alluding to a different one. The Igbo of Nigeria, according to Chinua Achebe, do not particularly like collections: "The pur- poseful neglect of the painstakingly and devoutly accomplished *mbari* houses with all the art objects in them as soon as the primary mandate of their creation has been served, provides a significant insight into the Igbo aesthetic value as *process* rather than *product*. Process is motion while product is rest. When the product is preserved or venerated, the impulse to repeat the process is compromised. Therefore the Igbo choose to eliminate the product and retain the process so that every occasion and every generation will receive its own impulse and experience of creation. Interestingly this aesthetic disposition receives powerful endorsement from the trop- ical climate which provides an abundance of materials for making art, such as wood, as well as formidable agencies of dissolution, such as humidity and the termite. Visitors to Igboland are shocked to see that artifacts are rarely accorded any particular value on the basis of age alone" (1984:ix).

that cultural or artistic "authenticity" has as much to do with an inventive present as with a past, its objectification, preservation, or revival. And in both of these discussions, the definition of cultural value is shown to be a matter of historical, political debate.

Since the turn of the century, objects collected from non-Western places have been classified in two major categories: as (scientific) cultural artifacts or as (aesthetic) works of art. Other collectibles—mass-produced commodities, "tourist art," curios, etc.—have been less systematically valued and appropriated; at best they find a place in exhibits of "technology" or "folklore." The separation of ethnography and art has not, however, been watertight. Certain classes of object have moved from one context to the other. But generally speaking, the ethnographic museum and the art museum have developed fundamentally different modes of classification. In the former, a work of "sculpture" is displayed along with other objects of similar function or in proximity to objects from the same cultural group, including utilitarian artifacts (spoons, bowls, spears, etc.). A mask or statue may be grouped with formally dissimilar objects and explained as part of a ritual or institutional complex. The names of individual sculptors are unknown, or suppressed. In the art museum a sculpture is identified as the creation of an individual. Its place in everyday cultural practices (including the market) is irrelevant to its essential meaning. Whereas in the ethnographic museum the object is culturally or humanly "interesting," in the art museum it is primarily "beautiful" or "original."

Elizabeth Williams' essay in this volume traces an important chapter in the shifting history of these discriminations. In nineteenth-century Paris it was, in effect, impossible to conceive of Pre-Colombian artifacts as fully "beautiful." *Ars Americana* was considered grotesque or crude by a dominant naturalist aesthetic. At best it could be assimilated to the category of the antiquity and appreciated through the filter of Viollet-le-Duc's medievalism. Williams shows how Mayan and Incan artifacts, their status uncertain, migrated between the Louvre, the Bibliothèque Nationale, the Musée Guimet, and (after 1878) the Trocadero. The latter institution, where they seemed at last to find an ethnographic home, treated them as scientific evidence. The Trocadero's first directors, Hamy and Verneau, showed scant interest in their aesthetic qualities.

With the modernist revolution—as Picasso and others began to visit the "Troca" and to accord tribal objects a nonethnographic admiration—the proper place of non-Western objects was again put in question. In the eyes of a triumphant modernism some of them, at least, could be seen as universal masterpieces. The category of "primitive art" emerged, along with its distinctive market and connoisseurship. This development introduced new ambiguities in a changing taxonomic system. In the mid-nineteenth century, Pre-

Colombian or tribal objects were antiquities or curiosities. By 1920 they were anthropologically meaningful and/or aesthetically valued. Since then, a controlled migration has occurred between these two institutionalized domains. Around 1930, for example, the Trocadero, under Rivet and Rivière, functioned primarily as a scientific collection but also served as an artistic resource in a Parisian climate of "modernist primitivism" (Rubin, ed. 1984). Some have regarded its successor, the Musée de l'Homme, as a kind of secret museum of tribal "art" (Vogel 1984). Other national traditions have seen less interpenetration of ethnographic and artistic domains; but there has usually been, from a distance, some degree of conversation. In recent years, the blurring of boundaries has markedly increased.

During the winter of 1984–85 in New York City, at least seven highly visible new exhibitions featuring tribal art were in progress. At the Museum of Modern Art a major body of African, Oceanian, and Eskimo artifacts was brought from ethnographic museums and private collections to be shown alongside works by Picasso, Giacometti, Brancusi, Derain, Henry Moore, etc.—modernist works that they had either directly influenced or that they powerfully resembled. At the Metropolitan Museum of Art (Mead, ed. 1984) Maori traditional objects were installed in a gallery adjoining the ruined Egyptian Temple of Dendur. While Ashanti treasures were on special display at the American Museum of Natural History, Northwest Coast artifacts from the Museum of the American Indian had traveled downtown to the more accessible IBM Gallery. There they were displayed in a darkened room to the sound of recorded chants. Outside stood a large totem pole, freshly carved for the occasion by the Kwakiutl artist Calvin Hunt. Simultaneously at the Metropolitan the recently opened Rockefeller Wing of tribal art continued to draw crowds. And to accommodate the overflowing interest and the burgeoning market, a new Center for African Art had just opened its doors. Its inaugural exhibit featured one hundred "masterpieces" from the Musée de l'Homme (Vogel & N'Diaye, eds. 1984).

The boundaries of art and science, the aesthetic and the anthropological, are not permanently fixed. In various anthropological museums (for example, the Hall of Asian Peoples at the Museum of Natural History), a new "boutique" style of display artfully arranges objects so that nothing could seem out of place on the wall or coffee table of a middle-class living room. And in a complementary development, the newly renovated Museum of Modern Art has expanded its permanent exhibit of cultural artifacts: furniture, automobiles, home appliances and utensils—even hanging from the ceiling, like a Northwest Coast war canoe, a much admired bright green helicopter.

Clearly the ethnographic/artistic object system, in connection with art markets and the world of commodities, is operating with a new inventiveness and flexibility. My concern is not to speculate on recent developments which may again be redeploying the categories of the beautiful, the cultural, and the authentic. Nor can I pursue here the shifting value of collected objects—whether "masterpieces" or "material culture"—within scientific anthropology (Sturtevant 1969, 1973; Jamin 1982; Reynolds 1983). I want only to underscore the unsettled, the nomadic, existence of these non-Western artifacts (Centilivres 1982:55). They have been diversely recontextualized, used as "cultural" or "human" evidence in the exhibit halls (or basements) of certain museums, made to stand for "artistic" beauty and creativity in others. They gain "value" in vaults or on the walls of bourgeois living rooms, are made and judged according to shifting criteria of authenticity, are brought from the Museum für Völkerkunde in Hamburg to hang beside a canvas of Joan Miró in New York. Where do these objects belong? I have been suggesting that they "belong" nowhere, having been torn from their social contexts of production and reception, given value in systems of meaning whose primary function is to confirm the knowledge and taste of a possessive Western subjectivity.

While these systems are institutionalized and powerful, they are not immutable. There exist possible standpoints from which non-Western objects can be encountered in ways that unravel self-evident, dominant, taxonomies. By way of conclusion, I would suggest three such positions, or modes of intervention.

1. Rather than grasping objects only as cultural signs and artistic icons (Guidieri & Pellizzi 1981), we can return to them, as James Fenton does, their lost status as fetishes. *Our* fetishes. This tactic, necessarily personal, would accord to things in collections the power to fixate, rather than simply the capacity to edify or inform. African and Oceanian artifacts could once again be "objets sauvages," sources of fascination with the power to disconcert. Seen in their nomadic resistance to classification they could remind us of our *lack* of self-possession, of the artifices we employ to gather a world sensibly around us.[5]

2. We can struggle to keep in view the historical relations of power in all collections of exotic objects. Who collects whom? How is another group's art or culture properly displayed? These have become openly political questions. In the New York exhibitions there were signs that the possession of the objects displayed was contested. A note in the Museum of Modern Art explained that a Zuni figurine would not be brought from Berlin because of objections raised by tribal authorities. The existence of living "tribal" peoples with ongoing relations to the art on display was clearly manifested in the

5. For a post-Freudian positive sense of fetishism see Leiris (1929, 1984); for the fetish's radical, critical possibilities see Pietz (1984), which draws on Deleuze; and for a semiologist's perverse sense of the fetish (the "punctum") as a place of strictly personal meaning unformed by cultural codes (the "studium") see Barthes (1982).

Northwest Coast installation. The show ended with work from living artists; wood chips were left around the freshly carved totem pole in the IBM atrium. The Maori and Ashanti exhibits both opened with active, ceremonial participation by non-Western groups to whom the artifacts "belonged" (in a sense not synonymous with private ownership). The conditions of collection and display were evidently negotiated—no longer in any one group's exclusive control. When relations of power among living political groups are manifested in exhibitions, the objects may seem to be less firmly "collected" within a single system of value.

3. It is important to resist the tendency of collections to be self-sufficient, to suppress their own historical process of production. The history of the collecting and recontextualization of non-Western objects is now, ideally, a part of any exhibition. It was rumored recently that the Boas Room of Northwest Coast artifacts in the American Museum of Natural History would soon be refurbished, its style of display modernized. Apparently (or so one hopes) the plan has been abandoned. For this beautiful, dated, hall reveals not merely a superb collection, but a moment in the history of collecting. The widely publicized Museum of Modern Art exhibit made apparent (as it uncritically celebrated) the historical circumstances in which certain ethnographic objects suddenly became works of high art. More historical self-consciousness in the display and viewing of non-Western objects can at least jostle and set in motion the object systems by which anthropologists, artists, and their publics collect themselves and the world. The essays in this volume are a step in that direction.

References Cited

Achebe, C. 1984. Preface. In *Igbo Arts: Community and Cosmos*, ed. H. M. Cole & C. C. Aniakor, pp. viii–xi. Los Angeles.

Barthes, R. 1982. *Camera lucida.* New York.

Baudrillard, J. 1968. *Le Système des objets.* Paris.

Bunn, J. 1980. The Aesthetics of British Merchantilism. *New Lit. Hist.* 11:303–21.

Centilivres, P. 1982. Des "instructions" aux collections: La production ethnographique de l'image de l'orient. In Hainard & Kaehr, eds. 1982:33–61.

Clifford, J. 1985. On ethnographic allegory. In *Making Ethnography*, ed. J. Clifford & G. Marcus. Berkeley (forthcoming).

Defert, D. 1982. The collection of the world: Accounts of voyages from the sixteenth to the eighteenth centuries. *Dialect. Anth.* 7:11–20.

Fabian, J. 1983. *Time and the other: How anthropology makes its object.* New York.

Fenton, J. 1984. *Children in exile: Poems 1968–1984.* New York.

Graburn, N., ed. 1976. *Ethnic and tourist arts.* Berkeley.

Guidieri, R., & F. Pellizzi. 1981. Editorial. *Res* 1:3–6.

Hainard, J., & R. Kaehr, eds. 1982. *Collections passion*. Neuchâtel.

Honour, H. 1975. *The new golden land*. New York.

Jamin, J. 1982. Objets trouvés des paradis perdus. In Hainard & Kaehr, eds. 1982:69–100.

Leiris, M. 1929. Alberto Giacometti. *Documents* 4:209–11.

———. 1984. *Manhood*. Trans. R. Howard. Berkeley.

Macpherson, C. B. 1962. *The political theory of possessive individualism*. Oxford.

Mead, S. M., ed. 1984. *The Maori: Maori art from New Zealand collections*. New York.

Mullaney, S. 1983. Strange things, gross terms, curious customs: The rehearsal of cultures in the late Renaissance. *Representations* 3:40–67.

Pietz, W. 1984. The problem of the fetish. Ms.

Rabassa, J. 1984. A Hand: The travail of Columbus. Ms.

Reynolds, B. 1983. The relevance of material culture to anthropology. *J. Anth. Soc. Oxford* 2:63–75.

Rubin, W., ed. 1984. *"Primitivism" in modern art: Affinity of the tribal and the modern*. 2 vols. New York.

Stewart, S. 1984. *On longing: Narratives of the miniature, the gigantic, the souvenir, the collection*. Baltimore.

Sturtevant, W. 1969. Does anthropology need museums? *Proc. Biol. Soc. Washington* 82:619–50.

———. 1973. Museums as anthropological data banks. In *Anthropology beyond the university*, ed. A. Redfield. *Proc. So. Anth. Soc.* 7:40–55.

Vogel, S. 1984. Introduction. *African masterpieces from the Musée de l'Homme*, 11. New York.

Vogel, S., & F. N'Diaye, eds. 1984. *African masterpieces from the Musée de l'Homme*. New York.

INFORMATION FOR CONTRIBUTORS

Future Volume Themes

Normally, every volume of HOA will be organized around a particular theme of historical and contemporary anthropological significance, although each volume may also contain one or more "miscellaneous studies." Potential contributors to announced volumes are encouraged to write to the editor before submitting drafts. Researchers on other topics are also urged to communicate about their work-in-progress, since later volume themes will be chosen in the light of such prior information. Volume themes already selected include the following:

HOA 4: *Anthropology Between Two World Wars: 1914–1945* (in press)

HOA 5: *Biological Perspectives in Anthropological Inquiry*
Although the origin of "anthropology" is often linked to the emergence of Darwinian evolution, and in the continental European tradition the term has usually referred (without any modifier) to the study of the physical characteristics of humankind, its relation to scholarly biological inquiry and to popular biological assumption has been recurrently problematic. At issue are some of the most deeply rooted and contemporaneously pressing anthropological problems, including the origin of humankind and its place within the natural world, the origin and social significance of "racial" differences, the relation of biological and cultural evolution, the biological and social significance of gender differences, etc.—as well as more specifically disciplinary matters having to do with the intellectual division of labor and institutional boundaries among the various human sciences and their component subdisciplines. We hope to elicit essays covering a wide range of intellectual and social history, which will help to illuminate present theoretical, methodological, ideological, and social concerns—although papers on the history of "physical anthropology" more narrowly conceived will also be welcome.

HOA 6: *Anthropology and the Romantic Sensibility*
Like much of Western intellectual life, anthropology has always been impelled by two contrasting energizing motives: the rationalistic and the romantic (polarities which correlate, perhaps, with others that are the staples of intellectual history: progressivism/primitivism; natural science/humanism, materialism/idealism, etc.). While anthropology is often spoken of as the child of the Enlightenment, reborn perhaps with Darwinism, the romantic current has run very strong, and the tension between the two continues to

the present (strongly to be manifested, for instance, in the Mead/Freeman controversy). Volume 6 will be devoted to the history of this tension, with special emphasis, as the title suggests, on the romantic current.

Manuscript Preparation

Manuscripts submitted for consideration to HOA should be typed twenty-six lines to a page with 1¼-inch margins. All material should be double spaced, including indented quoted passages in the text, as well as footnotes, which should be grouped together at the end, beginning on a separate sheet. Documentation should be in the anthropological style, with parenthetic author/ date/page references (Boas 1911:120) and a list of "References Cited" (begun on a separate sheet). For exemplification of stylistic details, consult previously published volumes; more extensive guidelines may be obtained upon request by writing to the editor. Please note that unsolicited manuscripts will not be returned unless accompanied by adequate postage. All communications on editorial matters should be directed to the editor:

> *George W. Stocking, Jr. (HOA)*
> *Department of Anthropology*
> *University of Chicago*
> *1126 E. 59th St.*
> *Chicago, Illinois 60637 U.S.A.*

INDEX

Abbott, Charles C., 62–70
Aborigines Protection Society, 21
Academic anthropology, 8, 36–37, 43, 52, 61, 69, 70–72, 75, 76, 88, 108, 112, 134, 135, 140, 197. *See also* specific universities
Achebe, Chinua, 241n
Aesthetic(s): and museum ethnography, 3, 146–63 *passim*; as dimension of museum, 6; instinct, 113, 161, 167; contrasted with ethnographic, 146, 147, 148, 164, 242, 243; non-Western, 152–53, 189, 241n; naturalistic, 152–55; classical, 153, 154; materialist, 154–55; values of pre-Columbian culture, 159, 160; reevaluation of, 163, 189; appropriation of primitive, 164, 240; and classification, 239. *See also* Art
Africa, 22, 25, 123–24, 135, 139, 140, 156, 163, 243, 244
Afro-American, 113, 118
Agassiz, Alexander, 57, 61
Agassiz, Louis, 49–51, 52–53, 61, 89
Algert, C. H., 176
Amateurs, 62–69, 202
American Anthropological Association, 12, 115, 130–31, 138, 141
American Antiquarian Society, 51
American Association for the Advancement of Science, 72
American Council of Learned Societies, 132
American Indian Movement, 185
American Indians. *See* Native Americans
Americanist(s), 146, 148–50, 162
American Museum of Natural History: founding, 83; Department of Anthropology staff, 84; administration, 84–85; anthropological halls, 90, 92, 94; building, 90–92, 94; mentioned, 72, 75–108 *passim*, 115, 120, 138, 243, 245
Andrews, E. P., 68
Angell, J. N., 116, 118
Angrand, Léonce, 156
Anteone, Gladice, 186
Anthropological Institute of Great Britain and Ireland, 30, 33, 115, 123, 124, 126, 141

Anthropological Society of London, 29
Anthropology: Anglo-American, 4, 8, 114–16, 139, 141; shift to behavioral, 8, 108, 114, 137, 140–41; demography of, 9, 12; rehistoricization of, 12; as science, 30, 51, 60, 115, 128, 137; as humanistic study, 51, 60; objects of, 108, 112, 192; political economy of, 112–16, 138–42; research priorities of, 133–34, 138; weakening of general anthropology, 141
Antiquarianism, 32, 221, 243
Antiquity of man, 20, 50, 53, 62–69, 70, 226, 227–28
Applied anthropology, 123, 126, 136, 137
Arapaho, 88
Archaeological Institute, London, 27, 28, 29
Archaeological Institute of America, 53–55, 56, 57
Archeology: and museums, 4, 9, 49–71 *passim*, 90, 92, 108, 170; "three age" system, 7, 26, 41, 225; prehistoric, 22, 23, 25, 219, 222, 226; Pitt Rivers and, 26–28; Paleolithic and Neolithic, 27, 41, 60, 220, 222, 226; at the Smithsonian, 50, 218; North American, 53, 55, 60–61, 70, 224; classical vs. prehistoric, 55, 56, 59–60; Mayan, 69–71, 140; training, 72, 108, 122, 228; support for, 140–41, 223; Southwest, 170, 171, 172, 175; recovery and interpretation of data, 218–19; and interpretation of human behavior, 219, 231, 232; radiocarbon dating, 220, 223; New Archeology, 223, 224, 225; mentioned, 202, 218–33 *passim*. *See also* Historiography of archeology
Art: "primitive," 9, 147, 148, 153, 155, 158–62, 163–64, 187, 242; fine art, 55, 58, 148, 189, 239; primitivist revolution, 146–47, 148, 159, 162–64, 242–43; *Ars Americana*, 146–63 *passim*; pre-Columbian, 146–63 *passim*, 242–43; Medieval, 152, 153, 154; classical, 152, 163; Renaissance, 152–53; decadence, 153, 154; evolution of, 153–55, 172; native artists, 167, 168, 174, 180, 183, 186; commercialization of, 167, 172, 176, 180, 181; preservationism, 167–

249